THE ECONOMICS OF URBAN WATER SUPPLY

THE ECONOMICS OF URBAN WATER SUPPLY

In Karnataka and Maharashtra

D.M. Madari

PUBLICATIONS

KALPAZ PUBLICATIONS

DELHI-110052

The Economics of Urban Water Supply in Karnataka and Maharashtra

Rs. 690

ISBN: 81-7835-556-6

Published in 2007 in India by
Kalpaz Publications
C-30, Satyawati Nagar,
Delhi-110052
Phone : 9212729499
E-mail: kalpaz@hotmail.com

Lasser Typesetting by: Rudra Computer Graphics, Delhi
Printed at: Salasar Imaging System, Delhi

Dedicated to my beloved

PARENTS

Contents

Preface

Studies on "Economics of Drinking Water Supply" in many parts of the world more specifically in water scarce zones and regions have attracted the attention of the policy makers and academicians as well. Researchers have engaged themselves in analyzing the micro-level studies of water during the last three decades. The significance of studies on water as an economic resource has been underscored by the uncertainties in the monsoons and recurring droughts as nearly one third of the total area of India has been susceptible for semi-arid and arid environment. Further there has been a marked contrast in the attention paid to the problems of electricity, road transport, public health and drinking water supply as economic overheads and public enterprises. The studies on public enterprises include not many water supply industries in Indian context.

The need for safe water is as old as the existence of human beings and improvements in health are associated with improvements in water supplies. Adequacy of water supplies plays a decisive role in the establishment and expansion of industries. Primary importance is to be given to water supply programmes for the success of industrial development plan. However, these programmes are to be supported by complementary programmes like education, health care, drainage and sewerage programmes etc, in an integrated approach at the global level. Community water supply is a basic need; access to safe drinking water is a human right and it is important to stress this human right because many people don't share it. Water remains no longer a free good and has become an economic good. If we fail to study,economics of 'water as a scarce resource' whose allocation should be governed by more rational decisions, our fault would not be condoned.

The World Health Organization initiated a programme for community water supplies in 1959 and resolved that "priority be given in national programme for provision of safe and adequate water supplies for communities. But, it was in 1960s that the benefits of adequate safe water were fully realized and a concerted effort was initiated in this direction. The WHO convened the first Expert Committee meeting in 1969 to consider specifically the problems of community water supplies and International Reference Center for Community Water Supplies (IRC-CWS) was set up. Further, WHO initiated steps to prepare guidelines and codes of practice in planning and design and management of community water supply and sanitation services with emphasis on public health aspects.

It has become a convention though the need for water is universal, to distinguish between rural and urban water supplies on the basis of differences in the structure, function, size, income and government of human settlements. Therefore public water supplies and water management assume greater importance. However, in a relative context the need for public water supplies appears to be greater and more urgent in urban areas. Water supply undertakings have certain obligations and are generally operated not for profit but are considered satisfactory if they cover the costs. These undertakings as public utilities will not have to maximize the profits per unit investment but will have to minimize per unit cost of supplies. The conventional cost-benefit analysis is rarely a tool that can be applied in practice in water supply and sewerage sector as the benefits from water supplies are intangible and cann't be measured in pecuniary terms.

Hence it is of greater importance to review the efforts made by International agencies, National and State Governments to provide this basic requirement. A great deal of data in a conventional sense, perhaps, is collected by various municipal and State Government agencies with regard to the provision, transmission and final distribution of water for various purposes in towns, urban and metropolitan areas. In some of the states separate Water Supply and Sewerage Boards are established to develop and pan water supply and sanitation. But, little is known about the economics, from planning to the pricing of water supply in other urban areas, more so in the case of small towns.

In the light of this, the present study deals with the economics of urban water supply systems in Karnataka and Maharashtra - A comparative study of Gulbarga and Sholapur Corporations and attempts to assess the utility and usefulness of the drinking water supply systems in these metropolitan corporations and to examine the prospects of improving the services of water supply in urban areas. At the micro level this book describes the procurement, purification and distribution of water supplies, the structure and levels of consumption of water by different categories of users. The costs and revenues from water supply in relation to output and the financial position of the corporations have been examined. The merits and demerits of the existing water rates or the pricing of water have been discussed and the alternatives have been suggested.

A study of this kind is novel in its subject matter and, it is hoped, would serve as an important step towards the more challenging and wider area of study viz, Economics of Urban Water Supply. In all, this book presents the management of municipal water resources in an organised form amenable for economic analysis and succeeds in identifying the areas for further research.

Prof. K. Nageswara Rao

Acknowledgements

At present, there is a loud and wide debate that in the days to come people or countries will have to fight the war because of water. This signifies the importance of water. Further as is well known, only less than 2 per cent of total rain water is available for human use. The floods, run-off of terrain water's, languishing lakes and ponds on the one side, the wells and tube wells facing reduction in ground water day by day has been a cause of great worry to mankind. In urban areas specially those cities which are not located on the bank of rivers face very serious problem of drinking water. The urban governments have to spend substantial amount of money and make proper arrangements for water supply for drinking, industrial and other purposes. The water charges go on increasing as the cities go on expanding and demanding more and more water which require more and more funds. On the other hand the households will not be able to get sufficient quantity of water. Water will not be supplied through out the day, it is supplied some time twice or thrice a week. If there is less rainfall, the reservoirs and sources of water supply cause further problems for urban governments. Therefore, the economics of urban water supply and its deep rooted study needs no further elaboration.

The present book is an outcome of the research work done at the Department of Economics, Gulbarga University, Gulbarga (Karnataka). It covers two highly expanding city corporation areas namely Gulbarga and Solapur. It has been a very vast area for an individual scholar. However, it has been possible to bring it to this due to the support, encouragement and help provided by many with whom I am associated.

I am highly grateful to the officials of Maharashtra Jeevan Prachikaran, Mumbai and Solapur, Karnataka Urban Water Supply and Drainage Board, Bangalore and Gulbarga, Planning Commission, Govt. of India, New Delhi, Gulbarga and Solapur Municipal Corporations who have been kind enough to provide data and information regarding the process of water supply in Karnataka, Maharashtra, Gulbarga and Solapur cities.

I am specially grateful to my parents, in-laws, wife, and son for their encouragement and moral support during the period of research work.

I am also thankful to Amit Garg, Director, Kalpaz Publicationss, New Delhi for their co-operation and help.

Dr. D.M. MADARI

List of Tables

1

Introduction

WATER SUPPLY AND ITS IMPORTANCE

Water is the vital fluid essential for human existence on the globe. Water, though a crucial component for the resource-environmental vector is a luxury for people living in semi-arid, arid, desert, hill, coastal and rocky regions, particularly of the third world. Drinking water is one of the primary human needs, water is required in households for numerous purposes such as, cooking, drinking, bathing, washing utensils and clothes[1]. It is told by experts that only tap water or water drawn from hand pumps and tube wells are safe to drink.

Water, though a gift of nature is becoming scarce, insufficient and unsafe for human consumption. A stage has come when humanity finds it necessary to make collective efforts to conserve the gifts of nature, even for its survival. Underdeveloped countries have a universal need for new and improved water supply systems. Thus, it has become the responsibility of governments in such countries to, collect, process and supply safe drinking water as a public service to the community through budgetary resources[2].

Water supply is a necessary part of the infrastructure required to attain the goals of social and economic development. Water supply is a public good because of its interrelationship with health status[3]. Diseases associated with contaminated water include gastroenteritis (inflammation of the stomach and intestines), a major cause of death in many developing countries due to parasitic disease, dysentery and typhoid.

A partial list of benefits from community water supply projects has been given by John Logan[4] namely, (i) health, (ii) economic development which includes (a) growth of commerce and industry, (b) production efficiency, (c) development of tourism, and (d) increase in food production; (iii) public cleansing, (iv) fire protection (v) savings in cost and time over use of primitive water supply facilities; (vi) encouragement of stable urban development, and (vii) increase in property values.

All these benefits do contribute directly or indirectly to economic development. The dialectic of public water supply engineers and public health officials tends to emphasize this view by ascribing to water supply a crucial role in economic development. Logan states "It can be argued that, if health is fundamental to development, water supply is fundamental to health, and therefore water is key to development". Similarly, Abraham Horowitz[5] has this to say: "If a single programme were chosen which could have the maximum health benefit, which would rapidly stimulate social and economic development and which would materially improve the standard of living of the people, that programme would be water supply with provision for water running into or adjacent to the house".

The water supply system is part of that category of economic activities subsumed under the caption of social infrastructure or social overhead capital which is not directly productive but is the necessary basis for the successful growth of productive activities. A number of questions have been raised about the level of investment necessary in social overhead or infrastructure facilities. Social overhead investment commonly accounts for over half the total of all investment in advance countries. A typical underdeveloped economy has only a small stock of social overhead capital in position and hence requires heavy initial investment for its augmentation to essential minimum levels[6].

In developed economies water supplies showed a permissive sequence-permissive in the sense that the expansions of the systems were made unassociated with evaluation of costs and benefits to be gained from an increased consumption of water.

Historically speaking, water for domestic supply was not treated as an economic commodity. Such an approach has doubtful validity or wisdom in underdeveloped countries with their shortage and high cost of capital[7].

There are no reliable and operational economic techniques ready for evaluating investment in public water supply. Hence, it is necessary to search the economic development literature for methodological guidelines for formulating a suitable evaluation technique applicable to public water supply schemes.

Urban water supply system in developing economies seems to be plagued by two major problems. First, the rapid growth of population in them places a great strain on already installed capacities. When new consumers are connected to an existing system at a pace more rapid than the expansion of its capacity, the service becomes less efficient and affects adversely all consumers, both already existing and the newly added[8]. The World Bank reports that in one city in South Asia, 40 per cent of the water entering an overloaded system was lost in distribution. Service was available only for a few hours a day in each of the neighborhoods it catered to. A second and related problem is that of poor management, a reflection both of under development of technical and managerial skills and of the difficulty or relating costs to benefits. A serious management shortcoming which has clear negative implications for public health is the inadequate attention given to maintenance and repair of existing public water supply systems.

Under conditions of capital shortage, a common problem for all underdeveloped countries, a principal which should plausibly pass muster in respect to rates would be the ability of the community to pay. The amount of revenue collected should be adequate to meet the operating and maintenance costs and to pay off capital debt, including service charges. Water supply, essentially a public utility service, should observe sound financial criteria. The strategy to be followed in the expansion of this utility would be the one which Hirschman[9] has called "development via shortages". In other words, it should be demand growth which should precede supply and demand should have grown to the extent at which a rate sufficient to cover the long run marginal cost of water supply could be chargeable on consumers.

It is possible to envisage two types of public water supply systems[10]: (i) water supply as public service and (ii) water supply as a public utility. Water supply could be considered a public service for social welfare reasons, a service which bestows public health benefits that contribute to economic development. Viewed from this angle, water supply would have to be made free of charge or at highly subsidized rates. All uses of water and all sources of water supply could not for practical economic reasons, be treated on this basis. The most important climate to this consideration would perhaps be the water taps for public use installed on public streets. The public water taps for public use installed on public streets. The public utility approach would suggest that water supplied should be charged at rates covering long run marginal costs. An obvious category for such treatment would be water supplied to households through private connections. An entirely different approach would tell that water supply should be made to those who can afford to pay. The rates fixed according to this criterion would be higher and would cover all costs-operating and maintenance costs and capital costs including service charges. It seems that all the three criteria will have to be simultaneously applied on the basis of distinctions drawn among types of consumers and nature of uses.

Urban water supply has now received attention of the nations of the world particularly since the United Nations has declared 1981-90 as the "International Drinking Water and Sanitation Decade". In connection with the observance of the decade, India has taken up massive investment in public water supply schemes[11].

Urban water supply systems are large in their size, designed for serving larger population through private house service connections and many public hydrants with elaborate the economies of scale available to a larger system, the responsibility of urban water supplies can be entrusted to municipal governments or to an independent agency. We propose to confine ourselves in this study to the analysis of urban water supply undertakings.

STATEMENT OF THE PROBLEM

There are multi-dimensional issues associated with the study of economics of urban water supply. For example, there is an incisive increase in the demand for water in urban areas. Because, the increase in population has put pressure on an increase in demand for drinking water. There is demand for water not only for domestic use but also industrial and commercial uses. Similarly, on the supply side, there are great many problems. Take for example, the natural rivers and tanks may not be close to urban areas and traditional wells do not have enough potential. The distance of water supply becomes expensive and difficult. The economics of urban water supply needs special attention because the individual (household) demand and supply cannot be met easily. The urban water supply will have to be a public utility. This, then open a pandoras box of pricing policy of public utilities. For example, if it is considered as a public utility, the pricing becomes economic, delicate and sensitive issue. Because the full cost pricing becomes inevitable. The households have to pay not only for the current but also the capital costs of water supply programmes. Do they pay for it or increasing water tax and rates on water supply is met with great resistance. It has been found in many cases that the opposition to increase in water tariff rates and taxes has achieved a great measure of success. Besides, the treatment of urban water supply as a part of basic infrastructure opens new issues of supply, maintenance and finance. This also becomes more of a state policy than the policy of urban water supply authorities.

The study of economics of urban water supply is important because of increasing disequilibrium between demand and supply. Because of this, more innovative methods will have to be supplemented for the existing methods of water supply. If we take specially, the occurrence of droughts and scarcity conditions, the supply of drinking water assumes a new dimension. The continuous decrease in surface water and underground water (water table) makes the supply problem all the more difficult. Therefore, the study of the scope for recycling wastewater treatment, reuse and rainwater harvesting are the methods presently under consideration. Similarly, the economics of urban water supply is a welfare-oriented activity. Hence, to maximise welfare of the urban dwellers, not only the quantity of water supply but its quality also becomes an important issue. Because, it is a well-known view that many people in India suffer from not only malnutrition but also from various water borne disease[12]. The water supplied in some places is said to be not worth for drinking. Accordingly for welfare maximisation purpose, attention also has to be focused on the quality of water. The filtration and treatment with chemicals are the immediate steps concerned with water supply authorities. But the treatment of diseases is a supplementing programme. The water supply, sanitation and health care considerations are no less important reasons for the study of economics of urban water supply.

As urban water supply is the most common and widespread activity in the country but there are area specific problems which call for their immediate solution. Therefore, providing an area specific solution to the problem of water supply is essential for the study of economics of urban water supply.

As the economic aspects of urban water supply remains a little researched area in Gulbarga and Solapur cities. The present study endeavors to make a modest contribution to overcome this lacuna. It covers all the major economic aspects relating to urban water supply in Gulbarga and Solapur drought prone areas of Karnataka and Maharashtra states.

JUSTIFICATION OF THE STUDY

There are number of well founded considerations for the special and comparative study of economics of urban water in Gulbarga and Solapur cities mentioned as below:-

1) Both Gulbarga and Solapur are the cities with geographical contagious and sharing the same socio–cultural heritage with near similar composition of population. The households needs, method of water use for various purposes are also similar in the study areas.
2) Geographically, Solapur is bigger than Gulbarga city and has more population and at the same time more advanced, in terms of trade and industry. Whereas the backwardness of Gulbarga and its relation to water supply is a very important comparative aspect for the study.
3) Both the cities have two historical religious tanks in the heart of the cities. Indeed it is surprising that the two religious tanks were at one point of time a source of drinking water

supply. But now the Sharanabasaveshwar tank and Sidheshwar tank are not utilised for drinking water supply. Symbolically, now there are historical religious tanks. Therefore, now it calls for the detailed study about the sources of water supply in these cities.

4) In terms of communication network and administrative status, the two cities are not only at the far end of the borders but also are the divisional head quarters (Solapur is district head quarter) of the two states. Therefore, more number of central, state and local government institutions are located in the two cities. As a supplement to the big size of government, more and more trade and business activities would come up. It is the responsibility of water supply authorities to meet additional but unavoidable demand for water which calls for a special study.

   All passenger trains stop at Gulbarga and Solapur and depend for repair, maintenance and water filling in the running trains. Hence, how to meet this demand is a special problem for Gulbarga and Solapur corporations.

5) Gulbarga and Solapur cities have surprisingly three sources of water supply each. The sources of water supply for Gulbarga city are Bhosga tank, Bennethora river and Bhima river. Solapur city has the water supply from Ekruk tank, Bhima river and Ujjani dam. Both the cities have a common major source of Bhima river. Bhima river is 25 km away from Gulbarga and 30 km away from Solapur.

6) Solapur is one of the industrial cities of the rich state–Maharashtra and Placed on the upper stream of the Bhima river. As a result, it has more advantage for utilising water from Bhima river. Whereas, Gulbarga being located in the downstream could get water only if released from the Ujjani dam (which will be at the mercy of Government of Maharashtra).

7) Both the cities have large number of bore wells. Sizeable parts of the cities and extension areas depend on bore wells for water supply. But there is a difference in the level of ground water tables. In both the cities many bore wells go dry during summer. But this problem is more intensive and

acute in Gulbarga when compared to Solapur city. Solving of the drinking water problem has become a very difficult task for the corporation of Gulbarga city.

8) It is worth to note that the Solapur city stands on better fruiting in terms of resources mobilization required for urban water supply. Whereas in Gulbarga, not only water supply is inadequate but also there is poor resource mobilisation. This becomes basis for our study.

9) In addition to availability and accessibility, utilisation of water is no less important comparative aspect. There are differences in the wastage in daily water supply distribution in Gulbarga and Solapur cities. There is reportedly 20 and 10 percent wastage in daily water distribution in Gulbarga and Solapur cities. The comparative study of wastages is essential in improving the quantity of water supply.

OBJECTIVES

The important objectives of the study are as follows:

1. To examine the state of art with respect to various important issues and aspects of urban water supply.
2. To identify the determinants of the quantity and quality of water supply in urban areas in India.
3. To analyse the inter–state divergences in the efficiency of water supply systems in Karnataka and Maharashtra states.
4. To evaluate the water supply position and distribution in Gulbarga and Solapur cities.
5. To examine the pricing pattern of water supply and its implications in the expansion of investment.
6. To explore the possibility of rain water harvesting and recycling waste water in the study areas in relation to their cost effectiveness.

HYPOTHESES

The study is designed to test the following hypotheses:

1. The present system of water supply has outlived the demand for water in the study areas.
2. The gap between demand and supply of water in Gulbarga and Solapur cities has been widening.

3. The financial performance of water supply accounts of the municipal corporations does not favour the expansion of urban water supply in both the cities.
4. The considerations of health and hygiene in water supply in the study areas have been greatly neglected.
5. There is an urgent need for rain water harvesting and recycling waste water in the study areas.

METHODOLOGY AND DATA SOURCE

In order to examine the economics of urban water supply for comparative purpose, besides the macro approach methodologically micro aspects have been adopted in the study. The study is based on both primary and secondary data fo examine the objectives of the study and to test the hypotheses. In the macro approach various elements of urban water supply in India, Karnataka and Maharashtra has been examined with the help of secondary data. While for evaluating the economics of urban water supply at a household level (micro level), the primary household survey method has been adopted.

The secondary data used in the study would comprise publications such as administrative reports of governments, other autonomous and semi-government agencies functioning in the area of water supply. Besides, books, articles and papers by individual researches have also been collected.

The primary data is collected from households having water connections by using questionnaire. Investigation also made into the use pattern of public taps through which water is distributed. The study covers Gulbarga and Solapur cities of Karnataka and Maharashtra states respectively. The sample of 150 households from each of these cities making a total of 300 households is drawn for the purpose of analysis. The sample covers various localities/ wards of the two cities. The personal interviews have been held with concerned officials of water supply authorities and collected ten years time series data for analysis.

The data have been arranged in tabular form and the statistical tools like percentages and averages have been made use of analysing the collected data.

STUDY PERIOD

The present study entitled "The Economics of Urban Water Supply in Karnataka and Maharastra: A Comparative Study of Gulbarga and Solapur Cities" covers the period from 1991-92 to 2000-01 for collection of secondary data. For collecting the primary data, the researcher undertaken the survey method in the year of 2000-01.

COVERAGE AND SCOPE

The urban water supply as it has assumed greater proportions, also many dimensions. The present study covers the two neighbouring and at the same time expanding cities such as, Gulbarga and Solapur of Karnataka and Maharashtra states. The study examines various important aspects of urban water supply such as, demand, supply, distribution, finance, cost, planning and management, quality of water and health, technology aspects in the study areas. The scope of the study is both micro and macro aspects of urban water supply in Gulbarga and Solapur cities.

CHAPTER SCHEME

In order to study the economics of urban water supply in Karnataka and Maharashtra; the researcher has made a comparative study of Gulbarga and Solapur cities. For convenience the entire study has been presented in eight chapters.

The Chapter - I includes importance of the study, the statement of the problem, justification, objectives, hypotheses, methodology, coverage and scope.

The Chapter-II is devoted to the review of literature and spells out the prominent research gaps. The important areas of review are a) infrastructure, b) demand, supply and distribution of water supply c) cost, finance and investment, d) planning, management and policy, e) household income and water consumption, f) pricing, g) technology, h) water supply and sanitation, i) health and environment etc.

The Chapter-III provides a glimpse of the drinking water aspects and their developments in India. The important aspects covered in this chapter are a) demand supply and distribution, b) cost and finance, c) planning and management, d) pricing, e) water use and consumption, technology, recycling and hygienic aspects.

The Chapter-IV examines the broad aspects of water supply situation and approaches in Karnataka and Maharashtra. The important aspects covered here are a) urban profile, b) accessibility of drinking water, c) funding pattern, d) physical performance and e) comparative assessment.

The Chapter - V examines macro analysis of water supply in Gulbarga and Solapur cities. The essential aspects covered in this chapter are locational history, growth of two cities and implications for drinking water, sources and systems of water supply, financial aspects, and critical look.

A primary survey carried out in Gulbarga and Solapur cities for understanding the economics of urban water supply at a household level has been discussed in Chapter-VI. The important survey aspects covered in the survey chapter are sample size and nature of questionnaire, profile of households, method and manner of water supply, behavioural findings, findings on management and health.

A critical analysis has been undertaken in Chapter-VII, while doing so the important points kept in mind which includes normative approach, household view, scope for remodeling, adoption of new techniques and technology, suggestions, limitations and scope for further study.

The brief summary and conclusions of the study has given in Chapter-VIII.

REFERENCES

1. Nageshwar Rao K., "The Economics of Water Supply", Himalaya Publishing House, New-Delhi, 1994.
2. Jacob John, "Economics of Public Water Supply System: with Special Reference to Kerala", Rawat Publications Jaipur, 1997, p.11.
3. Bhise, D.R., "Water Quality and Public Health", Quarterly Journal of Local Self Government, 1979.
4. John Logan., "The International Municipal Water Supply Programme: A Health and Economic Appraisal", American Journal of Tropical Medicine and Hygiene, Vol.9 No.5, September 1960, pp.469-476.

5. Abraham Horawitz, As quoted by A.Wolman and H.M. Bosch, "U.S Water Supply Lessons Applicable to Developing Countries", Journal of the American Water Works Association, Vol. 55, No.8, August 1963, p.954.
6. Agarwal, R.C., "Urban Water Supply: Issues and Approaches", In N.L.Gupta Ed. "Urban Water Supply", Rawat Publications, Jaipur and New Delhi, 1994.
7. Howe Charles., "Benefit Cost-Analysis for Water System Planning", Water Resources Management, No.2, 1971.
8. Scartato, R.F., "Time-Capacity Expansion of Urban Water Systems", Water Resources Research, Vol. 5, No.1, 1969.
9. Hirschman, A.O., "The Strategy of Economic Development", Yale University Press, New Haven, 1966.
10. Turneavre, F.E. & H.L. Russel, "Public Water Supply", John Willey and Sons, New York, 1960.
11. Warford, J.J., "Water Repayment: The Investment Decision in the Water Supply Industry", Manchester School of Economic and Social Studies, Vol.34, January 1966.
12. Anil Agarwal, James Kiwondo, Gloria Moreno, Jon Tinker., "Water, Sanitation and Health for All?", An Earth Scan Publication, London, 1981.

2

Review of Literature

Introduction

The urban water is essentially an age-old phenomenon; it is an indispensable aspect of urban life. As a result, there is an overwhelming amount of literature. Since the urban water is assuming greater importance and more complexities, one can expect more and more literature will emerge in the due course of time. But, as it is the important aspects of urban waters that would be found in the existing literature are as follows. For example, basic to urban waters, the literary issue is that, should it be treated as an infrastructure? If so, can that be given the status of a public utility? What is the philosophy of urban water are the important considerations. The next issues seriously discussed in the literature are demand, supply and distribution. There is ever increasing demand for growing cities, while the supply has many problems. "Supply creates its own demand" – the Say's Law is one but the efficient distribution is the other important issue. Similarly, the cost, finance and investment with regard to urban water is the modern unforgettable issue which has also found its roots in the literature. Who should bear the cost, how much has to be paid and what should be the nature of investment are the eye openers.

The planning, management and policy with regard to urban water supply have emerged in the recent past. Further, the pricing for urban water has assumed greater dimension. The resource mobilization and meeting the cost of water supply are very serious aspects. In addition to these, the household demand has many determinants. Added to this, the water supply is subject to the considerations relating to health and hygiene. The necessity is mother of invention. Hence, there is a great deal of discussion in the literature relating to the technology of urban water. It includes recycling, waste water treatment, rain water-harvesting etc. The urbanization and industrialization have forced on the thinking that the urban water is subject to various types of pollution. This is the latest aspect, which is the fore-front of the literature. Therefore, the purpose of this chapter is to review the literature and thereby find out the research gaps. For convenience, the chapter is divided into following sections.

The Section–I deals with the urban water as an ingredient of infrastructure. In the same way, demand, supply and distribution aspects have been discussed in **Section-II**. Cost, finance and investment aspects have been explained in **Section-III**. We have discussed the important literature of urban water supply, such as planning, management and policy in **Section-IV**. The **Section-V** has been devoted to discuss household income and water consumption. In addition to this, the pricing of urban water is discussed in **Section-VI**. The literature on water supply and sanitation aspects has been reviewed in **Section-VII**. The dynamic and most important aspect of urban water i.e. technology of water supply, in that recycling of waste water, rain water harvesting, waste water treatment have been discussed in **Section-VIII**. Water and environmental aspects have been taken into consideration in **Section-IX**.

SECTION - I
URBAN WATER : INFRASTRUCTURE STATUS

As a matter of consistency tied to urban life, the water supply began as a public utility. It is possible to envisage two types of public water supply systems:

1) Water supply as a public service, and 2) water supply as a public utility.

Water supply could be considered as a public service for social welfare reasons. A service which bestows public health benefits that contributes to economic development. The public utility approach would suggest that water supplied should be charged at rates covering long run marginal costs. An obvious category for such treatment would be water supplied to households through private connections. The studies by Garifield (1964), Coase R.H. (1970), Dajani, J. (1968) considered water supply as an important public utilities, such as power, communication, water supply, railways and others. For example, Keig N.G. (1970) considered water supply as an important public utility to be undertaken by the government. However if not the state, Badhe G.S. (1968) went further and took full note of the problems water supply and considered that it is essentially the task of municipal authorities. If municipal authorities have any power and role to play in the life of people, they should supply water as a public utility and collect the due charges. No longer the urban water supply being great and vast, American Water Works Association (1966), considered that urban water supply is an industry itself and it is subject to the economic laws. Indeed, unless water supply is done properly the cites have no life at all. When water supply to be considered as an industry, the public utility aspect still continue to be an important issue. Therefore, Bonbright James.C. (1961) went a step ahead and has discussed the principles of public utility pricing. Undoubtedly, there may or may not be acceptable aspect of Bonbright. But no body can deny the fact that, the water is a public utility and pricing is essential. Hirschamn, A.O. (1958) study discussed that, there is no doubt that neglect of public utilities can become a most serious drag on economic progress. However, the crucial issues in this context are that which principle of public utility pricing, (full cost–short run, long run, marginal cost) should be applied has kept the consideration of treating water supply as a public utility in the background. In modern days it is considered as lock stock barrel.

However, the urban water supply has come to be treated as an important ingredient of infrastructure. Accordingly, there is the general literature and some of the literature dealing with urban water supply as part of infrastructure. For example, the study by Kirman R.M. (1989), Anderson and Dannis (1989), Grimes O.F. (1988), and Lovei, Laszlo and Dale Whittington (1991). The aspects like a) finance for urban public infrastructure, (b) urban growth and infrastructural development in India, (c) urban infrastructure: problems and other associated issues, d) urban poor and basic infrastructural services. These studies are broad and vague. Further, from the review, it may be noted that they make only scanty reference to urban water supply.

Whereas, the studies by Agarwal (1997), Amitabh Kundu (1995), World Development Report (1994) and World Bank Research Study (1999) discuss the urban water as part of infrastructure, more specifically; the quality of life in a settlement is very much depends on the availability, accessibility and quality of infrastructure it provides. Adequate drinking water supply is one of the most important basic necessities having a bearing on health and the surroundings of human settlement. Acute scarcity of drinking water and also for agriculture and industry is a common problem in the hills which is due to location of human settlements along the ridge tops of arterial roads and gentle to steep slopes with limited availability of water imposing severe strain for fetching water from sources in valley bottom or from springs along the gently hill slopes as noted by Agarwal (1997).

Amitabh Kundu (1995) stated that availability of water is a basic necessity for the survival of human beings in both rural and urban areas. However, the provision of water for daily use is always not to the time of the demand as has been stated by Kundu. The World Development Report (1994) is of the view that, developing countries invest $200 billion a year in new infrastructure, 4 per cent of their national output and a fifth of their total investment, the result has a dramatic increase in infrastructure services, for transport, power, water and sanitation, telecommunications, and irrigation. During the past fifteen years, the share of households with access to clean water has increased by half, and power production and telephone lines per capita have doubled. Such increases do much to raise productivity and improving standards.

The World Bank study (1999) points out that, the effects of political and contracting institutions on the design and performance of contracts for reform of urban water supply, comparing different forms of private participation and reforms under public ownership. It examines the design and performance of reform (including the contractor selection process, contract design, and regulation frame work, looking at the how different types of reform addressed or failed to address, possible norms, problems of incentives, information asymmetries and credibility.

SECTION - II
DEMAND, SUPPLY AND DISTRIBUTION

Along with the growth and expansion of cities, the problems of demand, supply and distribution have become very important and forced for urgent attention of the authorities. Therefore, there is substantial amount of literature dealing with different dimensions of these aspects. Take for example, with respect to demand there are a number of studies such as Fort, (1958), Gottleb, (1963), Sharp, R.G. (1967), George W. Reid (1969) and Lee-Terence (1969). The study by Fort deals with forecasting the urban residential demand for water and Gottleb points out the urban domestic demands for urban water. Similarly, Sharp and George discuss the estimation of future demands for urban water. The modeling for municipal water demand and empirical aspect of the water demand problems have been discussed by Turhousky Stephen (1969). Besides, the future demand for urban water in India and some selected sectors of the state like Gujarat are noted in the studies by Nambiar (1977) and Panikar (1976).

As against demand, the supply side of urban water has received no less attention in the literature. It may be noted from the review that the important supply side studies are 1) Time capacity expansion of urban water systems, 2) Providing potable water how and why?, 3) Protected water supply, 4) The economies of scale and scope in water supply, and 5) Future water supply n Indian cities have been explained in the studies of Scartato (1969), Desai V.D. (1978), Pradhan, R.C. (1975), Kim H. Youn (1988), Brutan laor (1965).

In the wake of increasing demand and constraints of supply, for the purpose of our review distribution of water is a suitable issue. There are studies exclusively focused on distribution. These include Saha P.K. (1975), Planning inputs for water distribution system design in urban areas, Avadeshkumar (1976), selection of water distribution stations, Krishnamurthy (1976), a biological growths in water supplies some control measures with special reference to distribution systems. Param Shivam.R. (1986), unaccounted for water distribution system, Mukherjee (1989), a linear programming model for optimal water supply. CMDA Report

(1987), on water supply distribution network study, Raman.V. and others (1976) studies on preventive maintenance of water distribution system at Madras.

SECTION- III
COST, FINANCE AND INVESTMENT

The cost of water supply, how to finance and what should be the nature of investment have received sufficient attention in the literature. In so far as the cost is concerned the cost-benefit approach, marginal cost approach, the energy cost and transaction cost of water supply are very important. The following studies of Rogers Sheik (1964), Bradford (1970), Stober W.J. (1967), Turvey Ralph (1976), United Nations (1972), K. Pushpangadan and G. Murugan (1995), Bonem (1968), Saunders, Robert.J et al., (1977), Courtney Riordan (1971), Colby (1990), Steiner (1977), & Brnea Joseph (1965), discuss the important aspects of cost of urban water supply.

In addition to public finance and private finance, the financing urban water supply being very intricate issue has been subject a number of studies. For example, the study by Abhijit Dutta and Cremin (1993), discuss financing water supply and sanitation in urban India. Besides, the review of literature indicates a number of case studies. For example, the study by Bellubi (1979), P.K. Saha (1975) discusses financing and management of water supply and sewerage of Karnataka problems of management and financing of water supply in urban areas of Bihar, Uttar Pradesh and Madhya Pradesh. Vadodara water supply project – financial aspects and self financing urban water supply a model for Asansol Durgapur. Though the urban water supply requires huge amount of investment, how to invest and how best to maximize the benefits and optimize the investment has been elaborated in a number of studies 1) Warford J.J. (1996), water requirement: the investment decision in the water supply industry, 2) Riordan coutney (1971), general multistage marginal cost dynamic programming model for the optimization of a class of investment pricing decisions, Armstrong R.D. and Willis C.E. (1977), simultaneous investment and allocation decisions applied to water planning, Pyatt Edwin and Rogers Peter (1962), on estimating benefit cost rates for water supply investments.

SECTION - IV
PLANNING, MANAGEMENT AND POLICY

The planning for urban water has received good deal of attention in the literature. The important studies on planning are Leonard (1976), social well being of water resources planning, Lahiri .A. (1975), Planning water use for 2000 A.D., Howe Charles (1971), benefit cost analysis for water systems planning, Lauria., D.T. et al., (1977), models for capacity planning of water systems, Jacoby and Loucks, D.P. (1972), combined use of optimization and simulation models in river basin planning, Dal. A.K. (1979) Co-ordination of residual waters resource supply and demand planning model.

As far as management is concerned, the important literature here includes, World Bank (1993), water resources management, Aslam Parvaiz.M. (1986), why a national policy for water management, Postel Sandra (1984), rethinking management in an age of scarcity, Winpenny (1984), managing water as an economic resource etc.

The urban water supply was, is and will be an important policy matter this could be seen from the following literature. Milliman J (1963), policy horizons for future urban water supply, Smith S.C. (1964) & Castle E.N. (1964), economics and public policy in water resources development, Government of India (1987), Hubbel, L.K. (1978), Public policy for water supply, Grima A.P. (1973), Impact of policy variables on residential water demand and related investment requirement. Kuiper Edward (1965) water resources development, engineering, economics and policy, White, Gilbert et al., (1972) Water community wellbeing and public policy, William Sander (1983) Federal water resources policy and decision making, Vohra.B. (1975) a policy for water.

SECTION-V
HOUSEHOLD USE AND CONSUMPTION OF WATER

According to Prof. Lionel Robins, economics is the study of 'Scarcity and Choice'. In his own words: "Economics is the science which studies human behaviour as a relationship between ends and scarce means which have alternative uses". Similarly, the household behaviour in relation to water use and consumption is very important. Besides demand and supply, the household consumption and use, therefore acts as an equilibrating factor. There are number of studies dealing with the household use and consumption of water in the literature of the economics of urban water.

To start with for instance, the studies such as Andrews R.I (1989) and Arceivals S (1979) describe estimation of household consumption of water, per capita water consumption and losses. Whereas the studies made by Reddy V.R. (1993) and Rathore, M.S. (1993), Hanson. R and Hudson. H.E (1956), describe Bias in social consumption, Socio-economic factors affecting domestic water consumption, Trends in residential water uses. There are also according to our review, technical studies in relation to household use and consumption of water. For example, Altaf M. (1994), Mc. Phersal (1976), Schneider M.L. & Whittiach E.E. (1991), discuss a) Household response to inadequate water supply, b) Household water use, c) User specific water demand elasticity's.

In addition to these, there are also studies attempting to explain the important determinants of household water use and consumption. These are Hollamn and others(1973) Rees .A. (1971), Whittington Dale et al., (1990) and W.D.M. Mujwahuzi and others (1989) they try to specify price (further details see below) a) The effect of price and other selected variables on water consumption, b) Factors affecting metered water consumption, c) Estimating willingness to pay, d) Willingness to pay for water in Newala district. No doubt some of these are quantitative as well as qualitative variables. The literature recognizes the fact that willingness to pay is a qualitative variables suffering from various limitations.

SECTION - VI
PRICING POLICY

No doubt water is a natural good, but no longer it is true to say that it is a free good. The increasing demand and difficulties in supply in the wake of fast urbanization, the pricing of urban water has become a crucial factor to recognition with. However, there are as a nip in the bud, there are problems with the vary policies of pricing. As noted above, the first problem to encounter is treating water as a public utility or part of infrastructure. Thus, the policy issues pose serious philosophically multidimensional questions. Further, there are various technical methods of pricing. The question is which one has to be adopted in practice. The pricing is a crucial variable influencing and affecting the household residential demand. There are as per the review a number of studies in the literature bring out the issues relating to urban water pricing. These are noted in the following.

The urban water pricing policy, its importance, difficulties, and philosphic Konen Drums have been discussed in the literature. In this respect, for example, the studies of Murugan .G. (1993), Gopal Kishan (1994), K.S.R.N. Sarma, & Hubbel .L.K. (1978) and Cysi, et al., (1971), discuss the pricing policy aspects such as a) Pricing public utilities : a study of drinking water, b) Pricing of water supply in Indian cities, c) Pricing of urban water supply, d) Public policy issues in the pricing of water in urban areas of less developed countries, e) Some long run effects of water pricing policies respectively.

The next important aspect of urban water pricing policy as noted in the literature relates to the methods of pricing to be adopted. There are various methods both technical and non-technical. The following studies attempts to specify these methods of pricing policy to be adopted for urban water. For example, Riordan Courtney (1973), Hanke. S.H (1973), Meek.R (1963), Bonem .W.(1968), Brown, et al., (1969), Pushpangadhan and Murugan.G.(1991) Feldman S.L. (1975), Steve et al., (1975), Afifi (1969), try to examine a) Multistage marginal cost model of investment pricing decisions, b) An application of marginal cost pricing, c) On the marginal cost pricing, d) A socially optimum pricing policy, e) Pricing with changing welfare criterion, f) On the peak load pricing of urban water supply, g) Water rates: an assessment of current issues, and e) Economic evaluation of water supply pricing in Illinois respectively.

In the ultimate analysis, the pricing policy has great influence and impact on household responses to urban water, these needs to be taken in to account. If we see the literature, for example, the studies of Chicoine et al., (1986), Charles Howe (1967), P.L. Arora (2000), Crew M.A. (1970) and Gallagher .D.R. (1977) contemplate on the issues like a) Evidence on the specification of price in the study of domestic water demand, b) Some behavioural characteristics associated with residential water price changes, c) Impact of price on residential water demand, d) Pricing structure and demand management, e) Some problems of pricing under stochastic supply conditions and f) Influence of metering, pricing policies and incentives on water use efficiency.

SECTION - VII
WATER SUPPLY AND SANITATION

The people in cities needed drinking water. There are number of problems relating to demand, supply and distribution. The cost, finance and investment have also become serious issues. So, the attention has been focused on planning, management and policy aspects. However, the urban water supply has set with the problems of sanitation, sewage, sewerage and drainage. As a result, there are associated problems of health and environment. The big question is how to deal with the problems of sanitation. There are studies devoted for discussing this aspect. The important studies from our review are; a) Chandrashekar. S. (1969) Water supply and sanitation: integrated approach, b) Barnabas, A.P.(1978) Sanitation and drinking water supply, c) Patwardhan S.F.(1971) Setup for sanitation and water supply schemes needs an overhaul, d) Chhabria, B.C., (1970) From Sewage to clean water, e) Kshirasagar (1979) Environmental sanitation and safe drinking water, f) Chaturvedi. A.C. (1972) Water supply and sewerage; social service or development activity, g) Basu, Amit (1982) Some thoughts on water supply, sewerage and waste water systems, h) Raman. A. (1980) Norms and standards for urban water supply and sewerage services, i) Anand Krishna R. (1976), Water supply and sanitation in Bangalore.

Thus, it could be seen from the above that the need for proper approach to sanitation, integrated approach to water supply and sanitation, the required norms, quality of life and side effects of sewerage, sewage and drainage on water supply system have become all the more important keeping the water supply at the centre stage.

SECTION-VIII
TECHNIQUES AND TECHNOLOGY

The growing demand for water has forced the people to think about various techniques and developing technology for bettering the drinking water position. There is literature dealing with these aspects are as follows;

For example, some of the studies deal with the techniques of waste water treatment and recycling the waste water. But others deal with the direct issue of technology in relation to water supply. The studies by Hufsechmidt (1996), Lynn (1973), Muhich (1986), Reid (1966), Trivedi V.N. (1980), Hellman Associates (1969), Egypitan German Seminar (1982), Orlob (1958), Baale Rao,B. (1973), India Development Report 1999-2000 and Wadia, P.S. (1982) discuss a) Simulation techniques for design of water resources systems, b) Stage development of waste water treatment works, c) Capacity expansion of water treatment facilities, d) A mathematical model for predicting water demand, waste water disposal and cost of water and waste water treatment, e) Multi-stage marginal cost model of investment pricing decision, f) Water reuse - a flexible and efficient management alternatives for municipal water supply, g) Forecasting municipal water treatments, h) Water reuse in urban and rural areas, i) Cost of water treatment in California j) Cost estimates for various treatment systems in India and k) Pretreator and ancillary equipment for water treatment plant.

There are also few studies explaining the technology of water supply these are, Hirsheifer (1969), Kalbernatten (1989), Batchelor R.A. (1975), W.H.O. (1984) P.S. Rajawanshy (1996), Nanjunda Swamy (1983), Thomas Robert.H (1981), Unvala S.P. (1981), discuss a) water supply, economics, technology and policy, b) appropriate technology for water supply and sanitation, c) household technology and the domestic demand for water, d) low cast water supply and sanitation technology: pollution and health problems, e) economic and technological issues in water supply, f) appropriate technology for sanitation, g) importance of opportunities in urban water treatment technology and h) aspects of water treatment technology as applied to Indian public water supplies.

It may be noted from the review of literature in this aspect that there is birth of literature on the new technique and technology of urban water supply at macro level and micro level. This relates to the idea of rain water harvesting. For instance, in the recent past urban authorities have been attempting to open their eye on the issue of rain water harvesting. Because, where there is scanty and untimely rainfall, there is great prudence in adopting the new technology of rain water harvesting. Besides at a micro level, for example, households in Manipur and Kerala have developed the technology of roof water harvesting by the households during the rainy season. The households can store roof water underground during the rainy season and make use of it during the other seasons of the year.

SECTION - IX
WATER AND ENVIRONMENT

As noted above, the water supply has been associated or matched with the concern for sanitation, drainage, sewage, and other aspects. However, the pollution, especially in relation to water supply has become a subject of great concern. The review of literature points to the fact that some studies deal with pollution in relation to other aspects of water supply including health. Further, some of them have been exclusively concerned with environment as a influencing factor in the management and supply of drinking water in the urban areas.

For example, the study by Gaur, G. (1980), Munasigne Mohan (1992), Bowonder and Chettri (1987), Kshirasagar (1979), discuss the important environmental issues such as a) Water and environmental health, b) Water supply and environmental management, c) Urban water supply in India : environmental issues and d) Environmental sanitation and safe drinking water.

There is also a concern for environment in relation to water supply in the climatic conditions. This has been discussed by Michael (1980) who says there is water, wastes and health in hot climate. Similarly, the other studies by Kundu.A. (1991), and

W.H.O. (1984), have examined, a) Micro environment in urban planning, (b) Low cost water supply and sanitation technology : Pollution and health problems, respectively.

In addition to the general concern for environment there is also good amount of literature dealing with the environmental aspects of water supply in particular area or cities. The study of Calcutta Metropolitan Development Authority (CMDA-1988) explains environmental issues of water supply in eastern India and Chettri & Bowonder B. (1980) discuss environmental aspects of water supply in South India.

There are some studies relating to environmental aspects of water quality in north India. For example, the study by Sharma (1983) examines water pollution of Yamuna river and its influence on drinking water supply in Agra. In more specific terms the study by Srivastava (1978) exclaims the fact that Delhi water unfit even for gardening.

SECTION - X
CONCLUDING : THE RESEARCH GAPS

As per the review of literature attempted in this chapter, the important research gaps or the important aspects of urban water supply which need their incorporation or inclusion in our empirical study of "The economics of urban water supply in Karnataka and Maharashtra: A comparative study of Gulbarga and Solapur cities" have been noted in the following. Besides, since we have the empirical study the state of art question is kept in mind.

In terms of philosophy and practice, there are divergent views to consider urban water supply as a public utility within or one of the ingredient of urban infrastructure. This has a point blank problem of pricing, supply and maintenance of urban water. Besides, is it possible to have full cost pricing or supply? Urban water as a welfare measure is the fundamental issue.

The foremost aspect of urban water is its demand. The literature indicates that there is an ever increasing demand, and needless there are technical studies dealing with the forecasting and modeling aspects of demand for urban water.

If we look into the supply side, the important issues having an eye on our empirical study are providing potable water how and why, the economies of scale and scope in water supply, future water supply in Indian cities.

Besides, demand and supply the distribution is and has been treated seriously in the literature which need their reference in our present study. For example, planning inputs for water distribution, selection of water distribution stations, a biological growth in water supply, some control measures with special reference to demand systems.

The cost of water supply, how to finance and what should be the nature of investment have received sufficient attention in the literature, what is the situation specially in our study areas with respect to water distribution has to be taken into account. Similarly, as it is a public investment, how to finance (tax / charge collections, borrowing etc.) and how to recover this investment poses serious problem, specially if the water supply is considered either as a public utility or infrastructure. It is of almost interest if the disinvestment policy of the government in the recent past is taken into account. Needless to say, the municipal authorities have been compelled to think of devising the urban water supply plan to be handed over to private enterprises.

The growing urbanisation and increasing demand for water has been accepted as a subject of national planning. Further, the need for alternative sources of water supply, better utilisation of water are also treated very seriously. Under the circumstances, the governments have been forced to think on new, and newer policies as the days go by. What then is the idea of public authorities in our study areas is no less important aspect.

The review of our literature is clear that the pricing of urban water is and will be a million dollar question. The principles of economics will have to be thrown to the winds. Because the water charges, application of meter, cost recovery are the economic aspects. But the social welfare, supply of infrastructure and local political considerations loom large. Therefore, to gain salt from the review of literature, we will have to examine the question of pricing urban water in our study areas. The household use and consumption of water is related to its taste and preference. Besides, the income has its own influence. Hence, what sort of situation prevails in our study area is a gap that to be investigated.

The traditional method of water supply, its quantity and quality often have a crises cross underground relationship. In the modern days the underground electricity supply and telephone lines also get mixed up. How is the problem solved or to be solved in our study areas assumes greater importance. The drainage, sewage and sewerage also have to be looked into systematically.

With an eye to empirical research, there is need to study various techniques and technology of water supply in Gulbarga and Solapur cities. Because our review of literature points to the fact that reuse, recycling, treatment of supplied water, rain water harvesting have and will be serious aspects specially in our study area where there is irregularity, unseasonality and scanty rainfall.

REFERENCES

1. Garifield, "Public Utility Economics", New York, 1964.
2. Coase, R.H., "The Theory of Public Utility Pricing and Its Application", 1967.
3. Dajani, J.S. and Gemmel R.S., "Economic Guidelines for Public Utilities Planing", Urban Planing Journal and Dept Div, Sept 1973.
4. Keig, N.G., "Strategy of Policy: Funed Water Utilities", 1970.
5. Badhe, G.S., "Water Supply as A Public Utility Service in the Bombay City", Quarterly Journal of Local Self Government Institute, 1968.
6. American Water Works Association, "The Water Utility Industry in the United States", Journal of American Water Works Association, Vol.58, 1966.
7. Bonbright James. C., "Principles of Public Utility Pricing", Columbia, University Press, New York, 1961.
8. Hirschmann. A.C., "The Strategy of Economic Development", New Haven, Yale University Press. 1958.
9. Kirman, R.M., "Finance for Urban Public Infrastructure", 1989.
10. Asian Countries "World Development", Vol.17, No.14, April 1989.
11. Grimes, O.F., "Financing Urban Infrastructure in Developing Countries: An International Over View" in Doebele, W.Q. (Ed). Land Readjustment, Lexinston, Books, Lexington, pp.207-212.
12. Lovei, Laszlo and Dale Whittington, "Infrastructure and Urban Development", Discussion Paper 85, World Bank, Washington D.C. Processed, 1991.

13. Agarwal A.K., "Urban Infrastructure: Problems and Other Associated Issues: A study of Mizoram", Southern Economist, 1997.
14. Amitabh Kundu and Irudaya Rajan, "Urban Growth and Infrastructural Development in India", Productivity, Vol.36, No.2 July-Sept.1995.
15. World Development Report 1994, "Urban Infrastructure for Development" World Bank, Washington D.C.
16. World Bank Research Study, "Research Progress Abstracts of Current Studies", 1999.
17. Anderson and Dannis, "Infrastructure Pricing Policies and Public Revenue in African Countries", World Development, Vol.17, No.14, April 1989.
18. Fourt, "Forecasting the Urban Residential Demand for Water", (Unpublished Ph.D. Thesis), University of Chicago, 1958.
19. Gottleb, "Urban Domestic Demand for Water A Kansas Case Study, Land Economics, 39(3) 1963.
20. Sharp.R.G., "Estimation of Future Demands on Water Resources in Britain Journal of the Institution of Water Engineers, May 1967.
21. George W. Reid, "Multi-structural Municipal Water Demand Model", Water Resources Bulletin, Vol.VIII, No.5., 1971 p. 1238.
22. Lee, Terence R., "Residential Water Demand and Economic Development" Research Publication 2, Department of Geography University of Toronto, University of Toronto Press, Toronto, 1969.
23. Turhousky, Stephen., "The Demand for Water – Some Empirical Evidence: Once Consumers Response to a Commonly Uncertain in Supply", Water Resources Research, 1969, p.350.
24. Nambiar R.G., "Future Water Demands: the Impact of Growth on Water Use Pattern in Selected Sectors of Gujarat 1969-2000" ARTHAVIKAS Vol. XIII., No.1, 1977, p.13.
25. Panikar, J.T., "India's Water Needs for the Next 25 Years-Hope or Disaster?" Journal of Science, Today, Vol.II, No.2, 1976.
26. Scartato,R.F., "Time Capacity Expansion of Urban Water Systems", Water Resources Research, Vol.5, No.5 1969.
27. Desai V.D., "Providing Potable Water How and Why"?, 1978.
28. Pradhan, R.C., "Protected Water Supply", 1975.
29. KimYoung H., Clark Robert M., "Economies of Scale and Scope in Water Supply" Regional Science and Urban Economies, 1988, 18(4) November, pp. 479 – 502.

30. Brutan laor, "Future Water Supply in Indian Cities", Vol.3 No. 4 Decea, Geography, 1965.
31. Saha P.K., "Planning Inputs for Water Distribution System Design in Urban Areas", Journal Institute of Public Health Engineering (1) 1975.
32. Avadeshkumar and Sukhatankar G.A., "Selection of Water Distribution Stations", 1976.
33. Krishnamoorthi, K.P., Raman V. and Gadkaria.A., "A Biological Growths in Water Supply: Some Control Measures with Special Reference to Distribution Systems", 1976.
34. Paramshivam .R., "Unaccounted for Water in Distribution System" Paper Presented at The National Seminar on Water and Sewerage Tariffs, Organised by CPHEEO at Srinagar from Sep. 9–11, 1986.
35. Mukherjee et al., "A Linear Programming Mode or Optimal Water Transmission System: A Case Study for Ahmedabad", 1989.
36. CMDA Report, "Water Supply Distribution Network Study", Calcutta, May 1981.
37. Raman.V. et al., "Studies on Preventive Maintenance of Water Distribution System at Madras", Indian Journal of Environmental Health, 18 (4) 1976.
38. Rogers Sheik, "Benefit Cost Analysis for Municipal Water Supply", Land Economics, Vol.40, 1964, pp. 444-449.
39. Brad Ford, D.E., "Benefit Cost Analysis and Demand for Public Goods", KYKLAS, 23 (4) 1970.
40. Stober W.J. and Falk, L.H., "A Benefit Cost Analysis of Local Water Supply, Land Economics, Vol. 43, No.3, 1967, pp., 328-335.
41. Turvey Ralph, "Analysing Marginal Cost of Water Supply", Land Economics, Vol. 52, No.2, 1976, pp. 158-168.
42. United Nations, "Cost Estimates of Water Resources Projects", Water Resources Series, 42, U.N., New York, 1972.
43. Pusphagadan K and Murugan G, "Focus Cost Efficiency of Water Supply in Kerala", Productivity, Vol.36, No.2, July – September 1995, pp-228-235.
44. Bonem, Gilbert. W., "On the Marginal Cost Pricing of Municipal Water", Water Resources Research, Vol.4, No.1, 1968.
45. Saunders, Rober, J. et al., "Alternative Concepts of Marginal Cost for Public Utility Pricing : Problems of Applications in the Water Supply Sector", World Bank Staff Working Paper No. 259, Washington D.C. May 1997.

46. Riordan Courtney, "General Multistage Marginal Cost Dynamic Programming Model for the Optimization of a Class of Investment Pricing Decisions", WRR. Vol.7, No.2, 1971.
47. Colby, Bonnie, "Transaction Costs and Efficiency in Western Water", American Journal of Agricultural Economics, 5 (72) 1988, pp1184-92.
48. Steiner, H. "Regional Water Supply Capacity Expansion with Seasonal Demands and Energy Costs", Unpublished M.S. Thesis, University of California, Los Angels, November 1977.
49. Barnea Joseph, "Water Costs in Developing Countries", Dept. of Interior, Washington, 1965.
50. Abhijit Dutt and Cremlin, "Financing Water Supply and Sanitation in Urban India", IIP Publishing House, New Delhi, 1993.
51. W.H.O, "Self Financing Water Supply and Sanitation Services", 1964.
52. Bellubi, P.R., "Financing and Management of Water Supply and Sewerage" of Karnataka" by KUWS & DB paper presented in Govt. of India and W.H.O. Seminar held at KUWS & DB Bangalore, June 1979.
53. Saha P.K., "Self-Financing Urban Water Supply: A Model for Asansol Durgapur", Economic and Political Weekly, June 26, 1975, pp.1285-88.
54. Warford J.J., " Water Requirement: The Investment Decision in the Water Supply Industry", Manchester School of Economics and Social Studies, Vol.34, January 1996.
55. Riordan, Courtney, "General Multistage Marginal Cost Model for the Optimisation of a Class of Investment Pricing Decisions", Water Resources Research, Vol.7, No.2, June 1971.
56. Armstrong R.D. and Willis C.E., "Simultaneous Investment and Allocation Decisions Applied to Water Planning", Management Science, 23 (10), 1977.
57. Leonard .R. Brown, "Social Well Being of Water Resources Planning", WRB, Vol. XII, No.6, 1976.
58. Lahiri A., "Planning Water Use for 2000 A.D.", Commerce, 131 (3372), 1975.
59. Howe Charles W., "Benefit Cost Analysis for Water Systems Planning", Water Resources Management, No.2, 1971.

60. Lauria D.T. Schelenger, D.L. & Wentworth, R.W. "Model for Capacity Planning of Water Systems, Journal of Environmental Engineering Division, April 1977.
61. Jacoby, H.D. and Loucks, D.P., "Combined Use of Optimization and Simulation Models in River Basin Planning". Water Resources Research, Vol.8, No.6, 1972.
62. Dal .A.K., "Co-ordination of Regional Water Resource Supply and Demand Planning Model", 1979.
63. World Bank. "Water Resources Management", A World Bank Policy Paper, Washington, D.C. 1993.
64. Aslam Parvaiz. M., "Why a National Policy for Water Management, "Yojana May 1-15, 1986.
65. Postel, Sandra, "Water Rethinking Management in an Age of Scarcity", World Watch Paper No.62, World Watch Institute, Washington, D.C. 1984.
66. Winpenny J., "Managing Water as an Economic Resource, London Raut Ledge, 1994.
67. Milliman. J., "Policy Horizons for Future Urban Water Supply", Land Economics, 1963.
68. Smith S.C. and Castle E.N., (ed.), "Economics and Public Policy in Water Resources Development", Ames, 1964.
69. Hubbel L.K., "Public Policy Issues in the Pricing of Water in Urban Areas of Less Developed Countries", NAGARLOK, 10(2), April-June, 1978.
70. Grima A.P., "Impact of Policy Variables on Residential Water Demand and Related Investment Requirement", Water Resources Bulletin, Vol.9, No.4, 1973.
71. Kuiper Edward, "Water Resources Development Engineering, Economics and Policy", 1984.
72. White, Gilbert et al., "Water Community Wellbeing and Public Policy", 1994.
73. William Sander, "Federal Water Resources Policy and Decision Making", American Journal of Economies and Sociology, Vol.42, January 1983.
74. Vohra B., "A Policy for Water", QUEST (94), March-April, 1975.
75. Andrews, R.I., "Estimation of Household Consumption of Water", Water Resources Research, Central University of Hampshire, James Hall, Durham, U.S.A., 1989.

76. Arceivala, S., "Per Capita Water Consumption and Losses", E.E. Dept. Ankere, Turkey, 1879.

77. Reddy V.R. and Rathore M.S., "Bias in Social Consumption Case of Residential Water in Rajashthan", Economic and Political Weekly, August 7-14, 1993.

78. Hanson, R. and Hudson, H.E., "Trends in Residential Water Uses", American Water Works Association Journal, Vol.48, 1956, pp. 1347-1358.

79. Altaf M., "The Economics of Household Response to Inadequate Water Supplies Evidence from Pakistan", Third World Planning Review, 1994.16 (1), pp. 41-53.

80. Mc Pherson and Murray, B., "Household Water Use", American Society of Civil Engineers Monography, January 1976.

81. Schneider, M.L. and Whittalach E.E., "User-specific Water Demand Elasticities", Journal of Water Resources Planning and Management, Vol. 17. No.1, pp. 52-73, 1991.

82. Hollman, Kenneth. W. and Walter J. Primeanx. Jr., "The Effect of Price and Other Selected Variable on Water Consumption", Bureau of Business and Economic Research, University of Mississippi, Oxford, 1973.

83. Rees, J.A., "Factors Affecting Metered Water Consumption", Final Report to the Social Science Research Council, August 1971.

84. Whittington, Dale et al., "Estimating the Willingness to Pay for Water Services in the Developing Countries: A case study of Contingent Valuation Surveys in Southern Haiti", Economic Development and Cultural Change, 38(2), January 1990, pp.293-311.

85. Mujwahuz W.D.M., Mc Mohan G. and Kingakim Choe., "Willingness to Pay for Water in Newala District, Tanzania Strategies for Cost Recovery, Wash Field Reprot, 216, Water and Sanitation for Health Project, Washington D.C. 1989.

86. Murugan G. "Pricing Public Utilities: A study of Drinking Water", M. Phil. Dissertation (JNU), New Delhi, Centre for Development Studies, Kerala, 1993.

87. Gopal Krishan, "Pricing of Water Supply in Indian Cities", Maudhara Academy, Vol.3, No.2, 1984, pp.206-221.

88. Sarma K.S.R.N., "Urban Water Supply Tariffs: Issues in Determination and Administration", A study sponsored by

CPHEEO, Ministry of Urban Development, Government of India, IIPA, (Restricted), pp. 77-61, 1991.

89. Hubbel, L.K., "Public Policy Issues in the Pricing of Water in Urban Areas of Less Developed Countires", NAGARLOK 10(2), April-June, 1978.

90. Cysi, Marshall and Daneil Loucks P.. "Some Long Run Effects of Water Pricing Policies", Water Resources Research, Vol.7, No.6, Dec.1971.

91. Riordan Courtney, " Multistage Marginal Cost Model of Investment Pricing Decisions: Applications to Urban Water Supply Treatment Facilities", Water Resources Research, Vol.7, No.3 June 1971.

92. Hanke S.H., "Some Behavioural Characteristics Associated with Residential Water Price Changes", Water Resources Research, Vol. 9 No.4, 1973.

93. Meek R., "An Application of Marginal Cost of Pricing: The Green Tariff in Theory and Practice (Parts I & II respectively), Journal of Industrial Economics, Vol. X, No.3, 1963.

94. Bonem Gilbert, "On the Marginal Cost Pricing of Municipal Water", Water Resources Research, Vol. 4, No.1, 1968.

95. Brown, Gardner, Jr. and C.B.W. Mc. Guire, "A Socially Optimum Pricing Policy for a Public Water Agency", Water Resources Research, Vol.3. No.1, 1969.

96. Pushpangadhan, Murugan G., "Pricing with Changing Welfare Criterion : An Application of Ramsey Wilson Model to Urban Water Supply", Working Paper, Centre for Development Studies, Kerala.

97. Steve Hanke H., "Water Rates: An Assessment of Current Issues", Journal of American Water Works Association, Vol.67, 1975.

98. Afifi H., and BasseV.L., "Water Pricing Theory and Practice in Illinois University of Illinois Bulletin, Vol.66, No.142, 1969.

99. Chicone, David.L, Ganapathi and Ramamurthy, "Evidence on the Specification of Price in the Study of Domestic Water Demand", Land Economics, Vol.62, No.1, 1986.

100. Charles, Howe W and Linawaver F.P. Jr., "The Impact of Price of Residential Water Demand and Its Relation to Systems Design and Price Structure, WRR, Vol.III, No.1, 1967, p.13.

101. Arora P.L."Pricing Structure and Demand Management of Delhi Water Supply", Quarterly Journal of the AIILSG, Vol.70, No.3, 1999, pp.167-175.

102. Crew. M.A. and G. Robarts, "Some Problems of Pricing Under Stochastic Supply Conditions: The case of Seasonal Pricing for Water Supply", WRR, Vol.6, No.5, 1970.
103. Gallagher, D.R. and Robinson R.W., "Influence of Metering, Pricing Pollicies and Incentives on Water Use Efficiency", Australian Government Publishing Service, Canberra, 1977.
104 Chandrashekar, S. "Water Supply and Sanitation: Integrated Approach", Civic Affairs, 16 (II), June 1969.
105. Barnabas, A.P., "Sanitation and Drinking Water Supply", Indian Institute of Public Administration, New Delhi, 1978.
106. Patwardhan, S.V., "Setup for Sanitation and Water Supply Schemes Needs an Overhaul", Civic Affairs 19(I), August 1971.
107. Chhabria, B.C., "From Sewage to Clean Water", Civic Affairs, October, 1970.
108. Kshirasagar, S.R., "Environmental Sanitation and Safe Drinking Water" Southern Economist, 18 (7) 1 August 1979.
109. Chaturvedi, A.C., "Water Supply and Sewerage Social Service or Development Activity", Civic Affairs, 19 (7) February 1972.
110. Basu, Amit. "Some Thoughts on Water Supply, "Sewerage and Waste Water Systems", Urban India, 2(1) March 1982.
111. Raman, A., "Norms and Standards for Urban water Supply and Sewerage Services, Document", TCPO, Ministry of Works and Housing, New Delhi, November 1980.
112. Anand Krishna, R., "Water Supply and Sanitation in Bangalore", Civic Affairs, 24(5), 1976.
113. Hufsechmidt, M.M. and Fiering M.B., "Simulation Techniques for Design of Water Resources Systems", Harvard University, Cambridge 1966.
114. Lynn W.R., "Stage Development of Waste Water Treatment Works", Journal of American Water Works Association, Vol.65, No.9, 1973.
115. Muhich, A.J., "Capacity Expansion of Water Treatment Facilities", Ph.D. Thesis, Cambridge, 1986.
116. Reid, G.W. and Mulge, "A Mathematical Model for Predicting Water Demand, Waster Water Disposal and Cost of Water and Waste Water Treatment in Developing Countries", Background paper, 1966.
117. Trivedi, V.N., "Water Treatment in Hill Water Supply Schemes", Civic Affairs 27(11) June, 1980.

118. Hellman Associates, "Forecasting Municipal Water Treatments", United States of America, 1969.
119. Egyptian German Seminar, "Water Re-Use in Urban and Rural Areas", Cairo, 1982.
120. Orlob, Gerald, T. and Marvin R. Lindorf, "Cost of Water Treatment in California", Journal of American Water Works Association, Vol.50, 1968.
121. Baalerao, B.B. and Algarsamy, "Cost Estimate for Various Treatment Systems in India", Proceedings of the Symposium on Low Cost Water Treatment, Nagpur, 1973.
122. India Development Report 1999-2000, "Cost of Providing Drinking Water, Sanitation and Waste Water Treatment", p.17.
123. Wadia, P.S., "Pretator and Ancillary Equipment Water Treatment Plant", Civic Affairs, 29(6), January 1992.
124. Hirscheifer, J.J., Dattven and Mrilliman J.W., "Water Supply, Economics Technology and Policy", 4th Edition University of Chicago Press, Chicago 1969.
125. Kalbernatten, John M. and others., "Appropriate Technology for Water Supply and Sanitation – A Summary Economy Options", World Bank Report, 138, P.9. Vol (8), Washington, 1989.
126. Batchelor. R.A., "Household Technology and the Domestic Demand for Water", Land Economics, August 1975.
127. W.H.O., 1984 "Low Cost Water Supply and Sanitation Technology, Pollution and Health Problems", New Delhi, p.108.
128. Rajawanshi P.S., "Economics and Technological Issues in Water Supply", Rawat Publications, Jaipur, 1996.
129. Najunda Swamy P.L., and Ramaswamy M.V., "Appropriate Technology for Sanitation" paper presented in the National Seminar on Operation and Maintenance of Water Supply and Waste Water Systems, KUWS & DB, Bangalore, 25th. February 1983.
130. Thomas Robert. H., "Importance of Opportunities in Urban Water Treatment Technology ", Journal Indian Water Works Assocations, 12 (1) Jan-Mar, 1981.
131. Unvala S.P., "Aspects of Water Treatment Technology as Applied to Indian Public Water Supplies", Civic Affairs, 29(2) September 1981.
132. Gaur. G., "Water and Environment Health", 1980.

133. Munasinge Mohan, "Water Supply and Environment Management Developing World Applications", West View Press, Oxford, 1992.
134. Bowonder and Chettri, "Urban Water Supply in India: Environmental Issues", 1986.
135. Kshirasagar, S.R., "Environmental Sanitation and Safe Drinking Water" Southern Economist 18(7), 1 August 1979.
136. Michael, "Water, Wasters and Health in Hot Climate", 1993.
137. Kundu A., "Micro Environment in Urban Planning: Access of Poor to Water Supply and Sanitation", 1991.
138. W.H.O. "Low – Cost Water Supply and Sanitation Pollution and Health Problems", 1984.
139. CMDA Report, "Environmental Issues of Water Supply in Eastern India", 1988.
140. Chettri and Bowonder B., "Water Supply in Hyderabad: A case study Environmental Management Report", ASCI, Hyderabad, 1980.
141. Sharma "Water Pollution of Yamuna River and Its Influence on Drinking Water Supply in Agra", 1989.
142. Srivastava, "Delhi Water Unfit Even for Gardening", 1978.

3

Urban Water Supply in India

Introduction

Water is the vital resource of life and the root of all creation. It is essential for the health of the people and no single factor other than urban water could improve the wellbeing of the people in any country. It determines the mode and levels of living and all this must have made us to realise that water supply is something more than what we drink. Fresh water is more than an amenity, it is a treasure. By tradition, a tendency had been developed in India and in many developing and under developed countries that drinking water is a gift of nature and hence is free of cost. This notion was however slowly subsided particularly in urban centres consequent to the fast growth of urbanisation and industrialisation. Drinking water became scarce, contaminated and impotable causing health hazards. This lead to the intervention of public authorities inevitable and required to make necessary investments for production and distribution of potable water for consumption in urban areas as a public service. With the advent of scientific and technological innovation, the global phenomenon changed drastically, and enlighten all mankind about the safe drinking water[1] and its consequence on growth and welfare of the societies, irrespective of the countries of different ideologies and economic development. A land mark in this regard was United Nations declaration of the decade 1981-90 as the "International Drinking

Water Supply and Sanitation" during which period, all the member countries pledged to support to the action plan and implement the recommendations[2].

Given the idea above, the purpose of this chapter is to narrate the world wide situation relating to urban water position in different continents and sub-continents, the type of arrangements made and which are the areas calls for urgent attention. Similarly, followed by this the urban water position in India has been tailored to it. In this, the important aspects relating to India are demand, supply and distribution, cost, finance and investment, planning, management and policy, pricing, water supply and sanitation consumption and use, environment and health, techniques and technology etc. have been taken into account.

If urban water supply is treated seriously along with urbanisation in India, what are the programmes, plans and management aspects given important deserve attention. Therefore, for convenience to discuss and analyse urban water situation in India. This chapter has been divided into the following Sections. The global or world wide scenario as a prelude to Indian situation has been noted in **Section (I).** The urban water supply situation in India has been explained in **Section (II)**. The progress, programmes, plans and achievements (needs and deeds) have been analysed in this **Section (III)**.

SECTION-I
WORLD WIDE SCENARIO

History records that community life stabilized and civilization developed along the perennial sources of water. Water has been regarded as one of the most essential requirements of human life and the history of water and sanitation has been therefore as old as the history of mankind. Relies of water works structures have been found in the excavation of pre-historic ruins. Joseph's well at Cairo excavated in solid rock to the depth of 295 ft and with two lifts has been regarded as one of the most famous of ancient wells. Ancient Romans were perhaps the greatest water works builders of their times. Water supply for the city of Rome through several aqueducts is accepted as a master piece in the conception of water supply and the construction of net work for supply. Assyrian rulers had constructed large artificial lakes for the purpose of water supply.[3]

The fast growth of urbanization assumed a global phenomenon of which developing and underdeveloped countries have become major victims of drinking water supply and sanitation. The problem was identified in late fifties by the world organizations such as United Nations (U.N) and its subsidiary bodies.

Consequently, as early as 1962, World Health Organization (WHO) conducted a first global survey on urban water supply conditions and certain global standards and targets were set. In 1972, the U.N. conference on environment held on Stockholm gave international expression to the problem pertaining to the provision of safe drinking water and adequate sanitation particularly in developing countries. Subsequently, a second global survey was made in 1975 on community water supply and excreta disposal conditions in both urban and rural areas whose results led to the 25th World Health Assembly endorsing the revised targets. In 1976, the U.N conference on Human Settlements (HABITAT) held in Vancoover-Canada reiterated the gravity of the situation and recommended that safe water supply and hygienic waste disposal should receive priority from governments and international agencies with a view to achieve the targets for serving all the population at least by 1990. These recommendations of the HABITAT conference was adopted in the U.N. water conference at Mar-det Plata Argentina in March 1977 and to achieve the targets, 1981-90 was declared as the "International Drinking Water Supply and Sanitation Decade"[4]. The regional targets of urban water supply for the South-East Asian Region by 1980 were; coverage of 90 per cent of urban population of which 60 per cent through house connections and 30 per cent through public stand posts.[5]

The short supply of urban drinking water in third world cities is by and large a function of the increasing population growth, the widening gap in the distribution of urban income and an increasing reliance on the public sector to meet the rising demands on urban infrastructure. Some of the urban infrastructure such as drinking water, electricity and sanitation are marginally available in both rural and urban areas in the Third World. We occasionally come across remarks that in 1980, over half of the people of the Third World had no safe drinking water, three quarters had no sanitation at all not even single bucket of water for latrine. More than 100 million of third world people are drinking dirty water today than in 1975, and more than 400 million in 1975 have no sanitation. Diarrhea often caused by impotable water kills every year 25 million people in the Third World, and 16,000 children die every day[6].

According to the geographic view, the earth with its egg shape is surrounded by ¾ of water. But this is the oceanic or sea water. Nearly 97 per cent of all water is in oceans and about 2 per cent is covered under ice, while only one per cent is available for our direct use[7]. However, as our concerns for drinking water, the total water resources of the world, the global scarcity of drinking water, population without access to safe water in world and regions, population without access to safe water in developing countries are the important concerns in the context of world wide urban water scenario and situation existing in the days of globalisation have been discussed in the following.

Table-3.1
The World's Water Resources

Form of occurrence	*Volume in 1000 cubic kms*	*Percentage of total volume*
Oceans	1,370,323	94.20
Ground Water	60,000	4.12
Glaciers	24,000	1.65
Lakes	230	0.02
Soil Moisture	83	0.01
Atmospheric	14	Neg.
Pressure	01	Neg.
Rivers		
Total	1,454,651	100.00

Source: Nageshwar Rao, K., "Economics of Water Supply", Himalaya Publishing House, New Delhi, 1994, p.3.

Note: Neg- Negligible.

It may be observed from the following Table 3.1 that there are oceans, ground water, glaciers, lakes, soil moisture, atmospheric pressure, rivers are the important sources.

As noted above, so far mankind has not developed technology to convert ocean water for drinking purpose. If at all it is used to some extent for industrial or non-domestic purposes. The glaciers and soil moisture do not help much in the process of supplying drinking water. Therefore, of the total world water resources only 4.12 per cent is only for the drinking water. Further, even in the ground water, a sizeable percentage of it may not be of use for drinking purpose, because it contains many minerals and solvents.

In addition to the world wide water resources/sources, it may be seen from the Table 3.2 that Europe is the continent which has the great scarcity of water followed by Africa with their 8 and 11 per cent respectively.[8]

Table-3.2
Global Scarcity of Water

Region	*Percentage of World's Population*	*Percentage of World's Available Water*
Asia	60	36
South America	06	26
Central & North America	08	15
Europe	13	08
Africa	13	11

Source: Clarin News Paper, 11th January, 2000, United Nations, Wire Translation.

The Asia although with great amount of population also has 36 per cent of drinking water and is placed comfortably.

In the discussion of world wide drinking water scenario, it may be observed from the Table 3.3 that the regions differ in their population access to safe drinking water. As is expected, the Arabians[9] and South Asian countries have 82% of population access to safe drinking water.

Table-3.3

Percentage of Population without Access to Safe Drinking Water in the World and Its Regions during 1990-1997

The World and Its Regions	*Percentage of Population Without Access to Safe Drinking Water*
All Developing Countries	28
Least Developed Countries	41
Sub-Saharan Africa	50
Arab States	18
East Asia	32
South-East Asia and the Pacific	31
South Asia	18
Latin America and the Caribbean	22
Eastern Europe and the CIS	--
Industrial Countries	--
World	

Source: Human Development Report, 1999, p.78.

Table-3.4

Percentage of Population without Access to Safe Drinking Water in Selected Developing Countries During 1990-1997

Sl. No	*Country*	*Percentage of Population without access to safe drinking water*
1	Singapore	00
2	Hon Kong, China (SAR)	--
3	Korea, Rep of	07
4	Chile	09
5	Kuwait	--
6	Argentina	29
7	Bahrain	06
8	united Arab Emirates	03
9	Mexico	15
10	Malasia	22
11	Cuba	07

(Contd.)

(Contd. Table 3.4)

Sl. No	*Country*	*Percentage of population without access to safe drinking water*
12	Mauritises	02
13	Thailand	19
14	Philippines	16
15	Saudi Arabia	05
16	Sri Lanka	43
17	Maldives	40
18	Jordan	02
19	Iran, Islamic Rep of	10
20	China	33
21	South Africa	13
22	Indonesia	25
23	Viet Nam	57
24	Egypt	13
25	Iraq	19
26	Myanmar	40
27	Zimbabwe	21
28	India	19
29	Pakistan	21
30	Nepal	29
31	Bhutan	42
32	Nigeria	51
33	Bangaladesh	05

Source: Ibid., p.25

It is observed from the Table 3.3 that in all the developing countries having population without access to safe water during the period 1990-97 is 28 per cent[10]. It has been realized by the governments in the developing countries that inadequate supply of drinking water is one of the limiting factors for accelerated development.

For a simple world wide view of drinking water, an understanding of the position in developing countries will not be out of context. The facts relating to developing countries have been given in the Table 3.4.

In the selected 33 developing countries[11] (for which we have the data), the Vietnam comes on the top with 57 per cent of the population having no access to safe drinking water. The Nigeria with its 51 per cent of population having no access to safe drinking water comes as the second country in terms of drinking water supply (see Table 3.4).

According to Development and Environment Survey (1998) 'The next world war may be over water' about 40 countries will not have adequate water supplies in the near future'. The drought affected area in Africa is spreading at a rate of 2.3 million sq. miles a year'. 'The world wide irrigation boom is over' etc. may reflect the seriousness of the scarcity of water. The inadequacy of existing water supplies and the inequalities in use therein are indicated by these facts about 40,000 children die every day due to side-effects of the water crisis. It may be noted that fewer people have access to clean and adequate water in the 1990's than in the 1980; about 3.4 billion of the world's 5.3 billion population subsist on a per capita use of only 50 liters per day in other words, one seventh the amount used by an average American. Lastly, while in the recent past the situation predicted for India, China, West Asian Nations are enough to consider as the point of summing up. For example, "More than half of China's 600 cities suffer from water-shortages. In 1990, 20 countries suffered from chronic water scarcities with less than 1,000 cubic meters of water per capita per year and this number is expected to rise to 34 by 2025[12].

SECTION-II
SITUATIONAL ASPECTS IN INDIA

The important aspects of urban water supply in India as viewed in this section. India is surrounded by water on three sides with the 7,200 km-long coast line, an immense sea potential spreads out across 2.2 million sq. km. Yet, India is not a water abundant country, while only 3.5% of fresh water is available for use, the people tend to take it as if it is an unending source.[13]

It is said that the future wars would be fought for water, which is the life line of humanity. Water plays a crucial role in any country's welfare as well as economic development. India has indeed achieved significant strides in the water supply sector. However, in 1991 only about 82% of the urban households covering 85% of the urban population had access to safe drinking water. Against the national average target of supply of 140 liters per capita per day (LPCD) of water, the per capita consumption is too low and ranges from 165 LPCD in few larger towns to about 50 LPCD in most of the smaller towns. In fact, the availability in the urban slums is around 27 LPCD. The situation is critical in many large cities. For instance, in Chennai, the fourth largest city of the country, only 2 million of the 3.7 million residential consumers within the service area of the Water Supply and Sewerage Board are estimated to be connected to the system. On an average, they receive a supply of about 36 LPCD while the rest within the service area use the public taps which serve about 240 persons per tap. In respect of Kolkata too some three million are estimated to be living in basis and refugee settlements and about 2.5 million in urban blights which lack potable water. The consumption is low in many of India's over 3,700 urban areas. Urban water services are often characterized by impurities, distribution losses in many cases beyond 40 per cent[14] wasteful use and supply being un-metered in many parts.

Augmentation of water supply and mitigation of the above problems will require additional investment in the sector. An important dimensional issue particularly, in the recent past in India is that, India spends only 1.3 per cent of GDP on civic amenities, while America spends 4.6 per cent of Gross Domestic Product (GDP) on civic amenities. Should water supply be treated as a public utility? which is the responsibility of municipal governments or to be considered as a part of urban infrastructure, which is the national issue continues in India. If urban infrastructure is held high, the Rakesh Mohan Committee calculated Rs. 28000 crores in which the country spent only Rs. 2000 crores.[15]

Therefore, the important situational aspects relating to urban water in India are 1) demand, supply and distribution, 2) cost and finance, 3) planning and management, 4) pricing, 5) environment and health and 6) techniques and technology have been discussed in the following.

1. Demand, Supply and Distribution

Supply of safe drinking water in urban areas is one of the most stringent problems among the social consumption items, hence needs top priority.[16] Whereas, there is high elastic demand for water, specially in the context of growing cities. One side what alternative sources have to be tapped and how best the existing quantities may be supplied efficiently is a brain boggling issue for authorities. On the other hand, the urban people with increasing number, there is greater and greater demand for water for different uses. From the estimates of assessment and availability of water for diverse uses in the country, it is seen that the demand for fresh water for domestic, industrial and other uses will increase from 44 km^3 in 1990 to 77 km^3 in 2000 and 93 km^3 by 2050. If the population increases at medium variant of United Nations assessment is 100-200 LPCD norm, with other demands also increasing upward and limited production of usable water resource particularly when these are not distributed evenly in space and time, these resources will have to be treated as national asset and will have to be managed sustainable[17]. For example, the first is the demand for drinking water. There is also demand for different domestic and household uses. These include washing clothes, cleaning the floor, construction of house and watering the plants. Further, the equilibrium between demand and supply is very difficult to bring about. In addition to this, the further quagmire is about demand and supply in rural versus urban areas. Needless to say India has faced and is facing the problem of equilibrium between demand and supply.

There is no least exaggeration if one says, water is what water does.[18] Because similar to money, the water needs and its supply stretch to number of areas with differing dimensions. Who should pay, how much one should pay, who should collect and how much should be collected have become sundry problems regarding demand and supply of urban water in India. The demand and supply of water as it is prevailing in India has been given in Table 3.5[19].

It is seen from the Table 3.5 that the water is used in different quantities in different sectors. The important sectors are domestic, irrigation, energy and Industry. If we look into the figures for 1990, for example, agriculture requires the highest quantum of water followed by the domestic demand. Whereas, it is the sector in which there is a great short fall in supply, the shortfall is as

Table-3.5

Water Demand and Supply in Different Sectors During 1990 & 2000

Sectors	*Water Demand*				*Water Supply*			
	1990		*2000*		*1990*		*2000*	
	Cu Km	*%*	*Cu Km*	*%*	*Cu Km*	*%*	*Cu Km*	*%*
Domestic	25	4.5	128	9.6	13	3.9	80a	10.7
Irrigation	460	84.0	908	68.2	210	64.0	507b	68.4
Energy	19	3.5	208	15.6	10	3.0	115c	15.5
Industrial use	15	2.5	46	3.4	11	3.3	25d	3.3
Others	33	6.0	41	8.0	19	5.7	16	2.1
Total	552	100.0	1331	100.0	328	100.0	741	100.0

Source: Cited from Central Water Commission Reports 1990 & 2000, New Delhi.

Note: a) This does not include canal supply of drinking water, such as Narmada, Kaveri and others.

b) This does not include new dams and check dams and other sources which have not been commissioned.

c) The new projects with different new megawatt capacities planned by different states are not included.

d) The water treatment, recycling, purification, treatment of sea water and its quantity has not been taken into account. Further, the attempts of individual industrial house and its capacity are also excluded for want of informations.

much as 20 per cent and in 2000-01, it may be seen that the difference between demand and supply has increased. In other words, the supply situation is worsened. Furthermore, the sectoral findings are a) the demand for energy has increased, b) there is because of concentrated efforts, there is an improvement in domestic supply, c) there is an increase in demand for water in industrial use. It may be kept in mind that the railways, construction industry, and others have made their own effort. As a result the difference between domestic demand and supply is not reflected properly. The potable water, the borewells, lake water's and self help group efforts in increasing supply cannot be measured seriously.

Indeed, the domestic demand in the recent past is far greater than supply because more water is used by the energy sector. Energy is needed for urban water supply and domestic household water lifting for use or consumption. But it is of any body's surprise that there are no uniform rainfall in the country as a whole, as against demand and supply discussed above, the supply system is also important. It would help to understand the existing gap very systematically.[20]

Table-3.6
Source wise Access to Drinking Water by Urban Households in India

(%)

Round/Year	*Tap*	*Tube well and Hand Pump*	*Pucca well*	*Others*
28th Round (1973-74)	66.97	23.10	--	9.93
38th Round (1973-74)	70.50	15.30	--	14.20
42nd Round (1986-87)	73.57	13.98	9.38	0.60
Difference	6.6	9.2	9.38	8.0

Source: Sarvekshana, CSO, Vol. XII, No.2, Issue No.37, October 1988, Vol. XII, No.4, Issue No.43, April-June 1990.

Note: Others include the natural sources like canal, spring etc.

The important systems are taps, tube wells, bores, canals etc. The systems of supply and changes could be found in Table 3.6.

This is compliment to Table 3.7. It could be seen from table that, percentage of urban households having access to drinking water by tap source is increased from 66.97 to 73.57 percent between 1973-74 and 1986-87. Whereas by tube well and Hand pumps, the percentage of urban households having access to drinking water is decreased to 23.10 to 13.98 per cent between 1973-74 and 1986-87. Other sources also not covered more households between 1973 and 1986-87 that means decline by 13 per cent of households having access to drinking water by other sources.

Table-3.7
Population Not Served by Tap / Wells in Different Size Class of Towns In India During 1994

Size Class	*Percentage of Population Not Served by*	
	Tap	*Well*
Class-I	18.1	5.5.
Class-II	19.3	8.3
Class-III and below	29.8	14.1
All Towns	38.1	17.1

Source: Amitabh Kundu, "In the Name of Urban Poor Stage", New Delhi, 1994, p. 200.

It may be observed from the Table 3.7 that, there are also significant disparities between the size of towns and water supply in class-I and class-II towns have a much higher percentage of people served by a tap or well as compared to small towns. The important emerging points from the table are, a) in class I towns 18.1 per cent of people not served by tap supply and 5.5 per cent by well supply. b) Whereas in class II towns, the people not served by tap as well as well supply is 19.3 per cent and 8.3 per cent c) the class II and below towns are not served by tap and well supply by 29.8 per cent and 14.1 per cent, d) all the towns in India not served by tap supply and well supply of water by nearly 38 and 17 per cent respectively.

A considerable portion of the treated water is lost through leakages in the transmission and distribution system. Reduction in losses due to leakages through leak detection equipment has been found to be one of the most vital measures to minimise service cost and maximize service, but this aspect is still largely ignored. While there is considerable awareness about the need to reduce the leakages, there are no reliable estimates of the actual quantities lost. This problem has a direct linkage to the revenue generation and sustainability of the entire water supply system. Further, the awareness about use of water and conservation methods / equipments to ensure efficient use of water is generally services such as railways etc. Detailed investigations carried out by "National Environmental Engineering Research Institute" (NEERI) have revealed that about 17 to 44 per cent of the total flow in the distribution system is lost as unaccounted through leakages in main communication and service pipes and leaking valves. The major portion of leakage (about 82 per cent) occurs in the house service connection through service pipes and taps. The remaining 18 per cent are due to leakages in pipelines. Water supply is un-metered in major parts of urban areas and also a significant proportion is supplied, particularly in low-income areas through stand posts resulting in unaccountable losses.[19]

2. Cost and Finance

The cost and finance plays a very important role in the context of urban water supply. Who should bear the cost? and how the water supply schemes have to be financed? is one question, while its treatment of urban water as public utility or as a part of infrastructure is another problem.

Good operation and maintenance (O&M) can enhance the quality of service and extend the useful living facilities. This affects the financial performance of water utilities, and hence the resources available for investment in new services. To minimize the costs of operating a water supply system, competent management of capital and current expenditures, assets and liabilities are just as important as preventing losses of water from the system. Adequate cost recovery ensures that enough funds are available to pay for operation, maintenance, and debt service. The cost imposed on economies by poorly-run and maintained water supply and sanitation systems is not well documented but is clearly very large.

There is an ample evidence of poor quality water, unnecessarily sporadic service, large volume of unaccounted water, and inadequate collection, treatment, and disposal of effluent.

Financing of drinking water supply programme is crucial issue in urban areas in view of the massive investment required. These are beyond the scope of plan, but nevertheless, these would have to come into the sector to meet the goals of the plan and maintain the sustainability of the human settlements. Innovative financial strategies, including alternative leasing instruments and fiscal intervention are called for. Plan funds would be used not only for direct intervention but also as a leverage instrument, a strategy already introduced during the Eighth Plan in case of some urban infrastructure projects. This strategy has to be increasingly adopted to activate and sustain the funds flow from outside the Government Sector. Equally important is recovery of full cost. New strategies would be gradually developed, in terms of recovery of O & M cost in the first instance and total capital cost later, through subsidy in pricing will continue, more sparingly than in the past.

Maintenance of water supply, drainage and sewerage lines is of utmost importance because it helps in substantial service augmentation without additional investment on the facilities. It is estimated that about 30 per cent of water leaks through the distribution system. Where storm water and sewage disposal have common pipes, very often they get clogged due to sedimentation. Periodic cleaning of sewage mains would also increase their transportation capacity without additional investment on new lines.

The existing methods of plan allocation of soft loans for financing urban water supply and sanitation projects should yield place to a more realistic assessment of the needs for capital grants and market loans to finance capital projects. Capital grants could be wholly plan allocated, while loans could be made available through market and institutional borrowings, with required conditionalities.

In view of the massive investment required, it is obviously not possible for either the State Governments or the Central Government to go forward with this magnitude of funds. Institutional sources/externally aided projects, private sources and community sources would all have to come forward in case we have to provide every body with safe potable water within the stipulated time frame. The objective of 100% population coverage in urban area with safe drinking water supply could be achieved with an investment of about Rs. 20750 crores[20].

Given this financial performance of urban water supply schemes, the responsibilities of Local Government Undertakings (LGUs) and share of their spending for urban services are given in Table 3.8

Table-3.8
Responsibilities of LGUs and Share of LGU spending in India

Urban Services	*Type of Responsibility / Spending*
Water Supply	J
Slum upgrading	J
Health and Welfare Services	J
Low-income housing	P
Ratio of local government share to national Government share in total spending on urban Infrastructure	0.04[e]

Source: Computed from Elahi (1996), Mehta (1996), MohdNoh,(1996), Ninb (1996), Zhongping(1996), Pardo(1996).

Note: P- LGU is primarily responsible for providing service.
J- Service is jointly provided by LGU and state/central government
e- Municipal Government funds/state and central budget allocations.

Table-3.8 points out the prevailing situation relating to the responsibilities of municipal authorities. It is clear that drainage, traffic management, low income housing, are the areas complete in which municipal authorities alone are responsible. But, when we come to the water supply, the cost has to be meet jointly. The jointly includes the share of state and central government, but unfortunately the 70 per cent of the cost has to be borne by municipal governments which derive their revenues from house tax and user charges. As regard to the urban water, they are collecting only 8 per cent of total revenue from water supply. Therefore, it is evident that the hands of municipal authorities are tied up either to take new scheme or to maintain the existing level of water supply schemes.

3. Planning and Management

Most efforts at urban planning in the post-Independence period in India have been coloured by notions of ideal standards triggered by the visions of a newly emergent nation over time. However, these utopian exercises have been adopted albeit very gradually to the ground realities of fiscal and institutional constraints. However, incorporation of these constraints into the planning and management processes has not been very systematic. One of the most important sectors in this regard is urban infrastructure services notably water supply and sewerage. These become very important, particularly in the metropolitan context of high densities. Frequent epidemics and persistent health problems in urban areas are largely a result of the failure of urban governments in providing adequately these services.

While lacunae in urban services are widespread, equally important are the distributional issues. For example, while a metropolitan area boasts of very high per capita water supply almost a third of the population does not have access to adequate quantity and quality of water and a quarter of the population in certain areas does not have access to even a public toilet. Overflowing septic tanks and cesspools of untreated sewage are common sights even in upper income localities in the urban peripheries. These suggests that serious lapses in our planning and management.

The system of water distribution should avoid water disputes. All beneficiaries may get sufficient water. Water would be used economically. It will avoid unauthorised use of water. Govt. may get more revenue. The whole area of each urban city would be benefited by perlocation water, wells would work efficiently.[22]

The demand for water is increasing from various sectors of the economy. But our water resources are limited, none can increase them. Hence, it become a headache for water authorities particularly during hot weather. The demand for water for drinking and cleaning purposes is increasing rapidly in India. In recent years not only towns but villages are also facing the problem of shortage of drinking water in the hot weather. Therefore, they demand to release water from reservoirs in the river beds. The loses which the country is bearing on account of the poor water management are of staggering dimensions and contribute one of the important threats to our economic progress. The major problems of water management in urban areas and the possible strategies of over come the limitations are very important.

The losses which the country is bearing on account of poor water management are of staggering dimensions and contribute one of the important threats to our economic progress. The major problems of water management in urban areas and the possible strategies of overcoming the limitations are very important. According to one study, India has about 67 million hectare metres of surface water and 36.5 million hectare metres of ground water. There is natural and man made imbalances in these two water resources which call for a national policy for their exploitation.[23] Water resources management is so important matter that is cannot be left to the states alone in view of the inter state squabbles over use of surface water and their failure to meet the challenge.

As cities are increasing and existing cities are growing, providing safe drinking water to the slum areas is becoming very serious. In the process of planning and management of urban water supply in cooperating the slum dwellers is creating an overall problem of water supply. It may be noted in passing that an American Ambassador[24] to India making a grave comment pointed out that water in India is not drinkable. There is an urgent need for planning and management.

The examples of wastage or inefficient utilization of water resources are still more. In sharp contract to our fears of an approaching water crisis and food and agriculture report. Food and Agricultural Organisation (FAO) says that our land and water resources are capable of sustaining a population of 2.6 billion people provided they are properly managed. Government will therefore do well to lay more stress on management of this vital resources. Though with the existing gloomy picture, the governments are preparing long term plans and designing new methods of managing efficiently in the task of providing safe drinking water. This may be considered as a silver living in the field of planning and management of urban water supply.

4. Pricing

The pricing policies should be on the principle of full cost recovery. The pricing of drinking water in urban areas was, is and will be a serious problem in India. The root cause is its treatment as a public utility or part of infrastructure. The water supply for irrigation with the help of big dams with heavy investment (borrowed money) has been very different for the state governments to collect irrigation charges or taxes may be because they are not supplied properly or not supplied timely. Besides, there is a nexus between the farmers groups and politicians. This is also true in the case of urban water. The people resent the high water rates at large. The municipal authorities with political pressure also face the problems of collecting revenue. Therefore, what rate to be fixed, how much to be collected have become clearly the political issue. There is no regularity in supply, fixing meters and huge amount of arrears and backlogs provide a common picture with respect to pricing urban water in India.

Water tariff is a hotly debated topic in India today and one that needs repeated exposure until common sense prevails. A high-profile expose in June 2000-2001 witnessed a senior bureaucrat saying that the issue of water tariffs in India is a scandal. A respected Indian businessman responded from the floor that anyone advocating charging for water would come back in the next life as a "lizard in the desert" it is necessary to depolarize this water tariff issue.[25]

There is a consistency in the view point of consumers agreeing to pay more if there were improved service. Households were generally willing to pay up to 3.4 times more than the existing tariff. This was the cost they were necessarily incurring to augment supplied provided by the municipality Housing and Urban Development Corporation (HUDCO). What was perceived as true three years ago is even more so today. It is indefensible for state governments to perpetuate the myth that their voters are unwilling to pay more for an improved water service. The truth is that state governments appear unwilling to acknowledge that they provide poor municipal water service. These are unwilling to charge. Their actions result in a lack of funding and therefore in deteriorating municipal water service.

Some state governments promote free water, others a nearly-free service. There can be no support for the nearly-free service, because state governments should be persuaded by their political ideology to either provide free service or to recover the full cost direct from the consumer. The level of that service should be the same for both dogmas: to abandon intermittent supply (which is the cause of much waterborne disease distributed by the municipal authorities) and provide wholesome drinking water which is mandatory in the developed world. Free supplies lead to customer abuse. Taps are left on routinely all over India with the result that water that has cost the government dearly in abstraction, treatment, pumping and conveyance is allowed to spill over once the container is full. The customer is uneducated for the value of water, watches on without concern that fellow customers are being deprived from utilizing this precious commodity. The point is where there is no meter, no valves, and often no bill there is little incentive to conserve water, this is not peculiar to India.

The values associated with a water tariff should follow the same principles as for the provision of any other service. The Indian water tariff structures are very complicated and need to be greatly simplified. Tariffs should be defined to promote both economic efficiency and financial soundness of the water utility and should eventually cover all costs commented with operation and maintenance, debt servicing, the depreciation of existing assets and expansion of the service, the question of equity is no less important. Tariffs should not be discriminatory and should send a clear signal to consumers that reducing their consumption will reduce their bill.

Under the prevailing situation, circumstances and absence of a detailed study relating to water rates, tariffs and collections by authorities, the existing rates in few cities, followed by the rates applied for different uses of water about which the scarcity intimation, which is available has been noted in the following.

Table-3.9
Existing Tariffs in India Cost Recovery or Municipal Tax

Name of the City	*Tariffs*
Delhi	Rs. 1-5 per m^3
Mumbai	Rs. 2-7 per m^3
Thane	Rs. 1-10 per m^3
Bangalore	Rs. 3-33 per m^3
Mysore	Rs. 1-6 per m^3
Chennai	Rs. 2-25 per m^3

Source: Jessoprice. "The Water Tariff Debate", Indian Infrastructure, Vol.2, No.1 1st July 2000, p.47

The Information is not available for important cities and megacities, such as Kolkata, Pune, Hubli, Dharwad, Ahmedabad, Bhuvaneshwar, Bhopal, Gauhati, Alahabad, Lucknow to mention a few, these cities have different sources and quantity of water supply, but the information is available only for Delhi, Mumbai, Thane, Bangalore, Mysore and Chennai. However, the Table 3.9 shows clearly that tariff rate is highest in Bangalore, and lowest in Delhi, i.e. Rs. 3-33, per m^3 and Rs. 1-5 per m^3 respectively. An important point that could be reasoned is that Bangalore city does not have any great source of water supply in its vicinity. At the same time, the Bangalore and Bangalorians are considered as people of great awareness, the Cauvery water supply scheme may alter this situation. As regard to Delhi, the Jamuna river on the bank of which it is located, the supply cost is very low. The rates of Mumbai are also low just for the simple reason that Vihar lake is 20 km from Mumbai and is under the control and management of relatively efficient Mumbai Municipal Corporation. A noteworthy conclusion that could be drawn from the table is that, there are great differences and range of differences is also great among different cities in India an average tariff rate works out to Rs. 6 to 8 for 1,000 liters depending upon the location of source and lift involved. The tariff rate and its range in the city Mysore need to mention here as it has the cauvery as its pillow.

Besides low tariff rates, there are also very low rates for domestic and non-domestic uses. According to the information available for four cities (see Table 3.10) the average rates (minimum and maximum) are for domestic use Rs. 1.87 to Rs. 1.61 per kilo liter and for non-domestic uses, Rs. 14.75 to 25.25 per kilo liter. These rates are very low. If the information is seen very closely it appears that the lowest domestic rate is in Delhi and highest domestic rate is in Ahmedabad. Similarly, once again Delhi has the lowest non-domestic rate and highest is in Bangalore. The Kolkata is only city which imposes flat rate of Rs. 40 to 65 per month for domestic and Rs. 400 to Rs. 2200 per month for non-domestic uses. Therefore, the abysmally low rates (in particular the flat rates, and unmetered supply) will not fetch required amount of revenue to the municipal authorities. It is not possible to recover even the 25 per cent of the cost of supply. This may be attributed to the state governments interest for promoting industrialization at the expense of difficulties with municipal authorities. Thus, once again back to square, it is the problem of pricing the water[26].

Table-3.10
Comparative Water Rate Structure of other Mega Cities

Name of the City	*Domestic Water Rate*	*Non-domestic Water Rate*
Kolkata	Rs. 40 toRs.65 per month flat rate	Metered Rs. 7 per Kl and unmetered Rs. 400 to Rs. 2200 per month.
Mumbai	Rs. 1 to Rs. 2.75 Per Kl	Rs. 11 to Rs. 18 per Kls Rs. 22 to Rs. 35 per Kl.
Bangalore	Rs. 2.80 to Rs. 2.75 Per kl.	Rs. 30 to Rs. 58 Per kl.
Ahmedabad	Rs. 3 per Kl.	Rs. 8 per Kl.
Delhi	Rs. 0.35 to Rs. 0.70 per kl	Rs. 3 to Rs. 8 per Kl.

Source: Arora P.L. "Pricing Structure and Demand Management of Delhi Water Supply", Quarterly Journal of the AIILSG, Vol.70 No.3, 1999, p.170.

Note: The average domestic rates for 4 cities are Rs. 1.78 to 1.61 and for non-domestic Rs. 14.75 to 25.25 per kilo litre.

Debt recovery is a day to day activity of every finance department. So it should be in the municipal water business too. Failure to make prompt payment should attract a penalty that reflects the cost the defaulter has forced upon the utility through his act of negligence. That is only fair to consumers who do pay, who could otherwise fund the extra cost of defaulters, where efficient water utilities impose a disconnection policy, nearly 100 per cent payments are received within the month. Where the poor could be disadvantages by their withdrawal (or choice not to connect to) the distribution system, municipal authorities should have the right to provide a subsidy; based upon a clearly defined policy to help those who cannot help.

This would enable the utility to receive the predicted revenue for providing a service to the complete community rather than allowing a situation to develop where the utility does not serve those who cannot pay. Municipal water systems need major rehabilitation and investment. Today's low tariff regime across the water industry has constrained capital investment and ignored maintenance needs. A clear change in tariff policy is necessary to reflect "The Customer Must Pay" Philosophy, there is no other option in the long term and state government must be persuaded that this is the reality. Thus, quick action on tariff policy is necessary to prevent anarchy in the use of the dwindling water resources. There is an urgent need to revise the tariff rates for provides water supply and sanitation facilities as the present rates do not cover in the O & M costs in most of the cities. The rates should be revised periodically so that they cover not only the O & M costs but also a part of capital cost as well.

5. Health and Environment

In recent times, water quality has deteriorated due to rapid industrialization, population growth, as they generate increasing quantities of industrial waste water and domestic waste water respectively.

One of the indicators of quality of life is a clear environment. It can be further desegregated in terms of air quality, water quality, etc. Air in our cities has become highly polluted. Pollutant concentrations exceed limits considered safe by the World Health

Organization (WHO) by large margins. Water in most of our rivers is not fit to drink and in many rivers not even fit for bathing. Economic activities of production and consumption are accompanied by emissions and affluent of various by-products into the atmosphere.[27] Natural processes absorb these within limits and air and water quality are restored when these limits are exceeded, pollutants accumulate and water quality deteriorate.

How far have water quality deteriorated? what are the consequences? why do it deteriorate? who are the main polluters? what would it take to clean up our water? what are we doing to counter water pollution? why do our efforts not work? what policies can be effective? these are the questions to be considered seriously.

Water quality in most stretches of major rivers is below the Central Pollution Control Board (CPCW) prescribed best use category. Critical parameters affecting water quality are high biochemical oxygen demand and total coliform pathogenic water pollution due to domestic and human waste is the cause of many water borne diseases. Water quality degradation is increasingly becoming a source of conflict among upstream and down stream users.

Table-3.11
Burden of Water Related Diseases in India-1990
(In Millions of DALYS)

Diseases	*Male*	*Female*	*Total*
Diarrhea diseases	13.64	14.39	28.03
Intestinal helminthes	1.06	1.00	2.06
Trachoma	0.04	0.07	0.11
Hepatitis	0.14	0.17	0.31
Total water related diseases	14.88	15.63	30.51

Source: World Development Report 1993, pp. 216-19.
Note : DALYS-Disability Adjusted Life Years.

It is evident from the Table 3.11 that, the specific diseases are diarrhea, trachoma, intestinal worms, hepatitis, and the tropical cluster (schistosomaisis, leishmaniasis, lumpahatic filariasis in India). A quantitative measure that integrates premature death and temporary disability due to diseases is disability adjusted life years (DALYs). About 30.5 million DALYs are lost each year in India due to poor water quality and hygiene.

Excessive pumping of aquifers lowers ground water levels in coastal areas. This can cause saline infusion, rendering the water permanently unfit for human consumption. Inappropriate waste water disposal pollutes the receiving water and may render them unfit for abstraction and treatment.

The environmental related health problems concerned with water supply are very serious[28]. It is estimated that atleast 5 million urban dwellers lack access to clean drinking water and a far larger number of people do not have access to even the simplest of latrine facility. Degradation of water quality from industrial and domestic pollution is a major cause of environment related illness. In large cities such as Mumbai and Kolkata contamination of water in piped distribution systems due to inadequate maintenance has resulted in high rates of water-borne infections including diarrhea and enteric disease. The recent outbreak of cholera in Surat is a stark reminder that poor service can adversely affect health. In Surat (India) 0.9 million people affected by diarrhea reductions in disease occurrence attributable to improvements in the quality or availability of water exceeded 22 per cent in half the cases. Similar improvements are reported for other water-borne diseases.

Most of the water supplies are obtained from infiltration galleries and wells sunk in the beds of the main rivers or their tributaries. Despite chlorination, water supplied to the consumers, sometimes shows evidence of pollution. In many parts of the country, available water is rendered non-potable because of presence of iron, fluoride, nitrate arsenic or heavy metals in excess. Ground water supplies are also saline in many parts of the country. Water pollution becomes critical during the summer season when water availability also is scarce. Such water borne diseases as diarrhea, dysentery, Jaundice, typhoid, gastro enteritis, and cholera have come to be accepted as inevitable almost all over the country.[29]

In the present urban environmental situation, India faces although to a lesser degree, a grim health scenario with its vulnerable urban population under severe health risks connected with drinking water. These include widespread but preventable communicable diseases, moderate to serve malnutrition, particularly among growing children and women of reproductive age.

In India, water is essentially used as a onetime commodity, often treated and un-treated water is used indiscriminately.[30] There is substantial scope for segregated use of the water for appropriate uses and recycling of the waste water for further use for gardening, industries, street cleaning fire fighting, agriculture etc. This also brings another important consideration that the same quality of water use for drinking purposes need not be misused for large number of other activities like flushing, washing besides other uses and from that point of view, the possibilities or alternate water supply could also be kept in view for potable and impotable water.

6. Techniques and Technology

Development of new technologies and innovative total water system solutions for urban areas is needed to satisfy present human needs with respect to living standards and the present environmental goals. These future system solutions will encompass water supply quality dependent water consumption, reuse of rainwater, non-water borne sanitation and new methods of waste water re use in agriculture and non domestic uses. Decreasing availability of clean water implies that water-borne sanitation is not feasible solution for any country not equipped with effective wastewater treatment, and especially not for countries in dry climate conditions. Two important tasks can be listed in connection to sanitation issue, first of all safe, cost effective and socially acceptable water saving and safe sanitation alternatives or dry-sanitation technologies should be further developed and implemented. Secondly, it is necessary to facilitate smooth, long term transition in which water-borne and dry sanitation solutions exist parallel in the same city. Since sanitation is mostly lacking not in central parts of cities but in sub urban areas introduction of dry sanitation may bring rapid and low–cost alternative to satisfy the needs of those less wealthy. Wider introduction of dry sanitation (including separation sanitation) solutions will require increased research efforts to adopt already developed solutions to the local cultural and economical conditions of India.

In order to reduce the cost of operation and maintenance and the treatment of waste water, recently trends are emerging to adopt treatment technologies which are low on maintenance cost and at the same time are effective in taking care of and removal of the pollution caused by sewage from the waste water. The approach had therefore, been on an adoption of an aerobic system for treatment of the wastewater and also adoption of low cost sanitation technologies in the area where it is possible to find out sufficient land for construction of twin pits for leaching of waste water coming from cities.

One way to deal with the increasing demand for water is to have an integrated approach for water supply and waste water treatment to make the systems self sustainable. This would call for making modification in the conventional methods of treatment and to give more thrust on recycling and reuse of water.[31]

Rain water harvesting and ground water recharging are important. The need for the community based rain water harvesting or watershed development cannot be over emphasised. Suppose you had a hectare of land in dry barmer and you got 100 mm of water in the year, common even for this area. It translates to one million litres of water which should meet the drinking and cooking water needs of 182 people at a liberal 15 litres per day. The worst affected villages of Saurashtra too received 100-300 mm rainfall but they let the water go waste. The rain water needs to be harvested for its optimum use. Cheerapunji with about 11,000 mm annual rainfall, also suffers from safe drinking water shortages for want of effective harvesting systems.

There is an urgent need for adoption of techniques and technology for rain water harvesting at micro and macro level. It is demonstratively attempted by individual households in Munipur and Kerala. Why not the same be made a widespread programme in India? However, management monsoon rain is also a problem in sodic soils. As the rain water does not penetrate deep into the soils, it leads to water logging condition in a short period at the onset of rain followed by near drought condition if in between rains there is a long dry spell. Harvesting of rain water was practised in the grid parts of Rajasthan and Gujarat where facilities for rain water storage in the form of small cement lined and covered underground tanks in the basement of urban houses or tanks in courtyards offered stored water for use in lean periods. More recently, thought has been given to rain water harvesting in urban centres in other parts of the country[32]. To over come this and to conserve the excellent quality rainfall, system of water management should involve rainwater harvesting in urban areas.

SECTION-III
NEEDS AND DEEDS

After an understanding the situational aspects of water supply in India such as, demand and supply, cost and finance, planning and management, pricing, health and environment, and techniques and technology. For convenience, this section brings out urban access to safe water, percentage of urban population covered by safe drinking water supply, recommended water supply levels, plan outlays for water supply, central government expenditure on water supply have been discussed below. This would complete a match between needs and deeds of water supply in India. Besides, the time series data will take care of the growth aspects.

Though about 84 per cent of urban population has been provided with safe drinking water supply facilities as on 31st December 1990, the situation in most of the cities and towns is not satisfactory. The per capita water supply ranges between as low as 12 lpcd to as high as 460 lpcd, in Class-I cities. However, the national average for Class-1 cities is 147 lpcd. In the case of Class-II towns, the per capita water supply ranges between as low as 7 lpcd to as high as 600 lpcd with a national average of 78 lpcd for Class-II towns. Thus, there exists a wide gap in the per capita water supply in different urban areas of the country.

There has been a great concern placed on urban water supply in India. Table 3.12 indicates that, the urban population covered by protected water supply was 72 per cent at the time of launching of the decade programme in 1981. The entire population was to be covered by March 1991. The latest data received from the Central Public Health and Environmental Engineering Organisation (CPHEEO), and Ministry of Urban Development[33] reveals that the percentage of urban population covered by organised water supply, which includes piped water and tube-wells, has increased to 90 per cent in 1997. The latest data indicates that India is achieving high percentage to provide safe drinking water to urban population.

Table-3.12
Percentage of Urban Population Covered by Protected Water Supply in India

Year	*Access Rate*
1981	72.25
1985	72.88
1991	85.00
1997	90.00

Source: CPHEEO and Ministry of Urban Development, New Delhi 1999. As per CPHEEO, Government of India norms, the per capita supply level required for cities with different population are:

1) For cities having population upto 20000: 70 -100 LPCD
2) For cities having population 20,000-100000: 100-150 LPCD
3) For cities having population above 1 lakh : 150-200 LPCD

As per the Ministry of Urban Affairs and Central Public Health and Environmental Organisation (CPHEEO) recently recommended water supply norms is given in Table 3.13.

It is noted from the table that, population less than 20000, such cities should compulsorily provide water at least 40 & 70 litres per capita per day LPCD through stand posts and house connections. Class-I cities have to provide 100 & 135 LPCD of water with and without sewerage system. The cities with population above 10,00,000 have to provide atleast 150 LPCD. This points out that smaller towns require less quantity of water consumption whereas big cities require large quantity of water supply.

Water supply and sanitation is a state subject and funding of projects in this sector is essentially supported through the plan provisions to the state governments. Through the plan provisions for the sector steadily increased from 0.65 per cent of the total outlay in the Second Five Year Plan (1956-61) to 1.81 per cent in

Table-3.13

Recommended Water Supply Levels of Indian Cities

Sl. No.	*Population Range*	*Recommended water supply level (LPCD)*
1	Less than 20,000 a) Population served by stand posts b) Population provided with house connections	 40 70
2	20,000 to 1,00,000	100
3	1,00,000 to 10,00,000	a) 100 with no sewerage system b) 135 with sewerage system
4	10,00,000 and above	150

Source: CPHEEO & Ministry of Urban Affairs, New-Delhi, 1999.

the Seventh Five Year Plan (1985-90), this provision has been found to be highly inadequate. As a result, in urban areas against the target of achieving 100 per cent coverage (which was subsequently scaled down to 90 per cent) with safe drinking water and 75 per cent (which was subsequently scaled down to 50 per cent) with sanitation during the international drinking water and sanitation decade (1981-90), the coverage achieved in urban areas was only 85 per cent with safe drinking water and 45 per cent with sanitation.

The resources required to achieve 100 per cent coverage with safe drinking water and 75 per cent with sanitation are massive and call for recurring and non recurring investments of very high magnitude. The planning commission has estimated additional investment needs for water supply for the period 1996-2001 to be about US $3000 million. About one-third of the urban population lives below the poverty line. There has been a substantial understanding on the need to improve the water supply position in the country. There are a number of factors that inhibit achieving this objective.

Similarly, the importance of urban water supply in the planning process could be seen from Table 3.14 that it is true that the absolute amount spent on urban water supply has increased. For example, it was Rs. 43 corres during the First plan.[34] Without any increase in Second Plan, the amount on urban water supply increased to Rs. 89.37 crores in Third Plan. Whereas an appreciable absolute increase in urban water supply amount is experienced in Fifth Plan and it was doubled during the Seventh Plan placed at Rs. 2965 crores. Keeping with the requirements, the outlay on urban water supply increased from Rs. 5982 crores in Eight plan to Rs. 20750 crores in Ninth Plan. Therefore, there has been a four timkes increase in the outlay on urban water supply. Against this, however there has been as such no increase in the share of urban water supply in the total plan outlay throughout the period of First Plan to Ninth Plan.

Similarly, there has been considerable attention given to urban water supply during the plan periods in relative terms as well. For example, it was 1.28 per cent during the First plan and increased to 2.4 per cent during Ninth Plan period. It is quite disgusting to note that never the water supply amount has been atleast 3 per cent of public sector outlay.

When we consider the water supply outlay as a per cent of public sector outlay the emerging points are, a) Second, Third, Fifth, Seventh and Eight five years plans have experienced declined in the share, b) First, Fourth, Sixth and Ninth Five year plans have experienced increased in the share, and c) It is quite distinguishing to note that never the water supply amount has been atleast 3 per cent of public sector outlay[35]. Therefore, this is the reflection of uttter negligence shown on very important item i.e., urban water supply.

The urban water supply is a questionable issue in the Indian federal structure because should it be treated as centres responsibly or the responsibility of the state governments where the state governments consider that it is the responsibility of the local governments. Which have been recognized as third layer of government only in the recent past, though disregarding its constitutionality.[36] The following Table 3.15 describes the total expenditure of Central Government on water supply for the period 1990-91 to 1998-99.

Table-3.14

Plan Outlays for Water Supply and Sanitation Sector

(Rs in Crores)

Plan Period	*Total Public sector plan outlay*	*Total plan outlay water supply and sanitation sector*	*Percentage of public sector outlay*	*Plan Outlay for urban water supply and sanitation.*	
				Sector Amount	*Percentage of public sector outlay*
First Plan	3360.00	49.00	1.46	43.00	1.28
Second Plan	6750.00	72.02	1.07	44.00	0.65
Third Plan	8573.00	105.70	1.23	89.37	1.40
3 Annual plans	6664.97	106.42	1.58	N.A.	N.A.
Fourth Plan	15902.00	430.22	2.75	282.00	1.77
Fifth plan	39303.49	1030.68	2.62	549.44	1.40
Sixth Plan	97500.00	4302.20	3.43	1766.68	1.81
Seventh Plan	180000.00	4047.00	4.15	2965.75	1.65
2 Annual Plans	1370331.50	65224.70	3.62	1721.37	1.26
Eighth Plan	4341000.00	44272.90	3.23	5982.28	1.38
Ninth Plan	859200.00	N.A	N.A	20750.0	2.40

Source: Compiled from Various Five Year Plan Documents, Govt. of India, Planning Commission, New Delhi.

Note: NA- Not Available.

Table-3.15
Expenditure on Water Supply and Sanitation during 1990-91 to 1998-99

(Rs. in Crores)

Year	*Expenditure*	*Percentage*
1990-91	828	4.6
1991-92	934	5.2
1992-93	788	4.4.
1993-94	1262	7.1
1994-95	1351	7.5
1995-96	1756	9.8
1996-97	2957	14.5
1997-98	3449	19.3
1998- 99	4495	25.2
Total	**17820**	**100.0**

Source: Compiled from Various Budget Papers of Govt. of India.

There has been a considerable increase in the absolute expenditure of the centre on water supply from Rs. 828 crores to Rs. 4495 crores between 1990 to 1998, the total amount for this period was Rs. 17820 crores and the percentage change is also increased from 4.6 to 25.2 per cent from 1990-91 to 1998-99.

NOTES AND REFERENCES

1. World Health Organisation defines ' Safe Drinking Water ' as the "Treated surface water or untreated but uncontaminated water such as from protected borewells, sanitary wells, springs and natural conserved impoundments excluding all other water of doubtful quality". Community Water Supply and Excereta Disposal in South East Asia, W.H.O. Region Publications, South East Asia Series, No.14, WHO, New Delhi, 1977, p.2.
2. Planning Commission, Government of India. "Sixth Five Year Plan" 1980-85", p.397.
3. Nandedkar, V.G. "Water Supply a Public Utility Service" Regional Centre for Research & Training in Municipal Administration of All India Institute of Local Self-Government Bombay, 1976.

4. Bishnoi, O.P., "International Drinking Water Supply and Sanitation Decade Programme 1981-90", Civic Affairs, February, 1982, p.9.
5. Ibid., p.13.
6. Agarwal, et al., "Water Sanitation and Health-For All"?, Earth Scan, London, 1981.
7. Nageshwar Rao K., "Economics of Water Supply", Himalaya Publishing House, Mumbai, 1993, p.3.
8. Science and Environment Fortnightly. "Dirty and Thirsty", Down to Earth, February 29, 2001.
9. Even by the beginning of 21st century, the Arabian countries (specially OPEC) produce more of oil and suffer from drinking water and domestically and industrially usable water. It may be noted that the Arabians take bath on Friday to next Friday only. It is reported that they dip cloth and rub the body as a matter of taking bath. Because, there is acute shortage of water. Further, the drinking water issue has brought wars in Egypt, Israel and Turkey-Taiz in Yemen has piped water once every 21 days. For detail see, The Economist (London) "Water in the middle East", 1996 , p.63.
10. Human Development Report, 1999. p.78.
11. Ibid, p.110.
12. The Economist, "Development and the Environment Survey", March 21-28, 1998, p.14.
13. Nandalal Jotwani, "India Suffers the Centuries Worst Water Crisis", Swadeshi Patrika, May-2000, p7.
14. Sundar S and. Sarkar S.K., "Private Sector Participation in Water Supply",. The Hindu Daily News Paper, 16-7-2000.
15. Rakesh Mohan Committee, "The Committee on Urban Infrastructure Needs" Planning Commission, Govt. of India, New Delhi, 1996.
16. Rathore M.S., Ratna Reddy V. and S.Ramanathan, "Urban Water Supply in Rajasthan Problems and Prospects", Rawat Publications Jaipur, 1994, p.11.
17. Blake Nelson.M., "Water for the Cities" Sura Cuse University Press, Sura Cuse, New York, 1976.
18. Sheela Prasad, V.G., "New Economic Policy: Implications for water" EPW, May 22, 1999. p.1254.
19. Adhikeri M., and Gupta C.K., "Problems in Municipal Water Supply: Their Remedies", Social Culture 41(6) June 1975.

20. Planning Commission, "Ninth Five Year Plan 1997-2002", Govt. of India, New Delhi, p.271.
21. Ernesto M. Pernia and Stella Albastro I.E., "Aspects of Urban Water and Sanitation in the Context of Rapid Urbanization in Developing Asia", Asian Development Bank, Economic Staff Paper No. 56, 1997, p.23.
22. Meera Mehta and Dinesh Mehta, "Planning for Metropolitan Water Supply and Sewerage: A Case Study of Ahmedabad", Rawat Publications, Jaipur, 1993, p.260.
23. Aslam Parvaiz.M., "Why a National Policy for Water Management?" Yojana, May 1-15, 1986 p.10.
24. Daniel, Merihan American Ambassador to India 1977 to 1979, the government asked to him pack up and leave India, unfortunately, he was recalled.
25. Jessop Price, "The Water Tariff Debate", Indian Infrastructure, Ist July, 2000. Vol. 2, No.I, p.48.
26. Arora P.L., "Pricing Structure and Demand Management of Delhi Water Supply", Quarterly Journal of the All India Institute of Local self Government, New Delhi, Vol.17, No.3,1999, p.170
27. Munasinge Mohan, "Water Supply and Environmental Management: Developing World Applications", Forwarded by Donald lauria, Studies in Water Policy and Management, Boulder and Oxford, Westiview Press, 1992, p.447.
28. Logan, "Investment in Water Supply Program-A Health Economic Appraisal", American Journal of Tropical Medicine and Hygiene, Vol.9, No.5, September 1960.
29. Bhise, D.R., "Water Quality and Public Health", QRT J LSG, 1979.
30. Roma, "Treating Water for the City's ill-health", E.T, 21, Nov. 24(11) Jan. 1978.
31. Nandlal Jotwani, "India Suffers the Century's Worst Water Crises", Swadeshi Patrika, Vol. IV. No.5, May 2000, p.6.
32. Daksha Barai C., "The Augmentation of Water Supply to Meet the Needs of Rapidly Growing Metropolitan Cities of India", Rawat Publications Jaipur, 1993.
33. CPHEEO and Ministry Urban Development, New-Delhi 1999.
34. Data Compiled from Plan documents of various years, planning commission, Govt. of India, New Delhi.
35. If we compare this to GDP it will be abysmally low, See, Rakesh Mohan Report, Op. cit.

36. Can it be brought in the concurrent list or it is state responsibility is debatable However, though the responsibility is ultimately on municipalities or city governments.

4

Urban Water Supply in Karnataka and Maharashtra

Introduction

Water supply and sanitation is a state subject and funding of projects in this sector is essentially supported through the plan provisions to the state governments. In accordance with the main purpose of our study is namely, water supply in Gulbarga and Solapur cities, it is essential to have an insight into the water supply situation existing in Karnataka and Maharashtra states. It is no wonder to say that Maharashtra is a state with very high income and almost first place in terms of industrialization. It is also the state to have the second biggest city Mumbai in the country. Whereas, Karnataka has lower rank but the Bangalore is treated as fast growing city with its title as garden city of India. There are vast differences between Karnataka and Maharashtra if compared with several variables. The present chapter attempts to examine the process of urbanization and industrialization prevailing in these states and consequent demand, supply and impact on urban water only has been taken into account. What is the financial allocation, demand and supply position, the targets, achievements and the new schemes or programmes, administrative arrangements and funding system are very important. As a starting point for all this, the urban profile relating to water supply in the two states is inevitable.

For convenience, the present chapter is divided into the following sections. The urban profile of Karnataka and Maharashtra have been briefly noted in **Section-I**. The demand, supply and consequent disequilibrium situation in the two states have been discussed in **Section-II**. The funding pattern prevailing in the two states have been compared in **Section-III**. The targets, achievements and new schemes or programmes including ongoing schemes / projects of urban water in the two states have been treated in **Section-IV**. The plan-wise efforts and resulting imbalances have been evaluated in **Section-V.**

SECTION-I
COMPARATIVE URBAN PROFILE

All people, whatever their stage of development and their social and economic conditions have the right to have access to drinking water in quantities and of a quality equal to their basic needs[1].

Definition of urban area

In the 2001 Census of India, the definition of urban area[2] adopted is as follows:

a. All places with a municipality, corporation, cantonment board or notified town/area committee, etc.

b. All other places which satisfies the following criteria:
   i. A minimum population of 5,000.
   ii. At least 75 per cent of male working population engaged in non-agricultural pursuits;
   iii. A density of population atleast 400 persons per sq.km.

For the proper understanding of the magnitude of water supply situation and consequent issues emerging from the analysis in Karnataka and Maharashtra, an urban profile of the two states is a complimentary aspect. The urban profile consists of only a) Population and households, b) Geographical area and density, c) No. of industries, and d) No. of cities and towns etc.

It is noted from Table 4.1 that as per 2001 Census, the total population of the country is 102.71 crores. Karnataka population is 5.27 crores and that of Maharashtra is 9.67 crores.

Table-4.1
Total Population of Karnataka and Maharashtra States

(As Per 2001 Census)

State	*Total Population in crores*	*Percentage*	*Rank*
Karnataka	5.27	5.1	8
Maharashtra	9.67	9.4	3
India	102.71	100.0	-

Source: Compiled from Karnataka at a Glance 2002 and Maharashtra State Economic Survey 2002-03.

It is observed from the Table 4.1 that, the population of Maharashtra is nearly double of Karnataka as per 2001 Census. The states rank is eight and third respectively in the total population of the country.

As our major concern is for understanding the economics of urban water supply, the magnitude of urban population and household is essential to be kept in mind. The urban population of our study states has been noted in the Table 4.2.

Table-4.2
Urban Population of Karnataka and Maharashtra

State	*Urban population (in crores)*	*Percentage to total population*	*Difference*
Karnataka	1.79	33.96	6.14
Maharashtra	4.10	42.39	14.57
India	28.54	27.82	-

Source: Ibid, p.13 & 12

The urban population of Karnataka is 1.79 crore which is 33.96 per cent of total population of the country and the urban population in Maharashtra is 4.10 crore which is 42.39 per cent of the total urban population of India. It is above board that the urban population of Maharashtra exceeds that of India by 14.57 per cent. Similarly, the Karnataka urban population also exceeds that of India only by 6.14 per cent. The rate of urbanisation in Maharashtra is higher than all

India average. It is 8.43 per cent higher in Maharashtra compared to Karnataka.

Table-4.3
Urban Households in Karnataka and Maharashtra

States	Urban Households	Percentage
Karnataka	3556960	6.62
Maharashtra	7850000	14.62
India	53692376	100.0

Source: Ibid.

It may be noted from Table 4.3 that, as per 2001 Census, there are 53692376 urban households in India. Maharashtra has 8 per cent ahead of Karnataka in terms of urban households. It is true that Maharashtra state is far ahead in terms of urban households compared to Karnataka.

As against population, the geographical area is very important aspect of the urban profile. If we see the Table.4.4, it is clear that, the geographical area of Karnataka is 1.92 lakh sq.km which constitutes about 5.84 per cent and that of Maharashtra is 3.08 lakh sq.km. which is about 9.37 per cent. In terms of geographical area Maharashtra has second rank and Karnataka has the eighth rank in the total geographical area of the country[3] (see maps 4.1 and 4.2).

Table-4.4
Geographical Area of Karnataka and Maharashtra

State	Area (lakh sq.km)	Rank
Karnataka	1.92	8
Maharashtra	3.08	2
India	32.87	-

Source: Ibid, pp.15 & 25.

The density of population in Karnataka and Maharashtra have been given in the following Table 4.5.

MAP-4.1. KARNATAKA STATE

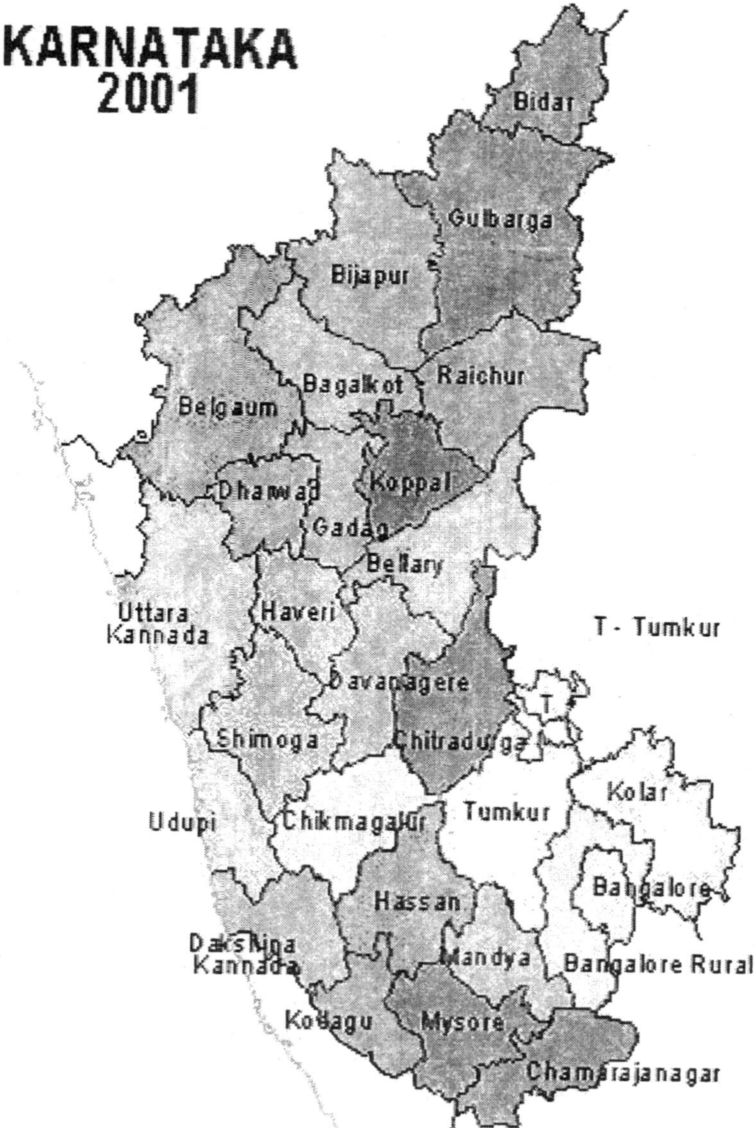

MAP-4.2. MAHARASHTRA STATE

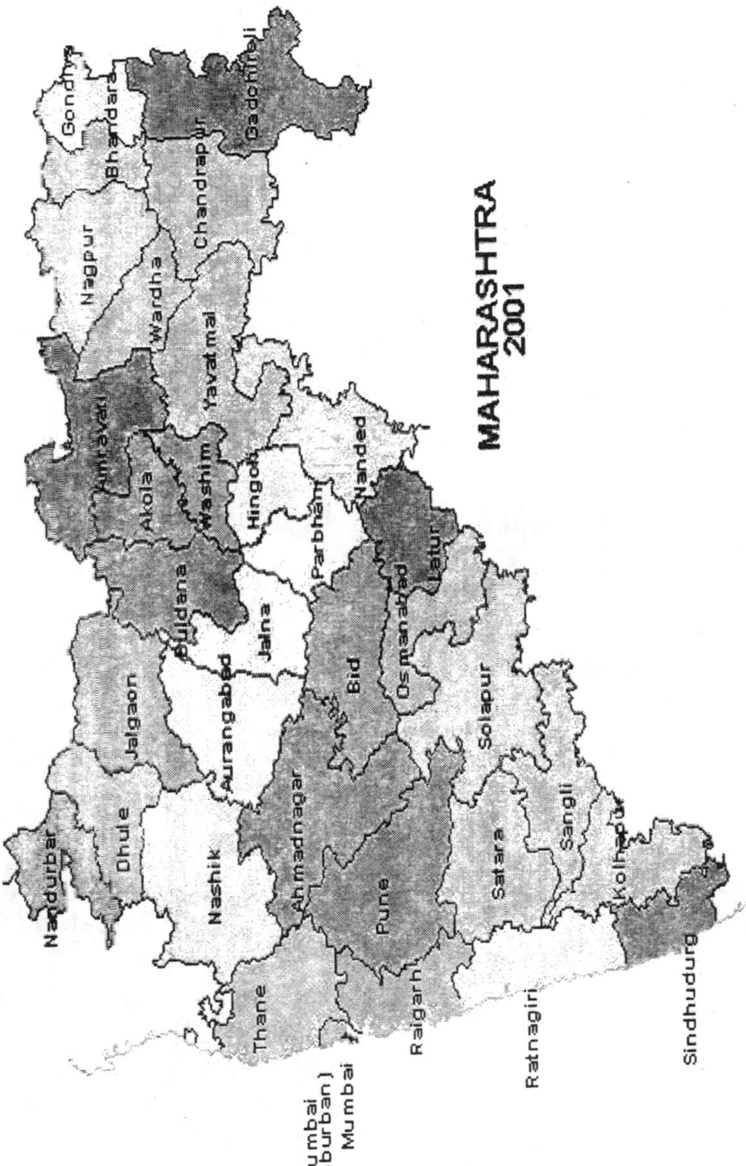

Table-4.5
Density of Population in Karnataka and Maharahstra

State	*Density*	*Difference*
Karnataka	275	49
Maharashtra	314	10
India	324	-

Source: Ibid. pp.16 & 20

The Karnataka has 275 persons per sq. km as against 314 per sq. km in Maharashtra. The density of population in Maharashtra is very closure to that of India and in terms of marginal calculation, there are 10 persons more per sq. km in Maharashtra. Therefore, it may be treated as not only highly but also thickly populous state of our study.

The water supply and providing other infrastructure facilities are contingent upon the administrative structure. The revenue divisions comprise of number of contagious districts. It is needless to say that each district needs its own independent services.

Table-4.6
Revenue Divisions of Karnataka and Maharashtra

State	*Revenue Divisions*
Karnataka	4
Maharashtra	6

Source: Ibid.pp19 & 21

If we see the Table 4.6 that Karnataka has only 4 revenue divisions[4] as against 6 revenue divisions in Maharashtra.

For the purpose of providing urban amenities, the geographical area needs a systematic division. That means towns, cities, big cities, urban agglomerations and corporations are the divisions conceive in the states. There are 3700 urban areas in the country.

Table-4.7
No. of Towns/Cities-2001

State	*No.of Towns/Cities*	*Percentage*
Karnataka	270	5.23
Maharashtra	435	8.42
India	5161	100.0

Source: Ibid p.28 & 32.

If we see the Table 4.7 that there are 270 towns in Karnataka and Maharshtra has 435 towns. That means there are 165 more towns and cities and urban agglomerations in Maharashtra.

By keeping in mind the problems, the state governments have attempted for decentralization of administration in urban matters.[5] Accordingly, giving vent to the area of and population, big cities (along with district head quarters) the states have created municipal corporations. The number of corporations (with greater independence and more state direct assistance) existing in Karnataka and Maharashtra are given in Table 4.8

Table-4.8
Categorisation of Urban Local Bodies

State	*Corporations*	*CMCs*	*TMCs*	*TPs*	*Total*
Karnataka	5	33	81	89	208
Maharashtra	15	47	96	87	245
India	-	-	-	-	3700

Source: KUWS & DB Bangalore, Annual Report 1998-99.
Note: CMCs-City Municipal Councils
TMCs-Town Municipal Councils.
TPs-Town Panchayats.

It is evident that not only there is higher rate of urban and better division of cities and towns, the Maharashtra has15 corporations as against only 5 in Karnataka, that itself speaks of the fact that number of corporations in Maharashtra are 3 times more than in Karnataka. As such, the Karnataka should think on this line of creating atleast few more corporations which will help providing better administration and urban amenities in the state.

The demand and supply of urban water is not only for drinking purpose but also for working of factories and industries. In this context, the following Table 4.9 points out very clearly that the Karnataka has 6952 industries and factories, whereas Maharashtra is having 19009 factories and industries.

Table-4.9
Industrialization in Karnataka and Maharashtra- 2000

State	*No. of Factories*	*Percentage of total factories*
Karnataka	6952	5.30
Maharashtra	19009	14.50
India	131094	100.00

Source: Statistical Outline of India - 2002-03, Tata Services Ltd., Dept. of Economics and Statistics, Mumbai.

These constitute about 5.30per cent and 14.50 per cent of the total figures 131094 of the country respectively. The industries needed great amount of water for their proper working.[6]

Furthermore, the difference between Karnataka and Maharashtra in terms of industrialisation and resulting implications for water supply could also be understood with the help of the amount of industrial production in them. Karnataka has industrial gross output of Rs. 42505 crore and Maharashtra has Rs.1,81,333 crore of industrial output. Therefore, there are number of factories producing output which need greater quantity of water.[7]

SECTION-II
ACCESSIBILITY OF DRINKING WATER

In urban areas, municipal authorities are the public bodies which take up the responsibility of providing water suitable for drinking purpose and for other requirements. In Karnataka and Maharashtra, drinking water supply falls under the category of obligatory functions of municipal councils within the municipality.

In Karnataka, "Urban Water Supply and Drainage Board" started functioning from 14th August 1974 and has been performing the functions of "investigating water supply and drainage facilities, planning and preparation of schemes, execution of schemes under phased programme, providing technical assistance or giving advice to urban local authority in the execution and maintenance of water supply and drainage works maintaining schemes incidental to urban water supply and drainage and any other matter which may be referred by government".[8] It also undertake capital works of urban water supply and drainage schemes in urban areas. The Board classifies the water supply schemes into:-

a) Piped Water Supply Schemes for towns whose population is below 20,000 and

b) Urban Water Supply Schemes for towns whose population is above 20,000.[9]

The policy of the government is that under 'piped water supply schemes', the town authority has to contribute 10 per cent of the total capital cost and the remaining 90 per cent will be borne by the state government as subsidy. In the case of 'urban water supply' schemes, the urban local authority has to bear the entire cost either by its own funds or by borrowing from Life Insurance Corporation (LIC) or State Government. However, even in the case of 'piped water supply' schemes, if the local authority is unable to contribute its share from its own sources of funds, the state government obliges to help by giving their contribution also as a long term loan or as a town development grant.

In Maharashtra, Maharashtra Water Supply and Sewerage Board (MWS & SB) was established under act of 1976, started functioning as full fledged implementing organisation in 1979. After functioning for about 17 years MWS & SB was restructured and renamed as Maharashtra Jeevan Pradhikaran (MJP)[10]. Maharashtra Jeevan Pradhikaran (MJP) a statutory body of Govt of Maharashtra is responsible for planning, designing and execution of water supply projects all over the state except Greater Mumbai in Maharashtra. The primary objective of MJP is to provide potable water supply and satisfactory sanitation facilities, so as to achieve and maintain clean environment operation and maintenance of water supply and sewerage schemes owned by the authority and giving technical advice to municipal councils for work carried out by them. As per Government Policy, after commissioning of the water supply/sewerage projects, these are to be handed over to the respective municipal corporations/councils for day to day operation and maintenance. MJP is also responsible for raising the loan from LIC, Open Market Borrowing (OMB) and repayment of the same on behalf of municipal corporations/councils. Government of Maharashtra stands guarantee for these loans. OMB is now discontinued by govt. since 1998-99. It is expected that the municipal councils will pay loan installment and interest promptly to MJP. The level of taxation is very low in Maharashtra wherever MJP supplies water directly to the consumers, the recovery is around 85%.

Supply of drinking water to urban areas in Karnataka and Maharashtra is basically determined by the sources of water itself. Geographically, many of the urban settlements are located near or on the banks of a river or stream. This facilitated drawing of water from this source both for consumption and for other purposes. If the settlement was not near a river or stream, sources like a tank or reservoir or a group of open dug wells were constructed which acted as artificial sources for drinking water. However, due to fast growth of urban centers, and consequent sanitation problems, these sources have become inadequate and un-hygienic to cater the needs of both domestic consumption and industrial purposes, with the advent of public health engineering, the raw water for consumption was restricted only to deep bore-well sources and all the surface and open well water sources were subjected to the treatment (purification) to avoid contamination and health hazards.[11] This resulted in high capital investments on machinery equipment and laying supply pipes up to the final consumer points.

In Karnataka, 37 per cent of the total towns have their source of drinking water from rivers/streams/canals and 10 per cent from tanks and reservoirs, and also, some towns (about 10 per cent) have these sources along with the ground water sources like bore wells. Ground water sources are found appropriate for small towns and flow water sources are common with medium and major towns due to their proximity to the source as well as the requirements of water to these towns. Deep bore wells yield uncontaminated water which does not require any treatment in most of the cases. This is also found ideal for smaller towns for limited uses of domestic purposes as deep bore wells reduce the burden of maintenance of capital intensive treatment plants. For bigger towns, where water is equally important for bulk consumers like industrial and other commercial establishments, natural sources like rivers, streams or tanks suit the purpose but with treatment.

The present section includes 1) Total and per capita water supply situation in class-I towns, 2) Total and per capita water supply situation in class-II towns, 3) Percentage of population covered by water supply system etc have been discussed in the following.

Table-4.10
Total and Per capita Water Supply Situation in Class-I Towns of Karnataka and Maharashtra States

Particulars	*Karnataka*	*Maharashtra*	*India*
No. of class-I towns			
1978	11	17	142
1988	14	29	212
1998	19	36	315
Total water supply (MLD)			
1978	467.61	2265.73	86382.18
1988	818.48	3547.19	15191.88
1998	1100	5102	19000
Per capita water supply (LPCD)			
1978	133	204	143.37
1988	110	176	147
1998	96	160	152

Source: Bidyut Mohanty "Urbanisation in Developing Countries", IIP Publishing House, New Delhi, 1993.

For the purpose of urban drinking water supply, the cities in every state have been divided into different classes. The supply of total water and per capita supply in class-I cities of Karnataka and Maharashtra state have been given in the Table 4.10.

If we look into the information, it is clear that there has been considerable increase in the number of class-I cities both in Karnataka and Maharashtra, between 1988 and 1998. There has been an increase of 8 class-I cities in Karnataka as against 19 in Maharashtra. Besides, there has been an increase in total MLD of water in Karnataka by 632 against 2836 MLD in Maharashtra. The two states total water supply is much lower compared to the all India figures.[12]

Whereas against total water supply, the per capita water supply gives us a different picture. For instance, there has been decline in Karnataka by 37 litres per capita per day (LPCD) as against 41 LPCD in Maharashtra. However, the poor water supply position in both the states in Class-I cities is evident from the Table 4.10. Against this, there has been an increase in per capita water supply in the country as a whole.

The type of water supply is an indicator of the system and its quality. For example, types of water supply are tap, tube well / hand pump, pucca well. The percentage distribution of persons across major sources of drinking water in urban sector could be found from the following Table 4.11.

Table-4.11
Percentage Distribution of Persons across Major Sources of Drinking Water in Urban Sector during 1986-87

State	*Percentage of Persons Across Major Sources of Drinking Water*				
	Tap	*Tube well/ Hand pump*	*Pucca Well*	*Others*	*All*
Karnataka	83.05	5.44	9.72	1.79	100.00
Maharashtra	92.83	1.54	4.72	1.21	100.00
All India	72.43	15.44	10.26	1.87	100.00

Source: National Sample Survey Organisation, 42nd Round, No. 361, 1986-87, p.153

The Karnataka and Maharashtra states are far ahead of the country in terms of water supply through the taps. Indeed Maharashtra is much more ahead of Karnataka and India. In this state, 93 per cent of the urban population is covered by tap system as against 83% and 72% in Karnataka and India respectively. Therefore, it is not difficult to imagine that tap is a source of water supply which is although sound and safe but is relatively costly. Thus, the data brings out the fact that being a rich state, Maharashtra is well ahead of other in providing safe drinking water to the urban people. In following the guidelines and criteria of classification of cities suggested by Urban Development Ministry, Government of India, as seen above no much ice, has been melt with regard to Class-I cities. However besides the above, keeping in mind the guidelines of planning department, further idea of classification of class-II cities have been adopted by state governments with regard to class-II cities/towns. The Table 4.11 gives the details of changes in number of class-II cities with the purpose of location of industries and tempering the process of urbanisation. The total number of class-II cities increased from 190 to 315 in the country. Similarly, there has been an increase in number of class-II cities in Karnataka and Maharashtra, 7 and 8 respectively between 1978 to 1998. This points to the fact that, the Karnataka has been more rapid in increasing class-II cities than Maharashtra with regard to the urban drinking water supply in India has increased from 1533 MLD in 1978 and 2335 MLD in 1998.

As against this, the Karnataka class-II cities experienced an increase in total MLD of water from 1978 to 1998. But there has been a decline in Maharashtra by 271 MLD of water during the period under consideration. The situation with regard to per capita water supply for the people of class-II cities has worked in the country as well as the two states of our study. For example, in India the per capita water supply is declined by 70 LPCD and 32 LPCD between 1978-98 and declined 234 LPCD in Karnataka and Maharashtra respectively.[13]

Therefore, it is above board from the Table 4.12 that due to large increase in population of class-II cities in the country, Karnataka and Maharashtra have been finding it difficult to provide drinking water to the people. The situation seems to be going out of hand as there has been steep increase in population on the one hand inability of the authorities in increasing total quantity of water.

No doubt, changes in the quantity of water supply, per capita water supply are the factors to be kept in mind, while understanding

Table-4.12

Total and Percapita Water Supply Situation in Class-II Towns in Selected Years of Karnataka and Maharashtra

Particulars	*Karnataka*	*Maharashtra*	*India*
No. of class-II towns			
1978	9	19	190
1988	12	22	241
1998	16	27	315
Total water supply (MLD)			
1978	44.47	381.75	1532.97
1988	64.37	191.82	110.00
1998	88.20	110.00	2335.00
Per capita water supply (LPCD)			
1978	75.75	310.49	125.27
1988	62.00	101.00	78.00
1998	43.35	76.00	55.00

Source: Ibid, p.156.

the economics of urban water supply, but the most important issue is the accessibility of water not to individuals but to the households. Because household is a unit which try to balance the per capita use of water within itself. This is so far the simple reason that some members of the household require small quantity of water and some members develop the habit of use in more and more quantity of water. As such the balancing factor for water use is not with the government but is left to the decision of the households.[14]

Table-4.13

Percentage of Households Having Safe Drinking Water in Urban Areas of Karnataka and Maharashtra

State	*Percentage of Households having Safe Drinking Water*		
	1981	*1991*	*Difference*
Karnataka	74.4	82.0	7.6
Maharashtra	85.6	90.5	4.9
India	74.1	82.0	7.9

Source: Compiled from Households Tables, Census of India, 1981 & 1991.

In this context, the percentage of households having safe drinking water is very important and has been noted in Table 4.13.

It is true that there has been a marginal increase in the percentage of households having access to safe drinking water between 1980 and 1990 decade. For example, Karnataka exhibit 8 per cent increase and Maharashtra by 5 per cent increase in number of households having access to safe drinking water. Similarly, there has been an increase of 8 per cent of the households from 74 per cent in 1980-81 to 82 per cent in 1991. Thus, some silver lining could be found during the decade 1980-90 in terms of progress made in the urban water supply to the households.

SECTION-III
FUNDING PATTERN

The financial pattern and performance of urban water supply schemes, which are of paramount importance and occupy a pivotal position in public sector institutions, particularly at state and local level. As stated in the chapters two and three above the financing of urban water supply has not been able to receive any systematic and clear-cut ideas and actions in the country as a whole. The central government is contemplating a scheme to implement in financing urban infrastructure with the co-operation and participation by the state governments. However, there is no certain idea with the state governments when they are dealing with urban local self-governments. Therefore, the situation differs from state to state. Similarly, there are differences in the financial targets and achievements. Added to these, there are also differences in financial position approved outlay and expenditure, capital receipts and expenditure have been accounted in the following.

The funding pattern of urban water supply schemes in Karnataka and Maharashtra is nearly the same but with some marginal differences. In some states, the local bodies have been permitted to borrow from the market and the state acts as a guarantee. While the local bodies have been granted permission to float bonds for collecting money to finance urban water supply schemes.

The existing pattern of funding in Karnataka and Maharashtra could be seen from the following Tables 4.14(a) & 4.14(b)

It could be seen from Table 4.14(a) for the towns with population upto 20,000 there is 100% grant. For the towns with population above 20,000 upto 75,000, 50% loan and 50% grant, the towns with population above 75,000 including corporations, loan from financial institution is 66.67% and government grant is 23.33%, and urban local body share is 10%. Indeed, how to provide 50% of loan and 10% of grant loan is a very big problem for the local authorities. This is also not clear regarding its application to the new schemes or on going schemes or with respect to maintenance.

Table-4.14(a)
Funding Pattern for Urban Water Supply Schemes in Karnataka

(Percentage)

Sl. No.	*Population Range*	*Loan from Financial Institutions*	*Govt. Grant*	*Urban Local Body Share*
1.	Up to 20,000	--	100.00	--
2.	20,000-75,000	50.00	50.00	--
3.	Above 75000 including corporations.	66.67	23.33	10.00

Source: KUWS & DB, Bangalore, Information Brochure, September, 2000.p.3.

The situation in financing urban water supply in Maharastra could be understood from the following Table 4.14 (b). For example, municipal corporations have 23.33% grant, and 76.67% loan, and 'A' class municipal council, 'B' class municipal council 'C' class municipal councils have 25%, 40%, 50% grant-in-aid and 75%, 60% & 50% loan amount.

Table-4.14 (b)
Financing Pattern of Urban Water Supply Schemes in Maharashtra State

Sl.No.	*Municipal Council Local Bodies*	*Funding Pattern (%)*	
		Govt. Grant	*Loan*
1.	Municipal Corporations Excluding Greater Mumbai.	23.3	76.7
2.	A-Class Municipal Councils	25.0	75.0
3.	B-Class Municipal Councils	40.0	60.0
4.	C-Class Municipal Councils (Population more than 20,000 as per 1991 census)	50.0	50.0
5.	Other 'C' class municipal councils having population less than 20,000.	100.0	Nil

Source: Maharashtra Jeevan Prodhikaran "Annual Report" 1997-98, CIDCO Bhavan Belapur, Navi Mumbai. p.10.

As per the Govt. of Maharashtra Order of 15th September 1994, the above financial pattern is revised in respect of Govt. Grant. The costs of the head works, main pipe line, pumping machinery, break pressure tank, etc., are provided with 100% grant in aid when these works are situated at a distance of 3,5, and 8 kms from the boundary of 'C'-class, 'B'-class & 'A'-class municipal councils respectively. In addition as per Govt. Order of 30 January 1996, cost of development of source or sharing the cost of dam is also eligible for 100% grant in aid.

Besides the norms or criteria, there is also a difference in financial targets and achievements in Karnataka have been given in Table 4.15. For example, in Karnataka budget allocation for piped water supply scheme is Rs.18 crores, and amount received Rs.13.6 crores and expenditure is Rs.11 crores. Therefore, for piped water supply schemes there is difference of Rs.4 crores between allocations and actually received and there is also Rs. 2 crores difference between received and actual spent. Therefore, this speaks of the existing problems in the management of financial resources. Further with regard to urban water supply, the budget allocation is Rs.66 crores and the actual amount received is Rs. 54 crores. The difference between budget allocation and actual amount received is Rs.12 crores and there is also difference

Table-4.15

Financial Target and Achievement of Water Supply Schemes, 1998-99

(Rs.in Lakhs)

Sl. No.	*Name of the Scheme*	*Budget Allocation*	*Amount Received*	*Difference*	*Expenditure*	*Difference*
1	Piped Water Supply Schemes	1800.00 (20.3)	1355.96 (18.8)	445.0	1104.84 (13.9)	251.12
2	Urban Water Supply Schemes	6646.40 (75.1)	5421.20 (75.2)	1224.8	6707.13 (84.5)	1285.93
3	Under Ground Drainage Schemes	400.00 (4.6)	425.00 (6.0)	-25.0	122.60 (1.6)	303.00
	Total	8846.40	7202.16		7934.57	

Source: KUWS & DB Bangalore, Annual Report 1998-99, Annexure-II.

between actual amount received and expenditure is Rs.14 crores. No doubt, the piped water supply schemes is problematic from the state, while in the urban water supply schemes, the local body's have spent more than that is actually received by them the local authorities have been very efficient in Karnataka from the fact that they have spent more than what is received and also spent more than what is allocated in the budget. The receipt of funds for urban water supply and sewerage schemes during last four years and the situation of funding urban water supply in Maharastra could be understood with the help of the following Table 4.16

Table-4.16
Financial Position of Maharashtra Jeevan Pradhikaran

(Rs.in Million)

Sl. No.	*Year*	*G.I.A*	*L.I.C. Loan*	*O.M.B*	*Total*
1	1995-96	434.30	164.90	500.00	1099.20
2	1996-97	770.60	154.90	434.30	1450.60
3	1997-98	1421.70	245.70	928.20	2849.90
4	1998-99	1200.80	500.00	-	1750.80

Source: MJP, Mumbai, Annual Report, 1999.

In Maharastra, there has been an increase in grant for urban water supply scheme Rs. 434.30 million to 1200.80 million in 1998-99, thus there is an increase of Rs.766.5 million.[15] There is also increase in loan amount and Open Market Borrowing during 1995-96 and 1998-99. For example, the loan amount increased by LIC Rs.385 million. But unfortunately, the OMB has been stopped during the year 1998-99. It may be seen from Table 4.16 that the receipt of the funds from Government, and loan from LIC / OMB is very meager compared to the programme taken up for municipal water supply and sewerage schemes. MJP is also operating and maintaining 35 urban water supply schemes (24 schemes up to consumer end 11 schemes upto bulk point). In addition 8 water works owned by municipal councils are being maintained as Full Deposit Works by MJP. As stated above, MJP is raising loan from

LIC and OMB and making repayment of the same to the financial institutions on behalf of the municipal corporations/councils. However, it is the experience of the MJP that municipal corporations/councils are not making repayment of these loans to the MJP. Huge amount of loan is outstanding with the municipal corporations/councils. MJP is repaying the loan with interest by diverting the regular grants received from government for capital works. Since government stands guarantee for these loans. Further, if MJP defaulters LIC may not grant loan for water supply schemes. These financial institutions are not willing to render financial assistance to the various municipal corporations/councils perhaps because of their un-sound financial position. It has also been observed that local bodies are not taking over the schemes after commissioning for one or the other reason and MJP is forced to operate and maintain these schemes. In urban areas 52 and 20 water works are maintained by MJP on ownership basis. The level of taxation is very low in Maharashtra and partial privatization is being tried by MJP in the form of entrusting of operations and maintenance of water works to private organizations / contractors.

Therefore, from the above it may be concluded that the pattern of funding is more efficient in Maharastra compared to Karnataka. Because not only the question of budget allocation, the release of amount allocated and actual spending by the local authorities create the difference between cups and lips which does not arise in Maharastra. The Maharastra local authorities will have to be efficient because the schemes are financed by loan which will have to be repaid with interest amount from the institutions like LIC.

A true grasp of nature and extent of funding in Karnataka and Maharashtra for urban water supply and the existing difference could be understand with the help of the following tables. If we take Karnataka, the Table 4.17 gives us the data on piped water supply, bulk water supply and deposit contribution works for the latest year 1998-99. Besides it also gives figures relating to opening balance, interest amount, demand (amount), and if these are put together, it becomes total demand of 3 aspects noted above. The actual collections are also given there in. The difference between demand collections provides us some analytical ideas on the pattern of funding.

Table-4.17

Demand, Collection and Balance of Water Charges, 1998-99

(Rs. in lakhs)

Name of the Scheme	*Opening balance*	*Total demand*	*Total collection*	*Difference*
1 Piped water supply	5.24	14.92	8.56	6.36
2 Bulk water supply	6077.94	8050.81	228.88	7821.93
3 Deposit contribution works	1285.59	1604.49	36.03	1568.46
Total	7368.77	9670.22	273.47	9396.75

Source: KUWS & DB Bangalore, Annual Report 1998-99, Annexure-II.

a) The total demand for piped water supply schemes is Rs. 14.92 lakhs during 1998-99, whereas the total collection is Rs. 8.56 lakhs and the difference is Rs. 6.36 lakhs, b) For bulk water supply, the total demand is Rs. 8050.81 lakhs and the total collection is Rs. 228.88 lakhs. The difference amount is Rs 7821.93 lakhs, and c) The demand from D.C. works is Rs. 1604.49 lakhs and collection is Rs. 36.03 laks only and the difference is Rs. 1568.46 lakhs. There has been increase in the differences of total demand and total collection from the three schemes mentioned in above Table 4.17. A noteworthy point with regard to funding in Karnataka is that, the bulk water supply indicates the largest difference of Rs. 7822.00 lakhs which is 83.25%. Therefore the bulk supply programme suffers from the problem of shortage of funds.

Table-4.18
Financial Performance of Maharashtra Jeevan Pradhikaran

Item	*1991-92*	*1995-96*	*Difference*	*Percentage*
Approved outlay	91.8	137.7	45.9	66.6
Receipts (Rs. in million)	63.7 (69.3)	109.54 (79.5)	45.8	58.1
Capital Receipts	24.0	38.0	14.0	63.1
Expenditure (Rs. in 000 lakhs)	18.0 (75.0)	30.0 (78.9)	12.0	60.0
Revenue Receipts	12.00	18.0	6.0	66.6
Expenditure (Rs. in 000 lakhs)	11.0 (91.6)	19 (105.5)	8.0	57.8

Source: MJP, Annual Report 1999.
Note: Figures in brackets indicates percentage of expenditure to receipts.

Similarly, in case of Maharashtra, Table 4.18 provides us data on approved outlay and receipts, capital receipts and expenditure and revenue receipts and expenditures. The important ideas which may be gathered from this table are a) the approved outlay for urban water supply schemes is Rs. 91.8 million in 1991 and it increased to Rs 137.7 million in 1995-96. The difference is Rs. 45.9 million, b) while the actual receipts increased from Rs.

63.7 million to Rs. 109.54 million between 1991-92 and 1995-96, c) Capital receipts and expenditure has been increased from Rs. 24000 lakhs to Rs. 38000 lakhs between 1991-92 and 1995-96 and Rs. 18000 lakhs to Rs.30,000 lakhs respectively period under consideration.

Lastly, between 1991 and 1995 these vast difference of Rs. 1000 lakhs between revenue receipts and expenditure.[16] Therefore, from an examination of data of Karnataka and Maharashtra, it may be concluded that the maintenance of water supply suffers from shortage of funds.

SECTION-IV
PHYSICAL PERFORMANCE

Though with difference, there has been a very fast rate of urbanization is taking place in both Karnataka and Maharashtra. In particular the 1980 and 1990 decades have indicated an unimaginable increase in the urban population. There is an increase in number of cities, towns and urban agglomerations in the two states. However, what is the achievement of the government under the given circumstances is a very crucial aspect. Therefore, the present part briefly describes the achievements of Karnataka and Maharashtra in terms of providing drinking water to the people, cities and towns. Accordingly, a) the comparative achievements, b) urban water supply schemes sanctioned and commissioned, c) physical and targets and achievements, and (d) the action plans of the two states have been noted in the following.

Physical performance of urban water supply schemes has been given in Table 4.19. It may be observed from the table that, for example, Karnataka state covered 194 cities and towns and provided water supply to 120 lakh urban population. In other words the state has been successful in providing water supply to 74 per cent urban population in the state.

While the Maharashtra state covered 242 towns and cities with the population of 295 lakhs, which constitutes 81 per cent of urban population. However, Maharashtra has a very small edge over Karnataka, but the two states have an undoubted task to providing water supply to nearly 26 and 19 per cent of total urban population. How far they are initiating the plans, programmes since 1991 could be understood from the following.

Table-4.19
Physical Performance of Urban Water Supply Schemes, 2000-2001

State	*Towns/cities covered*	*Coverage of population (in lakhs)*	*Total urban population (in lakhs)*	*Percentage*
Karnataka	194	120.00	162.0	74.00
Maharashtra	242	295.00	368.4	81.00
India	2200	2425.00	2700.00	90.00

Source: KUWS & DB Bangalore, and MJP Mumbai, Annual Reports, 2000-2001.

If we look at Table 4.20 that it is possible to understand the progress under KUWS & DB Schemes from 1990-2000.

Table-4.20
Progress under KUWS & DB Schemes 1990-2000

(Rs. in Lakhs)

Name of the Scheme	*No. of schemes completed*	*Total estimated expenditure*
1. Piped water supply	220	15868.26
2. Urban water supply	116	54666.95
3. Under ground drainage schemes	27	2726.84
Total	363	73262.05

Source: KUWS & DB Bangalore, Annual Report 2000-01.

It may be understood from the table that in Karnataka KUWS & DB has successfully completed 363 total schemes with Rs. 73262 lakhs expenditure between 1990-2000. Out of 363 schemes 220 are piped water supply schemes, 116 urban water supply schemes and 27 underground drainage schemes and the expenditure for piped water supply Rs. 15868.26 lakhs, Rs. 54666.95 lakhs for urban water supply and Rs. 2726.84 lakhs for UGD Schemes.

When we look at Maharashtra Table 4.21 between 1995-99, 171 urban water supply schemes undertaken, and completed only 72 schemes. The estimated cost is Rs. 31500 million and 155 urban water supply schemes are in progress for 151 towns / cities with the expenditure of Rs. 28500 million in 1999.[17]

Table-4.21
Performance of Urban Water Supply Schemes in Maharashtra (1995-1999)

Name of the Scheme	*Towns / schemes covered*	*Estimate cost (Rs. in million)*
Urban water supply schemes undertaken	171	31500.0
Schemes completed	72	21150.0
Schemes are in progress (9/1999)	155*	28500.0

Source: MJP Annual Report 1999.
Note: * indicates 155 urban water supply schemes for 151 towns / cities.

The efforts of two states is providing drinking water to the urban people could be understood with the help of the action plans, master plans, new schemes and re-innovating the old schemes in the two states could be seen from the Tables 4.22(a) and 4.22(b) for Karnataka and Maharashtra respectively.

As regards Maharashtra, it is seen from Table 4.22(b) that, the action plan 2000-01 gives the water supply position of Maharashtra state a) there are 60 continuing schemes and 3 new schemes are backlog municipal water supply schemes and the probable expenditure is Rs. 32040.14 lakhs during March 2000, b) under non-backlog municipal water supply and sewerage schemes are 175 continuing schemes and 103 new schemes, the total schemes 278 and the estimated cost is Rs.693722.17 lakhs, c) there are 123, and 78 continuing and new schemes under external aided municipal water supply and sewerage schemes and d) 22 and 4, continuing and new schemes, are comes under accelerated urban municipal water supply schemes. The total cost is Rs. 10144.16 lakhs. The action plan points out that, non backlog municipal water supply and sewerage schemes are highest in Mahrashtra i.e., 278 during 2000-01.

Table-4.22

Performance of Urban Water Supply Schemes in Karnataka

Sl. No	*Schemes*		*Estimate cost*
I	New schemes sanctioned and commissioned during October 1999 to September 2000		
	a. No. of now schemes sanctioned	25	318.50
	b. No. of schemes commissioned	15	115.05
	c. No. of ongoing schemes	62	516.44
II	Master plan for water supply schemes (2000-01 to 2007-08)		
	a. Master plan for 194 towns / cities		1033.0
	b. Master plan for 208 towns / cities		2973.0
III	Action plan for water supply schemes (2000-07)		
	1. Urban areas covered under international assistance.		
	a. Ongoing KU'D project under ADB assistance		4
	b. Proposed KCEMUD project under ADB assistance		10
	Total		14
	2. Balance urban areas requiring improvements to water supply (208-14)		194
	3. Ongoing schemes		52
	4. Balance fund required to complete above on going schemes (Rs in crores)		358.56
	5. Towns / Cities requiring augmentation of source		76
	6. Approximate cost to meet the above augmentation (Rs. in crores)		303.18
	7. Towns / cities requiring remodelling of distribution and additional storage facilities.		66
	8. Approximate cost to meet the above requirement (Rs. in crores).		370.95
	Total cost for 194 towns/cities (Rs. in crores)		1032.69
	The loan amount for action plan for water supply schemes (Rs in crores)		826.13

Source: KUWS & DB Bangalore, Information Brouhure, Sep 2000.

SECTION-V
THE COMPARATIVE ASSESSMENT

As a matter of continuity, before the understanding of economics of urban water supply in the study areas, a comparative macro level assessment in Karnataka and Maharashtra is essential. The urban profile, demand and supply patterns, targets, achievements and new schemes which have been discussed above are the important. Therefore, the latest demand for water, the norms of water supply, and the plan outlays in two states have been considered here for the purpose of the comparative assessment.

If we look into the latest demand for water, for example in Karnataka a) The demand for water for drinking purpose is 20 billion cubic meter, b) The demand for agriculture is highest that is 490 billion cubic meter, and c) The industrial demand for water is 26 billion cubic meter, which could be seen from the Table 4.23. Whereas in Maharashtra i) The water demand for drinking purpose is 33 billion cubic meter, ii) The highest water demand for agriculture is 630 billion cubic meter and iii) The industrial water demand is 30 million cubic meter.

If we compare the two states the emerging points are, i) drinking water demand difference of two states is 13 billion cubic meters, ii) the highest difference from agriculture is 140 billion cubic meter, iii) lowest difference of industrial demand is 4 billion cubic meter. A noteworthy point is that Maharashtra is the leading state in terms of latest water demand when compared to Karnataka. No doubt Karnataka is making serious efforts to increase the water supply situation in the affore mention sectors in recent years. The Maharashtra being the rich state is far ahead of Karnataka. Besides, it may be recapitulated that Government of Maharashtra have taken a policy decision to accord first priority for reserving a water source for drinking purpose.[18] Nation as a whole, the present scenario as regards demand of water for various usage, the share of allocation of water for drinking purposes is going to marginally increase from present 4.5% to 5%. Thus at macro level, these appears to be adequate availability of water, and serious problem is anticipated. However, at the micro level there is large variation of rainfall in the state. Particularly there are some drought prone areas, which need to be tackled on priority, presently reservation of water in the storage has been agreed up to 15% of net storage. In case of drought prone areas, highest reservations would be necessary.

Table-4.23
Sectoral Water Demand in Karnataka and Maharashtra During 2000

(Demand in billion cubic meters)

Type of Use	*Karnataka*		*Maharahstra*		*Difference*
	Demand	*Percentage*	*Demand*	*Percentage*	
Drinking	20	3.56	33	4.4	13
Agriculture	490	86.4	630	84.0	140
Hydropower Generation	21[a]	3.7	27	3.6	6
Industrial use	26[b]	4.5	30	4.0	4
Other miscellaneous usages	10	1.7	30	4.0	20
Total	567	100.00	750	100.0	--

Source: KUWS & DB and MJP Reports, 2000, p.36 & 25.

Note: a) Includes efforts of generating through river waters and extension of stages existing hydal power projects.

b) Includes efforts in establishing units funded by private institutions and Non-Resident Indians (NRI).

Similarly, the attempt for renovating tanks in a phased manner has been taken up by the Government of Karnataka and the purpose of this programme is to increase tank irrigation, on the one side and provide drinking water to the rural and urban areas alike. It is a hilarious task requiring very huge amount of money. In an estimated more than 50,000 tanks in the state only 5000 tanks has been taken up during the current price, there is progress but for from expectations.

As against water demand, the desired litre per capita per day (LPCD) norms assumes (water supply policy) greater significance in the two states which could be seen from the Table 4.24.

Table-4.24
Water Supply Position

Sl. No	Population Range	Water Supply Level (LPCD)		
		India[a]	Karnataka[b]	Maharashtra[c]
1	Less Than 20,000 a. Population served by stand posts b. Population provided with house connection	 40 70	 40 70	 50 70
2	20,000 to 1,00,000	100	100	125
3	1,00,000 to 10,00,000	a) 100 with no sewerage system b) 135 with sewerage system.	- -	- -
4	10,00,000 and above	150	135	150

Source: a) Data from Central Public Health and Environmental Engineering Organisation & Ministry of Urban Affairs and Employment, New Delhi, 1999-2000. p.87
b) Data from KUWS & DB, Bangalore, Annual Report 2000-01.
c) Data from MJP, Mumbai, Annual Report, 1999-2000.

There is greater demand for water in Maharashtra compare to Karnataka as seen above. But, it may be hypothesized that richer the state higher the norm for good quality and quantity of drinking water. Given the demand for water as explained in the table above, the following data points to the details of LPCD norms transposed in all India.

It may be reaffirmed that in almost all the states the per capita supply is much below the desirable norm set by different authorities.[19] The national average supply is 140 litres per capita per day (LPCD) in the 133 class-I cities surveyed as against the International Standard and norm of 200 LPCD. Govt of India norms for quantity of water are 40-250 LPCD for urban areas and 55 LPCD for rural areas. It is observed from the Table 4.24 that in Karnataka the level of water supply in 208 urban areas ranges from 40 LPCD to 135 LPCD. In Maharashtra the level of water supply in 245 urban areas ranges from 50 LPCD to 150 LPCD compared to all India Maharashtra is ahead by 15 LPCD Karnataka.

Table-4.25

Plan Outlay for Urban Water Supply in Karnataka and Maharashtra

(Rs in Lakhs)

State	*Plan Period*								
	I	*II*	*III*	*IV*	*V*	*VI*	*VII*	*VIII*	*IX*
Karnataka	75.0	195.3 (38.5)	600.0 (32.5)	1300.0 (46.1)	3300.0 (39.4)	6700.0 (49.3)	15500.0 (43.2)	33533.0 (46.2)	55000.0 (60.9)
Maharahstra	300.0	450.0 (66.6)	1221.0 (36.8)	5955 (20.5)	11420 (52.1)	37400 (30.5)	69700.0 (53.7)	97127.0 (71.8)	154000 (63.0)
Difference	225.0	225.0	621.0	4655.0	8120.0	30700.0	54200.0	63594.0	99000.0
% change	25.0	43.4	49.1	21.8	28.9	17.9	22.3	34.5	35.7

Source: Compiled from Various Plan Drafts of Karnataka and Maharashtra States.

Note: Figures in the parentheses indicates the percentage change ineach state during the plan period.

A comparative picture of plan outlays can give a supportive idea of the match between means and ends. For example, during the First Plan there was Rs. 75 lakhs in Karnatka and Rs. 300 lakhs in Maharashtra and the difference was Rs. 225 lakhs. In Karnataka the Second Plan allocation was Rs. 195.3 lakhs and in Maharashtra it is Rs. 450 lakhs and the difference was Rs. 255 lakhs which is 43.4% like that, during the Third Plan, the Karnataka plan outlay on urban water supply was Rs. 600 lakhs and of Maharashtra was Rs. 1221 lakhs, the difference was 621 lakhs which is 49.1 %. more. Similarly, in Eighth Plan (see Table 4.25), the plan allocation in Karnataka was Rs. 15500 lakhs and in Maharashtra it was Rs. 69700 lakhs, the difference was Rs. 54200 lakhs and 22.3 per cent. There has been a reduction in the gap between Karnataka and Maharashtra that means 22.3 per cent more than Karnataka in the plan outlays on urban water supplying during VIIth plan by 10.5 per cent. When we switch to the Eighth Plan, the plan allocation in Karnataka is Rs. 33533.0 lakhs and in Maharashtra it is Rs. 97127.0lakhs, the difference is Rs. 63594 lakhs as such difference between Seventh and Eighth plan needless Maharashtra is ahead of Karnataka but Maharashtra state has maintained only a status quo in terms of plan allocation measured in percentage points.

A comparison of allocations for urban water supply in the two states under consideration provides a different picture. It was Rs. 55000 lakhs in Karnataka and in Maharashtra it is Rs. 1,54,000 lakhs, the difference is Rs. 99000 lakhs and the percentage difference is 33.7%. This clearly shows a sharp declined in the plan outlay on urban water supply in Maharastra.

When we see the situation of plan allocations within the two states the emerging points are a) In Karnataka there is an increase of 38.5 per cent in Second Plan, b) between IIIrd and IVth Plan the difference is 13.6 per cent, c) there has been 6.1 per cent difference during VI and VII Plan, d) between VII and VIIIth Plan, the difference is 3 per cent, and such difference between VIII and IXth plan is 14.5 per cent. Therefore, it should be noted that no doubt there are fluctuations in plan allocations for urban water supply in Karnataka, but there is a greater move for increasing allocations to urban water in Karnataka. Similarly in Maharashtra, a) there was an increase of 66.6% in Second Plan, b) between IIIrd and IVth Plan, the difference was 16.3%, c) there is difference of 23.2% between VI and VIIth Plan, d) between VII and VIII the Plan the difference is 18.1%, and such difference between VIII and IX Plan is 8.8 per cent.

Thus, the inter state and intra state plan allocations on urban water supply in Karnataka and Maharashtra brings us to the conclusion that a) there is no doubt an increase in absolute amount of investment in two states, b) Karanataka has registered only 14.7 per cent increasing during VIII and IX plan, c) While Maharashtra state has an increase in plan outlay by 9 per cent during the same period.

NOTES AND REFERENCES

1. United Nations Water Conference (1977), "Resolution on Community Water Supply".
2. Govt. of India, "Census Report 1991".
3. In the recent past the states like Madhya Pradesh, and Uttar Pradesh and Bihar have been divided and new states, chattigarh, uttar anchal and Jarkhand have been created and as a result the ranks may alter substantially.
4. In the recent past, for better administration geographically, new districts such as Koppal, Haveri Davanger, Bagalkot, Chamargjnagar, and Udpi etc have been created. But there is not increase in number of revenue divisions by so far. This is a shortcoming for estimating the needs of water supply and infrastructural facilities.
5. The central government is thinking of issuing guidelines to the state with respect to the creation of bigger cities into corporations.
6. Annual Survey of Industries, 1996-97 (Factory Sector) Vol. I, CSO (Industrial Statistical Wing), Ministry of Static's and Programme Implementation, Govrnment of India, Calcutta.
7. For example, food, beverages, chemicals, storage and ware housing, electricity etc are the industries which require great textiles, the also require to some extent small quantity of water. In all, besides domestic there is water demand for industrial use.
8. Nageshwar Rao M. "Urban Water Supply", Studies in Urban Public Sector, Ashish Publishing House, New Delhi, 1985, p.170.

9. However, in subsequent discussions in urban water supply except otherwise emphasized, the term 'urban water supply ' is used covering both piped and urban water supply schemes.
10. M.J.P., 'Annual Report 1997-98, CIDCO Bhavan, Belapur, Navi Mumbai.
11. Ibid.
12. Bidyut Mohanty, "Urbanisation in Developing Countries", IIP Publishing House, New Delhi 1993, p.153.
13. Ibid, p.156
14. Within each household each member acts as decision maker independently if he or she has access to other sources. Further each member is independent in the use of water but is accountable to the total quantity of water available to the household for the day.
15. Such figures for 2001 are yet to come from the census data.
16. See, Report of MJP, "Private sector participation in urban water supply and sewerage projects", 1999.
17. According to the report of MJP, 1999, the estimated cost of Rs. 28,500 million in under consideration. The expenditure during 1999 is Rs. 10,400 mn. The balance funds required would be to the tune of Rs. 18100 mm this is about 63 per cent difference the planned and exactly spent expenditure. Though for a rich state it is a demanding problematic issue.
18. See, KUWS&D Board Bulletin, p.18 & Maharashtra Jeevan Pradhikaran Report. Op.cit, p.25
19. Archana Ghosh, "Status of Water Supply and Sanitation Sacilities in Urban India an Overview", IIP Publishing House, New Delhi, 1993.

5

Macro Analysis of Urban Water Supply in Gulbarga and Solapur Cities

Introduction

The water is lifeline for all creatures, including all the tulchar.[1] For reaching the depth of economics of urban water supply, a macro analysis of water supply in Gulbarga and Solapur cities is an essential step. This would also help in understanding the similarities and differences between the two cities and their implications to policies and programmes to be framed for the cities under consideration. Historically, the two are having apparent similarities but differ significantly in their growth, system of water supply, sources of water supply and financing of water supply. Therefore, the purpose of this chapter is to examine the macro level aspects of water supply in the two cities. For convenience, it is divided into the following sections. **The Section–I** describes locational history, The **Section–II** describes the growth of two cities, implications for drinking water and improvements to water supply schemes. **Section–III** is devoted for the discussion of sources and systems of water supply existing in Gulbarga and Solapur cities. The **Section-IV** discusses financial aspects which is crucial for water supply. A critical analysis of the problems and prospects for the future has been attempted in **Section-V**.

SECTION-I
LOCATIONAL HISTORY

Location

The Gulbarga is fast growing city and the Divisional Head Quarter of the districts of Bidar, Gulbarga, Raichur, Bellary and Koppal with a big business centre.[2] It is situated on the Mumbai-Madras central line and about 640 kms from Bangalore. The Gulbarga city is linked by broad guage railway line to states capital and the capitals of the neighbouring states namely Andhra Pradesh and Tamil Nadu. The Bangalore-Humnabad state highway passes through the city. The other important state highways which link the city are Gulbarga-Sedam, Gulbarga-Aland & Gulbarga-Afzalpur roads. The nearest Aerodrome is at Hyderabad, which is at a distance of 298 km. The city is in the Northern Plains of Karnataka in the Krishna river basin.

The first Gulbarga Municipality was established in 1945. During 1961, the population of Gulbarga was 97,159. Gulbarga Municipal Council was upgraded to a corporation on 2-10-1981, present municipal corporation area is 65.15 sq. kms. Population of city in 1991 was 3.4 lakh and at present it is nearly about 4.50 lakh. The city is divided into 55 wards for the convenience of municipal administration and the water supply arrangements are made in the division of the town into Ground Level Service Reservoirs / Elevated Service Reservoirs.

Solapur is the fourth largest town in Maharashtra state and is situated about 455 km from Mumbai towards south National Highway No. 9.[3] It has a number of rail and road link to some of the important towns in Maharashtra and neighbouring states. Road transport facilities are quite good. It is a biggest centre of education as well as business. Solapur is essentially an industrial town. The major economic activities of Solapur city are Textile Mills, Dal and Oil Mills.

Solapur municipality was established on 1st August 1852. In the year 1965 the population of Solapur was 28,646, the first general census was held in the year 1872 and the population numbered 53,403. Solapur municipal council was upgraded to a corporation on 1st May 1964. Present municipal corporation area is 180 sq.kms. Population of the city in 1991 was up to 6.44 lakh, including urbanising area and at present it is nearly about 10 lakh soul. Up to 1992 the city limit area was 33 sq.kms. By 5th May 1992 the municipal city limit area extended up to 180 sq.km and the city spread all around the original one during that time 12 adjoining villages and habitats were included. The city has been divided into 90 wards for the convenience of corporation administration and the water supply arrangements are made on the division of the city into Ground Level Service Reservoir and Elevated Service Reservoir/High level Service Reservoir Zone.

The major economic activities in Solapur are due principally to textile mills, handlooms and powerlooms constituting the cotton industry engaged in spinning and preparation of yarn, weaving and finishing.[4] The other important industries are Shivaji Works Ltd., manufacturing iron castings and Siddheshwar sugar factory. M.I.D.C. has set up an industrial estate covering 445 hectares of land on eastern border of the town. Solapur is a major commercial centre for the states of Maharashtra, Karantaka and Andhra Pradesh.

Brief History of Gulbarga and Solapur Cities

Historical importance of Gulbarga city back to Bahamani period, the city was made the first capital of Hasan Gangu Bhamani in 1347. The city has its glory until the end of the Bhamani Kingdom in 1874. Later Gulbarga was one of the Subha in Nizam Kingdom, until it was made over to Karnataka state during the reorganisation of states in 1956.

As per the Gulbarga District Gazetteer, the modern name Gulbarga derived from 'Gul' 'burg', which means, a huge muddy round shaped landscape. The name Gulbarga means, 'a leaf with flowers', as it is derived from Persian language the 'Gul' means flower and 'Burg' mean leaf. However, since its geographical identification (blue hard rock) it is called as 'Kalburgi'[5], which means "a stony land" or "stone roofing" or a "heap of stones" in Kannada language.

The Gulbarga is an ancient urban agglomeration, but founded on the Jagat tank located by the side of Sharanbasaveshwar temple. Therefore, this tank might have been the source of drinking water supply, the muddy table was used for agricultural cultivation, as the black soil was fertile. In the due course, the Veerashaivism (which was popular during 12 and 13th century A.D) attracted number of people for Sharana Basveshwar temple and its annual Kar festival. At the advent of time, the Muslim invasion took place during 1347 and became the kingdom of Hasan Gangu Bahamani Shah who built his fort on the South bed of Jagat tank.[6] The interfued among the Muslim rulers led to the downfall of Bahmani and the Gulbarga fort was surrendered to Adilshah of Bijapur and later it came under the Nizam of Hyderabad. Thus, the basic historical and locational inference is that the Gulbarga city is not located on the bank of any river and the Sharana Basveshwar tank added only a cluster of households alongside the fort which was named after Adilshah and is presently known as Shahabazar, as it continued under Bahmani dynasty and later over taken by Adilshah and further brought under the rule of the Nizam of Hyderabad. The Sharan Basvashweshwar tank was the only source of drinking water. A nearby river let Bhosga came into prominence for drinking water supply to the people of present Gulbarga city which is knows as Bhosga Tank.

Similarly, Solapur probably formed part of the territories of the Shatakarni or Andhrabhritya dynasty whose capital was Paithan on the river Godavari. A sanskrit inscription dated, Shaka 1238 after the down fall of the Yadavas town was known as Sonalipur, later called as Sonalapur and Sandalapur.[7] Hence it is probable that during the course of time the name Solapur was evolved by dropping 'na' from the original name Sonalapur. Solapur is one of the ancient cities in India with a history traceable to the year 90 B.C. centrally situated Siddeshwar tank was constructed in the twelfth century and the fort in the year 1358. Solapur was ruled by Marathas till 1818. After the battle of Asti of Marathas in the same year, Solapur was surrendered to the British. Similar to Gulbarga, the present Solapur city is not located on the bank of any river but there is an ancient temple Siddharameshwar located in the midst of Siddashwar tank, which has been the only source of drinking water to the inhabited people of Solapur urban agglomeration and people attending the Siddharam Kar festival on Makara Sankaranti day. The people of Solapur urban agglomeration faced with the problem of drinking water started depending on Ekruk river let which is known as Ekruk tank. Thus, it is evident from historical records that two cities defy the usual theory of location[8] (see Maps 5.1 and 5.2).

Map-5.1 & 5.2 Gulbarga And Solapur Cities

SAMPLE WARDS IN GULBARGA

1. Station Baazar
2. Jagat
3. Gajipur
4. Maktampur
5. Raja
6. Mominpura (A)
7. Mominpura (B)
8. Aasifgunj
9. Shahabazar
10. Brahmapur (A)
11. Brahmapur (B)

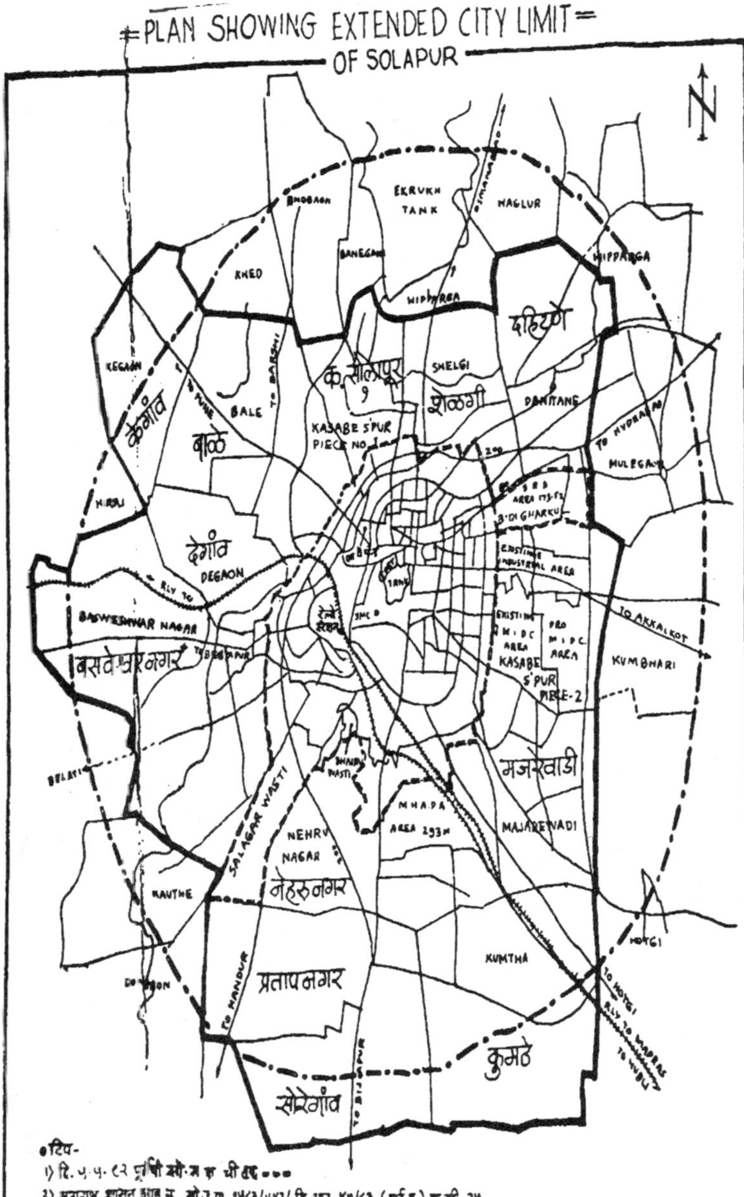
PLAN SHOWING EXTENDED CITY LIMIT
OF SOLAPUR
EKRUKH TANK
HAGLUR
KHED
HIPPARGA
KEGAON
BALE
SHELGI
KASABE S'PUR PIECE NO. 1
DEGAON
BASWESHWAR NAGAR
TO AKKALKOT
KUMBHARI
KASABE S'PUR PIECE-2
EXISTING INDUSTRIAL AREA
MAJAREWADI
MHADA AREA
SALAGAR WASTI
NEHRU NAGAR
KAUTHE
KUMTHA
TO NANDUR
TO BIJAPUR
TO HOTGI
RLY TO MADRAS
MULEGAON
DAHITANE
TO HYDRABAD

Configuration and Topography

Configuration and Topography may be considered as the most useful latent aspects in the context of research in urban water supply. Because, besides the traditional, the most modern source of water supply which is gaining currency is rain water harvesting.[9] The configuration and topography of Gulbarga and Solapur may be understood with the help of the following Table 5.1. The Gulbarga city is situated between northern latitude of 17^0-20' and eastern longitude of 76^0-56'.

Table-5.1
Configuration and Topography

City	*Latitude*	*Longitude*
Gulbarga	17^0-20' North	76^0-56' East
Solapur	17^0-11' North	75^0-54' East

Source: Compiled from Gulbarga and Solapur Regional Metrological Centres Registers 2000-01.

Whereas, Solapur, the city is situated between northern latitude of 17^0-11' north and eastern longitude of 75^0–54' East. Thus, it is clear that, Gulbarga is on the top in topography by 9 inches in latitude and 1^0-2' in longitude if compared to Solapur.[10] The levels in the Solapur city and extended areas varies from 440 mtrs to 490 mtrs. the general slope is from north–east to south–east.

Temperature and Climate

The temperature and its portogue i.e.,climate are highly influential in providing drinking water to the urban people. The high temperature and prevailing hot climate acts as a catalyst in evaporating the water in the reservoirs and storage tanks.[11] It is needless to add that the hot climate also greatly reduces the level of ground water. In other words, the water table gets affected very seriously. Under this background, the temperature prevailing in Gulbarga and Solapur have been noted in the Table 5.2.

Table-5.2
Temperature and Climate

City	Highest	Lowest
Gulbarga	41.3°C-45°C	14.8° C-16.2°C
Solapur	41.5°C- 43.5°C	15.3° C

Source: Ibid

The temperature in Gulbarga varies from 45°C and 43.5°C in summer season. The highest temperature prevailing in Gulbarga city varies from 41.3°C to 45°C and the lowest temperature is varies from 14.8°C to 16.2°C in winter season. While in Solapur, the temperature varies from 41.5°C to 43.5°C in summer to about 15.3°C in winter. It is important to remember that save the finger count days[12] during winter, the maximum average temperature in the two cities is between 35°C to 40°C. Further, the two cities have similar temperature and climatic conditions.[13]

Rainfall

The rainfall[14] is the key to urban drinking water supply. No doubt, the system and technology are important but act only as complement to the rainfall. Besides, the technological change and application of modern techniques are highly dependent on urban water supply. Against this, the rainfall situation may be understood with the help of following Table 5.3

The average rainfall in Gulbarga city is 624.1 mm. The lowest rainfall is 410 mm in 1991, the highest rainfall recorded in Gulbarga city is 843.8 mm in 2000 and if we look at the rainfall of Solapur city, the highest rainfall has been recorded is 1249 mm in 1998, the lowest rainfall is 448 mm in 1992, the average rainfall recorded in the city is 707 mm and there has been poor rainfall during 1991, 1992, 1994, 1997 and 1999 respectively.

It is disheartening to note that the two cities due to poor rainfall face the problem of drinking water supply. And the two cities being away from big dams are also found to be ineffective in providing drinking water to the people with the help of good railway network.[15] Most often, the people of Gulbarga city migrate to Chennai and

Table-5.3
Rainfall in Gulbarga and Solapur Cities

Year	*Rainfall (in mm)*	
	Gulbarga	*Solapur*
1991	410.3	587.2
1992	617.3	448.4
1993	645.8	851.7
1994	426.4	450.9
1995	576.1	930.3
1996	764.4	820.1
1997	548.0	593.8
1998	711.6	1249.2
1999	696.4	477.3
2000	843.8	660.1
Total	6240.1	7069.0
Average	624.1	706.9

Source: Gulbarga and Solapur Regional Meterological Centres.

Mumbai and people of Solapur migrate to Mumbai with the whole family. The droughts are the common place experience of the people of Gulbarga and Solapur. As a practical problem, the drinking water supply for Gulbarga is irregular i.e., oftenly twice or thrice a week. However, if rainfall is matched too topography, Solapur stands in a better position in the context of drinking water supply.

SECTION -II
GROWTH OF CITIES AND IMPLICATIONS FOR DRINKING WATER

Alongside the locational history, the history of Gulbarga and Solapur differ sharply in terms of their medieval, political, growth structure. It is the common place experience and the feeling of patriotism and political freedom and independence that which has the main difference between the growth of Gulbarga and Solapur cities. The Gulbarga city (also some part of Maharashtra-

Marathawada), excluding Solapur was under the rule of Nizam of Hyderabad against this, the Solapur came under British rule as early as in 1838, the growth of two cities differ by more than a century(110 years). If this being the case the growth of cities and contingent drinking water aspects differ but only historically. The Gulbarga city under the Nizams rule did not experience any works, while change and had only a regimented growth with differing religious groups and settlements. But the neighboring Solapur city had a phase wise British attention and development for water supply.

Structure of the Cities

Gulbarga

The ancient fort and the central business area from the nucleus part of the city on the northern side of a larger water sheet (Jagat Tank). The city has grown in north-south direction with Bangalore-Humanabad state highway as axis. The city has also grown towards east along the Sedam road. Brahmpur is an old extension on the southwest of Jagat tank with Sharanabasaveshwar temple as a land mark. Similarly the holy tomb of Khaja Bande Nawaz forms another important land mark amidst residential area in the north-east. The city has also grown on the Afzalpur road and Jewargi road. The Madras-Bombay railway line passes from south-east to western part. (South of Heerapur village).[16]

Solapur

The ancient fort and MIDC area, Kasabe Solapur are the part of the city on the northern side of a larger water sheet (Siddeshwar Tank). The city has grown in north-south direction with Akkalkot road an axis. The city has also grown towards south with the areas of Nehrunagar, Kumtha, Soregaon, Salgarwasti, Pratapnagar, Japur, Nandur roads. The Ekruk tank is towards north of the city and nearest to city, the extension areas like Bale, Khegaon, Degaon, Basaveshwar nagar towards western part of the city and Dahitane, Kasbe, Kumbhari east, Majarewadi, Kumtha towards eastern part of the city respectively. Soregoan, Shelgi, Hipparga, Badegoan, Khed, Hagulur grown towards north of the city, the fort, and Siddeshwar tank exists in the heart of the city.[17]

In the process of expanding the geographical limits of the two cities of our study there has been change in the inclusion of surrounding adjusted villages. The following Table 5.4 provides the coverage of villages in Gulbarga and Solapur cities during the year 1992. The Gulbarga city covered under its limit only 8 villages,

Table-5.4
Urbanized Villages-1992

City	*Urbanized Villages*
Gulbarga	08[a]
Solapur	12[b]

Source: Records from Gulbarga and Solapur Municipal Corporations.
Note: a) 8 Villages are covered under Gulbarga city namely, Vakkalgera, Brahampur. B, Rajapur, Dariyapur, Biddapur, Shaik-Roza ,Kapnoor& Badepur.
b) 12 villages are covered under Solapur city namely Kegaon, Bale, Kasbe Solapur 1 & 2, Shelgi, Dahitane, Basaveshwarnagar, Degaon, Pratapnagar, Nehrunagar, Soregaon, Majrewade and Kumthe.

Whereas, the Solapur city incorporated 12 villages. These villages have different sources of water supply and their consequences for city authorities cannot be made a wild guess. Indeed, Solapur covered more villages under its limit than Gulbarga.

Existing Water Supply Arrangements

Gulbarga city has three sources[18] of water supply namely, a) Bhosga reservoir, b) Bennithora river and c) Bhima river (See Map 5.3).

The Sharanabasveshwar tank was the only source of drinking water in earlier period. A nearby river let Bhosga came into prominence for drinking water supply to the people of present Gulbarga city which is known as Bhosga tank.

I[st] Stage Water Supply Scheme with Bhosga Reservoir as Source

An earthen embankment with R.C.C. was executed to store the water and supply to Gulbarga city for 30,000 population. This

MAP-5.3 SCHEMATIC DRAWING OF GULBARGA EXISTING WATER SUPPLY SCHEME (I, II & III STATE)

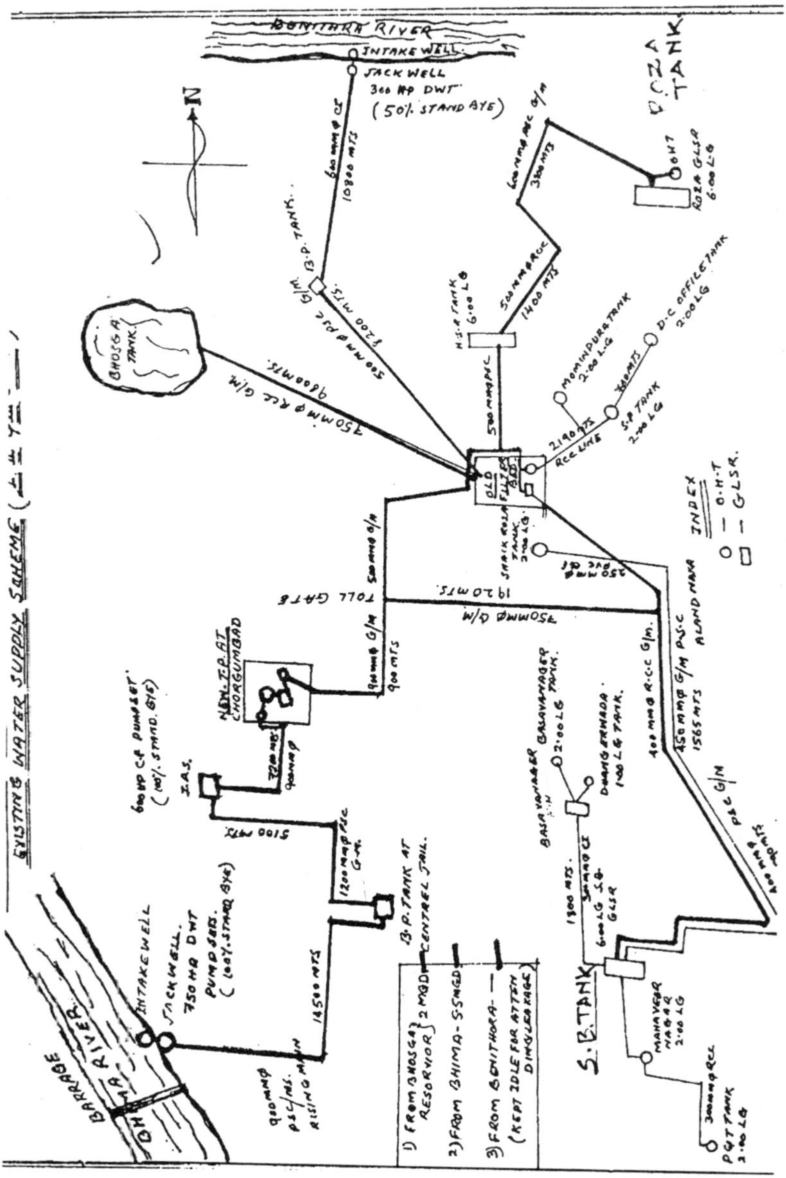

reservoir is situated at a distance of 9.6 kms from the city, catchment area of the tank was 90.23 sq. kms. The gross capacity of the tank was 418.6 MC ft. This water was drawn to filter bed for filtration and further distribution. The system runs on gravity force only. The maximum storage level was 18 feet. Due to scanty rainfall during last monsoon the tank was not received the full level of water. The present water level is 1616.50 (as on 20-10-1999), during its full capacity, the water is drawn to city at the rate of 2.0 Million Gallons Per Day (MGD) only as against 4.0 MGD due to silting up of Reinforced Cement Concrete pipe (Gravity main). The scheme has been remodeled under comprehensive water supply scheme to Gulbarga city I stage (estimated cost Rs. 97.00 lakh) of the Bhosga tank was increased from 289 Million Cubic feet to 418 MCft. A new 30 gravity main (8 kms long has been laid in place of open channels) additions to treatment units of 2 MGD located on the town towards north and improvements to distribution system. The scheme has been completed during 1970 for designed a prospective population of 1,00,000. The outlay of the scheme was Rs. 84.40 lakh. The water was drawn during power failure or any other problem at Bhima source. Owing to the abnormal increase in population, additional source i.e., Bennithora river is considered for IInd stage water supply scheme for the city.

IInd Stage Water Supply Scheme with Bennithora River as Source

Second stage water supply scheme to Gulbarga city is designed and executed with Bennithora river as a source which is at distance of 20 km. Under this scheme river head works have been constructed near Kurikota village, rising main of 600 mm dia Cast Iron (C.I) Pipe 10.70 Kms long has been laid to convey water from head works to break pressure tank at Salamtekdi with 300 House Power (HP) 3 Nos. Deep well turbine pumps, gravity main with 600 mm dia and 500 mm dia Pre–Stressed Concrete (PSC) pipes, 8.2 kms. long has been laid from break pressure tank to treatment works. The scheme has been completed during 1978 and the outlay of the scheme was Rs. 143.00 lakh against the estimated cost Rs. 161.00 lakh with the above two schemes about 4.5 MGD of water can be supplied to Gulbarga city which is sufficient for a population of 1.80 lakh at the rate of 25 Gallon Per Capital Per Day. The capacity of the existing treatment works is also 4.5 MGD. The scheme is useful only when there is flowing water in the river, no storage arrangement is there. The water is drawn to make good of short supply from Bhima source.

The Gulbarga City is divided into 11 municipal administrative wards and distribution of water is done by 5 Ground Level Service Reservoirs (GSLRs) and 11 Elevated Reservoirs (ESRs). In addition to above, the city is having 1145 borewells fixed with hand pumps, and 145 bore wells fixed with suitable submersible pumps. Due to scanty rainfall during last mansion, the ground water is dwindling and causing failure of hand pumps. During recent survey, it is observed about 100 hand pumps dwindled in the city, causing drinking water scarcity.

IIIrd Stage Water Supply Scheme Bhima River as Source

This scheme was administratively approved vide on 21-5-1987 and technically sanctioned by the board in 1988 for Rs. 12.86 crore. It is situated 25 km away from the city. The above scheme is nearing completion and targeted for commissioning by the end of December 1992. Due to increase in population, third stage water supply system to Gulbarga city is designed and executed during 1993. The scheme has a designed to the pumping capacity of 5.5. MGD. To store the water at river, a barrage is constructed and 2750 HP DWT pumpset are erected at jack well to pump the water at a rate of 2,75,000 gallons per hour through a rising main of 900 mm dia. The second stage pumping is done at I.P.S. Kotnoor having 600 HP 2 centrifugal pumpsets. A new treatment unit of 5.5 MGD is constructed for further distribution of water to city. The present population of city is 4.30 lakh and water supplied to Gulbarga city is 6.75 MGD, and per capita water supply is 15.7 GPCD (as against 35 GPCD).

Solapur City:

Solapur city obtains its water from two old sources Ekrukh tank and Bhima river and one new source Ujjani dam[19] (see Map-5.4).

Ist Stage Water Supply Scheme with Ekrukh Tank as Source

Till 1880 Sidheswar tank was the only public source of water supply to the town apart from private wells. In 1882, water

MAP-5.4 SOLAPUR WATER SUPPLY SCHEME (UJJANI DAM)

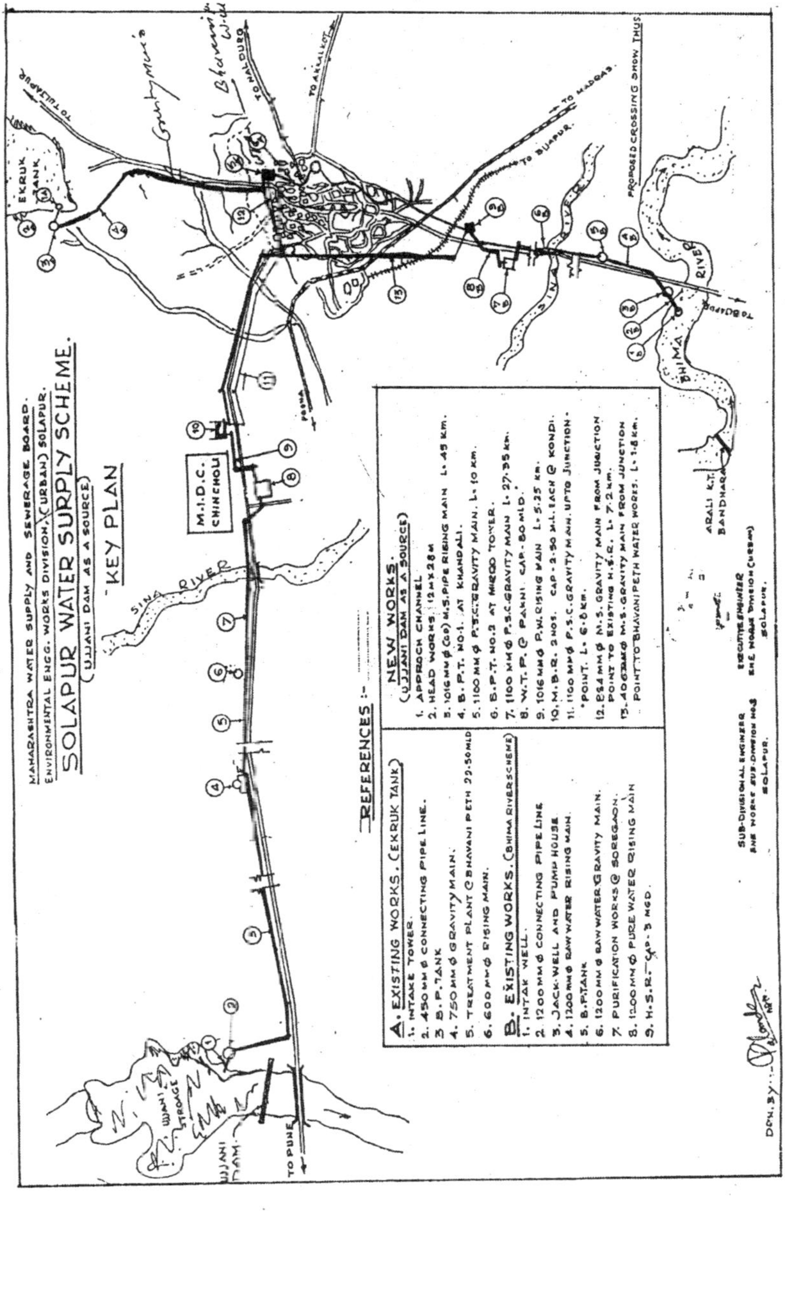

from Ekrukh tank (6 km to the north of the town) was supplied to the town through pipes, and it was first developed source and it comprises an earthen dam with storage capacity of 2160 Mc ft, as a source of water supply. Initial capacity of the treatment plant was 4 Million Litres per Day (MLD). Subsequently, this capacity has been enhanced to 22.50 MLD in 1932. From this Ekrukh tank 22.50 MLD water is abstracted through dam outlet of 750mm dia pipe conveyed through 750 mm dia RCC gravity main to Bhavani Peth Water Treatment plant. The filtration units introduced and commissioned from 1943. Treated water from Bhavani pet is pumped to several service reservoirs (ground and elevated) for distribution in the city. The capacity of water treatment plant was 22.50 MLD. It has been experienced in the past that scanty rainfall during last ten years, the Ekruk tank goes dry and solapur city had to face scarcity of drinking water.

IInd Stage Water Supply Scheme Bhima River as Source

A scheme for drawing water from Bhima river at village Takli, about 30 km south of Solapur town on Solapur-Bijapur road (National highway No.13) was implemented and commissioned in 1968. It is provided for a supply of 45 MLD (in 20 hours) filtered water to town. This scheme was further augmented in 1987 to supply additional 45 MLD and has been commissioned against its total capacity of 90 MLD, the supply at present being drawn is in the order of 90 MLD. Head works consisting of intake well, 1200 mm diameter connecting pipeline, jackwell and pump house are located on Bhima river at Takli. Raw water is pumped through a 1200 mm diameter. Still rising main to a break pressure tank and from break pressure tank to water treatment plant at Soregoan. Treated waters is pumped to a master balancing reservoir called Hill Service Reservoir which is a ground structure situated at the highest elevation in the vicinity of the city. From the Hill Service Reservoir supply gravitates to the various sumps and pumped to the elevated service reservoirs and ground service reservoirs for distribution in the city. Total cost of this scheme is Rs. 303 lakh.

In addition to the above sources, there are about 2300 borewells with handpumps located at different locations in town which together give a supply of 4 MLD water.

IIIrd Stage Water Supply Scheme Ujjani Dam as Source

The population of the Solapur city is 9.75 lakh, and water supplied by two sources is 112.50 MLD (22.50 MLD from Ekruk tank and 90 MLD from Soregoan water works with Bhima river). Considering the rapid development of the city-being a famous trade and pilgrim centre and for providing water supply to extended limits of the corporation, the demand in immediate stage (2011) would be about 183 MLD. Therefore, for meeting this increased requirement scheme of 80 MLD capacity with Yeshwant Sagar (Ujjani Dam) as a source has been sanctioned by the Government on 27-5-92 to be aided by OECF Organisation for Economic Corporation-Japan through Housing and Urban Development Corporation (HUDC).

This scheme is located at 100 km away from city and designed to supply 70 MLD. The scheme under execution envisages of situated on the submergence of Ujjani dam which includes raw water pumping machinery comprises 600 H.P.V.T pumps-6 Nos. Raw water is conveyed through 1016 mm dia M.S. pipe rising main of length 45 km to B.P.T. at Khandali having capacity 2 lakh from this BPS water gravitates through 1100 mm dia PSC pipe 8 kg to 18 kg. raw water gravity main of length 37.35 km water treatment plant of capacity 80 MLD, including pure water sump and pump house, pumping machinery of 250 HP-6 Nos, 1016mm dia M.S. pipe pure water rising main of length 5.25 km. Master Balancing Researvior of capacity of 2.5 MLD, (2 Nos) 1100 mm dia P.S.C. pipe gravity main up to junction point of length 6.8 km, 864 mm dia M.S. gravity main from junction point to existing Hill Service Reservoirs of length 8.61 km, 406 mm dia M.S. pipe gravity main from junction point to Bhavani Peth Water Works of length 2.77km. Miscellaneous works like electric connection, land acquisition, telephone arrangement, staff quarters, wire fencing, wireless system, approach road. The water from Bhavani Peth Water Works at Hill Service Reservoir shall be distributed to the city through existing transmission lines, Elevated Service Reservoir and distribution system.

The expected scale of water supply on completion of this scheme 140 LPCD for city, 50 LPCD for stand post, 70 LPCD for urbanisable village. Gross water requirement of water immediate stage (2011) 182.50 MLD and total water supply including existing scheme (2011) 180 MLD. The population for the year 2011 will be

13.00 lakh and rate of population growth 8.57% per year. Gross cost of the scheme (Ujjani) is Rs. 9072.38 lakh. Funding from G.I.A. 23.33% which is Rs. 2116.58 lakh, loan from OECF Japan through HUDCO is Rs. 6608.80 lakh(66.67%), paid up to Dec.1995 and public contribution received up to Dec 1995 is Rs. 347.00 lakh. These three sources will meet the immediate stage (2011) requirements 182.50 MLD from

Bhavanipet water works	22.50 MLD
Soregoan water works	90.00 MLD
Ujjani water works	70.00 MLD
Total	182.50 MLD

SECTION - III
SOURCES AND SYSTEM OF WATER SUPPLY

An enquiry into the economics of urban water supply is dependent on the sources and quantity of water supply. Further, the systems (house service connections, public stand posts and non-domestic connections) are very important in the drinking water supply to the urban population. It is an established hypothesis, that more and bigger the sources of water supply and better quantity and sufficiency in the water supply. The greater is the source better quantity and quality of water supply. If the sources are large, there would be no problem as regards the quantity of daily water consumption. The system of water supply is as important, as that of the source and these are equally important to ensure the better supply and household consumption. Therefore, the sources and systems of water supply existing in Gulbarga and Solapur cities have been examined in this present section.

The growth of population and per capita availability of water in Gulbarga and Solapur cities shown in Table 5.5. According to 1901 Census, the population of Gulbarga and Solapur cities was 29288 and 75288 respectively.

The population increased from 0.29 lakh to 4.30 lakh in Gulbarga and 0.75 to 9.75 lakh in Solapur during 1901-2001. Thus, the population of Solapur is double the population of Gulbarga. Besides population, drinking water supply also has to be doubled. It is noted from table that, the per capita availability of water per

Table-5.5

Growth of Population, Water Supply and Per Capita Availability of Water in Gulbarga and Solapur Cities

	Population		Decadal growth rate		Daily Water Supply (Lakh gallons)		Per Capita Availability of water per day (gallons)	
	Gulbarga	Solapur	Gulbarga	Solapur	Gulbarga	Solapur	Gulbarga	Solapur
1901	29,288	75,288	--	--	7.0	12.0	23.9	15.9
1911	32,437	89,434	10.75	18.78	9.0	17.5	27.7	19.6
1921	35,820	1,13,931	10.43	27.39	12.0	27.0	33.5	23.7
1931	41,083	1,35,574	14.69	18.99	16.0	35.0	29.9	25.8
1941	53,551	2,03,691	30.34	50.20	25.0	48.5	46.7	23.8
1951	77,189	2,66,050	44.14	30.61	35.5	55.0	45.9	20.7
1961	97,159	2,96,050	25.87	11.27	43.0	70.5	44.3	23.8
1971	1,45,588	3,80,000	49.84	28.35	44.5	95.0	30.5	25.0
1981	2,18,621	5,11,000	50.16	34.47	66.0	93.0	30.2	18.6
1991	3,03,139	7,04,000	42.22	37.76	70.5	210	23.1	29.8
2001	4,30,000	9,75,000	43.16	38.49	67.5	265	15.7	27.1

Source: For col.2, Government of Karnataka and Maharashtra, DistrictCensus Hand Books. For col.3, Reports on Water Supply Improvements Schemes in Gulbarga and Solapur Municipal corporations.

Note: Deducted 20% & 10% distribution losses in Gulbarga and Solapur respectively.

Table-5.6 (a)

Source wise and Zone wise Distribution of Water from Service Reservoirs in Gulbarga City, 2000-01

Source of supply	*Quantity of Water Supply (Lakh Gallons)*	*Service Reservoirs*	*Capacity of Service Reservoirs (Lakh Gallons)*	*Areas / Zones Served*
Bhima river	55.0	5 Nos. GLSR	22.0	I, II and III
Power pumps	0.85	11 Nos. ELSR	32.0	Part of I, II & III
Hand pumps	0.40	Direct pumping		(Extension areas where regular water supply is not available that places power pumps and hand pumps are working.)
Total	67.5		54.0	

Source: Compiled from Gulbarga City Municipal Corporation Records, 2000-01.

Note: When there is power failure at Bhima Head Works, the water supply to city from Bhosga reservoir at the rate of 20 lakh gls, and only when there is flow in river Bennithora, 0.50 MGD of water is being received at filter bed, near Taj Sultanpur Road Gulbarga.

In Gulbarga city 55 electoral wards have been divided into 3 zones. Each zone includes 18 wards for proper administration.

day is 15.7 gallons and 27.1 gallons in Gulbarga and Solapur respectively during 2000-01. This is not half of the quantity suggested for the residents of class-I cities. There are differences in the drinking water supplies of the two cities. Thus, though only being a district head quarter the daily water supply and per capita water supply of Solapur (197.5 lakh gallons and 11.4 gallons) more than that of Gulbarga.

It is coincidental that there are three sources of water supply in both the cities. For example, in Gulbarga city a) Bhosga, b) Bennethora and c) Bhima river and for Solapur city, Ekruk tank, Bhima river and Ujjani dam. The Bhima river is common to both the cities. The source wise water supply in two cities could be understood with the help of the Tables 5.6 (a & b).

Table-5.6 (b)

Source wise and Zone wise Distribution of Water from Service Reservoirs in Solapur City

Source of supply	*Qty of water supplied (lakh gls)*	*Service Reservoirs*	*Capacity of Service Reservoirs (lakh gls)*	*Area / Zones Served*
Bhima river	176.7	5 Nos GLSR	110	II, V & VI
Ujjani Dam	88.3	18 Nos ELSR	45	I, III & IV
Power Pumps & hand pumps	–	Direct Pumping	--	Part of all zones covered
Total	265	–	155	–

Source: Compiled from Solapur Municipal Corporation Records and MJP (MWS and SB) Solapur, Remodelling of City Distribution System Report, 2000.

Note: 1. In Solapur city 90 electoral wards have been divided into six zones. Each zone includes 15 wards for proper administration.

2. Water supply from Ekrukh tank is only during rainy season.

The daily quantity of water lifted to Gulbarga city is 67.5 lakh gls and for Solapur it is 265 lakh gls. There are 16 service reservoirs (GLSR & ELSR) existing in Gulbarga city for daily distribution of water and the capacity of these service reservoirs is 54 lakh gls. Likewise, the Solapur city has 3 sources for water supply to city. The daily quantity of water lifted to Solapur city is 265 lakh gallons and 23 service reservoirs are existing in Solapur city for drinking water distribution and the capacity of these service reservoirs is 155 lakh gallons. It is pertinent to note that Solapur has 35 more wards, 7 more service reservoirs, 197.5 lakh gallons more quantity of water lifted and also 101 lakh gallons of more capacity of service reservoirs (see Map-5.5 and 5.6).

MAP-5.5 WATER SUPPLY DISTRIBUTION NETWORK IN GULBARGA CITY

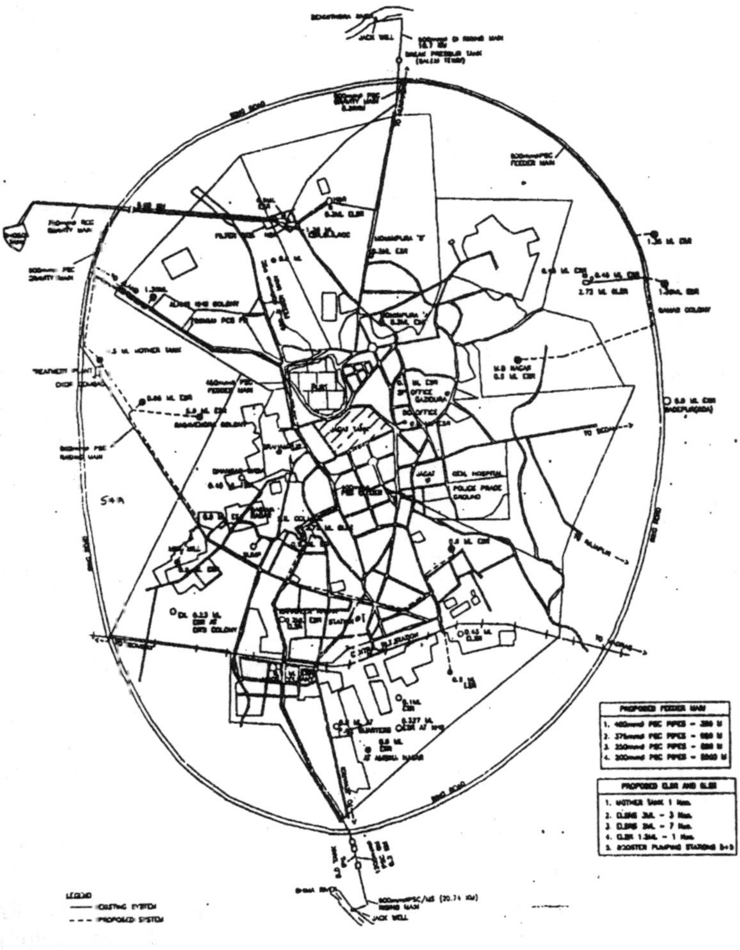

MAP-5.5 WATER SUPPLY DISTRIBUTION NETWORK IN GULBARGA CITY

The protected water supply system maintained by Gulbarga and Solapur Municipal Corporation and supplies drinking water to the population of the town. In addition to this there are public and private wells in the cities. House service connections, public taps and non-domestic connections are the important means through which water is supplied to the cities. A zone wise distribution of these installations in 2000-01 is shown in Table 5.7. There are 1301 and 2300 borewells[20] catering to the domestic needs of the population other than drinking. A better perspective of water supply

Table-5.7
Zone wise details of population, HSCs, PSPs, NDCs and Borewells in Gulbarga and Solapur Cities 2000-01

Particulars	*Zones*						*Total*
	I	*II*	*III*	*IV*	*V*	*VI*	
Population 2001							
Gulbarga	120282	109837	199881	-	-	-	430000
Solapur	143250	111275	128750	293250	100250	198225	975000
No. of Households							
Gulbarga	24056	20467	36727	-	-	-	81250
Solapur	28650	22255	25750	58650	20050	39645	195500
HSCs							
Gulbarga	6828	4395	8440	-	-	-	19663
Solapur	8560	5250	4355	15550	2850	11755	48300
PSPs							
Gulbarga	925	650	425	-	-	-	2000
Solapur	587	410	349	189	472	293	2300
NDCs							
Gulbarga	85	110	150	-	-	-	345
Solapur	455	680	750	588	475	552	3500
Borewells							
Gulbarga	304	450	547	-	-	-	1301
Solapur	310	604	505	280	351	250	2300

Source: Compiled from Gulbarga and Solapur Municipal Corporations.

means not only the system of water supply but also the number of people that these systems cover. In other words for water supply it is the people who matter most. Viewed in this context, the table brings out the difference between Gulbarga and Solapur in terms of population covered during the year 2000-01.

The Table 5.7 exhibits clearly that Solapur having six zones covers the population of 9.75 lakh as compared to only 3 zones and 3.40 lakh population in Gulbarga. Hence, in terms of population covered, households served, the Solapur stands high in attitude in the covering of water supply. Even with the respect to borewells, Solapur is far ahead of Gulbarga having 1000 more borwells to serve the people than Gulbarga city.

However, the most astonishing fact is that the two cities lag behind in terms of households to be covered by each public stand post, when the government norm coverage of 25 households for each stand post is taken into account. There is not much of difference between the two cities in terms of households covered by each public stand post.

House Service Connections

The first water supply scheme for Gulbarga and Solapur Municipal Corporations was completed in before 1947 in Gulbarga and 1882 in Solapur and water was supplied to the town through house service connections. Bhima River and Ujjani Dam sources are commissioned in 1993 and 1998 and improvement works (remodeling) were completed in 1997 to meet the increased demand for water.

For example in Gulbarga, there were 13017 House Service Connections (HSCs) during 1990 and this has been increased to 19663 in 2000. There is an increase of 6646 HSCs (66.2%) in Gulbarga. The annual additions were highly fluctuating and ranged from 350 to 1050, 2379 and 261 during the decade. While in Solapur there were 25514 HSCs in 1990-91 and they have nearly doubled between 1990-91 and 2000-01. The annual additions were highly fluctuating and ranged from 535 to 10746 during the decade. There are large number of connections in Solapur during 1999-2000 and 2000-01, i.e. 2400 and 10746 and the percentage change is 36.6 during this period (see Table 5.8)

Table-5.8

Number of HSCs, PSPs and NDCs in Gulbarga and Solapur Cities

Particulars	Year (1990-91 to 2000-01)										
	90-91	*91-92*	*92-93*	*93-94*	*94-95*	*95-96*	*96-97*	*97-98*	*98-99*	*99-00*	*00-01*
Number of HSCs											
Gulbarga	13017	13367	13952	14602	14987	15267	15620	15973	16500	19402	19663
Solapur	25514	26049	26769	28414	30159	32014	32764	33664	35154	37554	48300
Annual Additions											
Gulbarga	-	350	585	650	410	280	353	296	1050	2379	261
Solapur	-	535	720	1645	1745	1855	750	900	1490	2400	10746
Public Stand Posts											
Gulbarga	592	767	1977	1122	1232	1357	1753	1808	1893	1940	2000
Solapur	2025	2055	2080	2090	2120	2150	2195	2210	2235	2265	2300
Annual Additions											
Gulbarga	-	175	210	145	110	125	396	55	85	47	60
Solapur	-	30	25	15	25	30	45	15	25	30	35
Non-Domestic Connections											
Gulbarga	260	265	274	275	284	289	293	300	302	304	345
Solapur	1340	1450	1575	1725	1890	2110	2305	2480	2735	3050	3500
Annual Additions											
Gulbarga	-	5	9	1	9	5	4	13	8	18	17
Solapur	-	110	125	150	165	220	195	175	255	315	450

Source: Compiled from Gulbarga and Solapur Municipal Corporation Records.

If we see the difference between Gulbarga and Solapur HSCs are concerned, Solapur is ahead by 12497 HSCs during 1991 and 28637 HSCs in 2000. It may be observed from Table 5.8 that HSCs are concerned, there was 51 per cent difference between Gulbarga and Solapur during 1990-91 and if compared to the figures for the year 2000-01, such difference was 40.7 per cent this points out the fact that there is a leap forward in Solapur in HSCs as compared to Gulbarga.

Table-5.9
Zone-wise Percentage of Population Served by HSCs in Gulbarga and Solapur Cities, 2000-01

Zone Number	*Percentage of Population Served by HSCs*		*Difference*
	Gulbarga	*Solapur*	
I	28.4	29.9	1.5
II	21.5	23.6	2.1
III	23.0	16.7	6.3
IV	-	26.5	-
V	-	14.2	-
VI	-	29.6	-
Total	24.2	24.8	0.6

Source: Compiled from City Municipal Corporations Records, 2000-2001.

It may be noted from Table 5.9 that in Gulbarga total percentage of population served by HSCs is 24.2 per cent. If we see the zone wise coverage, Zone-I covered 28.4 per cent of population, Zone-II 21.5 per cent, and Zone-III 23.0 per cent of population served by HSCs. Whereas in Solapur, total population served by HSCs is 24.8 per cent. Zone wise coverage is 29.9 per cent in Zone-I, 16.7 per cent in Zone-III, 14.2 per cent in Zone-V and 29.6 per cent in Zone-VI.

If we see the difference between Gulbarga and Solapur, Solapur is 0.6 per cent ahead in terms of population served by house service connection than Gulbarga during 2000-2001. That means Solapur covered more household connections than Gulbarga.

Public Stand Posts

The number of public stand posts[21] installed in Gulbarga and Solapur is shown in Table 5.8. During 1990, there were 592 Public Stand Posts (PSPs) in Gulbarga city, this has been increased to 2000 in 2000-01 and the change during this period is 30 per cent. Where as in Solapur city there were 2025 PSPs during 1990-91 and increased 2300 in 2000-01. There are only 275 PSPs have increased during 10 years period. The authorities of Gulbarga and Solapur city roughly estimated 150 and 200 people for one public stand post.

If we see the difference between Gulbarga and Solapur PSPs are concerned it is clear that, Solapur city has 1433 more PSPs than that of Gulbarga and such difference is 86.9 per cent in 2000-01. Thus, Solapur registering a significant growth in water supply.

Slums are a curse on modern civilization. The slum people are vulnerable to many diseases, problems and difficulties. They also need access for safe drinking water. The Table 5.10 provides the information on the number of slum people dependent on each PSP in Gulbarga and Solapur cities.

Table-5.10
Population Dependent on Each Public Stand Post in Slum Localities of Gulbarga and Solapur Cities

Slum Zone No.	*1995-96*		*2000-01*	
	Gulbarga	*Solapur*	*Gulbarga*	*Solapur*
I	175	275	225	315
II	280	200	275	250
III	320	205	355	160
IV	--	175	--	150
V	--	245	--	275
VI	--	210	--	190

Source Gulbarga and Solapur Municipal Corporations Records, 1995-96 and 2000-01.

It may be noted from the Table 5.10 that in all slum zones except zone-II, the population dependent on each tap increased between 1995 to and 2000. The excess population dependent on each public tap was highest in Zone-I & III in 1995. That means, there are 175, 280, 320 population dependent on each public tap in Zone I, II and III respectively. During 2000, the population dependent on each public stand post in Zone- I, II and III is 225, 275, 355 in Gulbarga city respectively. Where as in Solapur, highest population dependent on each public tap in Zone-I is 275 and the lowest population dependent is 175 in Zone-IV for 1995-96, while 2000-01 population dependent on each public tap has increased from 275 to 315 in Zone-I, 200 to 250 in Zone-II and 245 to 275 in Zone-V, but such population is declined in Zone-III, Zone-IV, and Zone-VI respectively.

If we compare the two cities, in Gulbarga population dependent on each stand post is highest in Zone-III during 1995-96 and in Zone-I during 2000-01. Whereas in Solapur Zone-I has highest population dependent on each public stand post in 1995 and in 2000. However, Solapur stands on better footing in serving slum people through stand posts if compared to Gulbarga.

Non-Domestic Connections

Water supply to Non Domestic Connections(NDCs)[22] is also very important and essential. For example, during 1990-91 Gulbarga city has 260 NDCs, this has been increased to 345 in 2000. There is an increase of 85 NDCs during the decade (see Table 5.8). Whereas in Solapur, there were 1340 NDCs in 1990-91 and it is increased to 3500 NDCs in 2000-01. There has been a nearly 3 times increase of NDCs during the decade. Between 1990-91 and 2000-01 there is an increase of 2160 NDCs in Solapur.

If we see the difference between Gulbarga and Solapur, there is 19 per cent difference during 1990-91 and such difference for 2000-01 is only 9.8 per cent. Therefore from these standards it is evident that system of water supply in Solapur is far better and satisfactory than Gulbarga.

It is not just the importance and growth of NDCs but the type of NDCs signifies the background of developments taking place, have background of developments taking place, have taken place and will take place in a city. Given this back ground.

Table-5.11
Non-Domestic Connections in Gulbarga and Solapur Cities

Category	*1995-96*			*2000-01*		
	Gulbarga	*Solapur*	*Difference*	*Gulbarga*	*Solapur*	*Difference*
State, Central Govt. Offices[1] and Others[2]	256	1990	1734	306	3090	2784
Commercials	26	85	59	36	345	311
Industries / Factories	2	25	23	3	65	61
Total	284	2100	1816	345	3500	3155

Note: 1) The Railways and its demand for water has been included, connections/supply under central government offices.

2) Others include, banks, educational institutions, hospitals etc.

The importance of water supply and its distribution in Gulbarga and Solapur would be understood from the Table 5.11. There are 256 NDS for state and central government offices, 26 and 2 non domestic connections for commercial and industries / factories respectively in Gulbarga in 1995-96. While during 2000-01, non-domestic connections for offices increased to 306 and commercial and industries 36 and 3 respectively. Where as in Solapur city there are 2100 NDCs in 1990-91, out of this, 1990 NDCs for state and central government offices, 85 NDCs for commercials and 25 NDCs for industries and factories. During 2000-01 this has been increased to 3500.Out of this, State and Central Government office connections are 3090, 345and 65 are commercial and industries respectively.

The difference between Gulbarga and Solapur for NDCs are concerned, there was difference of 1816 NDCs in 1995-96 and such difference for 2000-01 is 3155. It may be noted that with regard to demand for water in the two cities exhibit the same background i.e., between 1995 to 2000, there has been an increase of commercial and industrial water connections in Gulbarga. Undoubtedly, there is an increase of these two sectors but only marginally. Same is true of the changes that have taken place in Solapur city. To say in brief, both the cities are leading towards more and more commercialization and fall by industrilization. Besides, there has been a decline in the percentage of NDCs connections provided to Central and State Government offices.

SECTION - IV
FINANCIAL ASPECTS

The finance is the life blood of an institution for undertaking any activity. The sound financial account forms the basis of efficiency in water supply. The financing water supply is a part of overall finances of the corporations. The method or system of account keeping i.e., to take note of opening balance and closing balance is the procedure adopted for general finance and that of financing water supply. Therefore, a) Total receipts and payments of the corporations, and b) Its opening balance and closing balance have been treated as the starting point for the purpose of comparing

Table-5.12
Receipts and Payments of Gulbarga and Solapur Municipal Corporations

(Rs. in Crore)

Year	Receipts			Payments		
	Gulbarga	Solapur	Percentage	Gulbarga	Solapur	Percentage
1991-92	3.94	34.28	11.5	3.97	34.28	11.6
1992-93	4.45	42.02	10.5	4.56	42.18	10.8
1993-94	4.48	48.37	9.3	4.06	48.37	8.4
1994-95	4.66	54.75	8.5	4.18	54.75	7.6
1995-96	7.67	69.98	11	7.66	63.31	12.1
1996-97	8.31	74.33	11.2	7.04	79.33	8.9
1997-98	8.39	72.12	11.6	9.89	77.89	10.7
1998-99	12.36	81.43	15.2	13.02	81.43	15.9
1999-00	8.91	104.94	8.5	7.84	104.94	7.5
2000-01	15.08	127.95	11.8	16.96	125.8	13.6

Source: Gulbarga and Solapur Municipal Corporation Records for Various Years.

Gulbarga and Solapur Municipal Corporations. Furthermore, the water supply receipts and payments and opening and closing balances regarding water supply only have been discussed in the following.

An attempt is made here to analyse the annual accounts and financial datas available with the Gulbaraga and Solapur Municipal Corporations to disclose their importance and relevance. If we compare the receipts of Gulbarga and Solapur, it is evident that the receipts of Gulbarga corporation was only 11.5 percent of Solapur corporation during the year 1991-92. This did not increase or it has remained constant over a decade, thereby suggesting that there is no improvement in the receipts of Gulbarga corporation.

The total receipts (capital and revenue) of the Gulbarga corporation were Rs. 3.94 crore in 1991-92 and the highest amount of receipts is Rs. 15.08 crore in 2000-01. It may be noted from Table 5.12 that the receipts of Gulbarga corporation have registered a near 3 fold increase between 1991 to 2000. Whereas in Solapur the receipts have increased from Rs. 34 crore in 1991-92 to Rs. 128 crore in 2000-01, that means there has been a four fold increase in total receipts of corporations.

The total payments (Revenue and Capital) of Gulbarga Corporation were Rs. 3.97 crore in 1991-92 and this has been increased to 16.96 crore during 2000-01. There has been, four times increase in the total payments of Gulbarga corporation. Whereas in Solapur, the total payments were Rs. 34.28 crore in 1991-92, and it is increased to 125.8 crore during 2000-01. There has been nearly four times increase in the total payments.

The growths of receipts have registered a four time increase in both the Gulbarga and Solapur between 1991 and 2000-01. What is significant is that the receipts in Gulbarga were only Rs. 4 crore as against Rs. 34 crore. That means Gulbarga receipts were only 11.5 crore of the receipts in Solapur during the year 1991-92. While in the year 2000-01, the receipts of Gulbarga Corporation were Rs. 15 crore as against 128 crore in 2000-01, which means they have been about 12 per cent of the receipts of Solapur Corporation. The comparison of growth of receipts in the two cities indicates that during 10 years period, the receipts of Gulbarga

Corporation very low as a percent of the receipts of the Solapur Corporation. If we see the comparison of payments, Gulbarga Corporation payments were only 11.6 per cent of Solapur Corporation during 1991-92 and this has been increased to 13.6 per cent in 2000-2001.

The two cities opening and closing balances are given in Table 5.13. It may be observed from table 5.13, that, Gulbarga corporation opening balance was Rs. 0.50 crore in 1991-92 and this has been increased to Rs.1.85 crore in 2000-01. It is three times increase in opening balance of Gulbarga corporation. While the closing balance was Rs.0.34 cores in 1991-92 and it is increased to 4.37 crore in 2000-01.

Where as in Solapur, the opening balance was Rs. 1.40 crore in 1991-92 and this has been increased to Rs. 15.87 crore during 2000-01 and it increased more than 9 times but the closing balance of Solapur Corporation was Rs. 2.5 crore in 1991-92 and it is increased to Rs.19.10 crore in 2000-01.

The intercity comparison of opening balance and closing balance and their growth between 1991-2000 demonstrate that the Solapur Corporation has exhibited a phenomenal growth both in opening and closing balance during the period under consideration. This speaks of the fact that Solapur collects and spends more amount than that of Gulbarga Corporation.

Given this scenario, the Table 5.14 gives the picture of receipts and payments of Gulbarga and Solapur cities on water supply accounts. The water supply account is maintained separately by the two corporations. If we look into Table 5.14, it is evident that, for example during 1991-92 the receipts from water supply accounts were Rs. 0.35 crore, it is Rs.0.80 crore in 1994-95 and this has been increased to Rs.1.03 crore in 1996-97. Between 1996 and 2000, it increased from Rs. 1.03 or to 1.19 crore. There has been six times increased in water supply receipts during 1991 to 2000. The payments of water supply account in Gulbarga city were Rs. 0.65 crore in 1991-92, Rs. 1.50 crore in 1994-95 and it is increased to Rs. 1.60 crore in 1996-97. Further this has been increased from Rs. 1.60 crore to 2.40 crore in 2000-01. There has been about four times increase in payments of Gulbarga water supply account. Whereas in Solapur, the receipts

Table-5.13

Opening and Closing Balances of Two Cities Municipal Corporations

(Rs in crore)

Year	*Opening Balance*			*Closing Balance*		
	Gulbarga	*Solapur*	*Percentage*	*Gulbarga*	*Solapur*	*Percentage*
1991-92	0.50	1.40	35.7	0.34	2.05	16.6
1992-93	0.34	2.05	16.6	0.25	3.68	6.8
1993-94	0.25	3.00	6.8	0.13	6.15	2.1
1994-95	0.13	6.15	2.1	0.62	8.15	7.6
1995-96	0.62	8.15	7.6	0.66	12.61	5.2
1996-97	0.66	12.61	5.2	1.60	12.46	12.8
1997-98	1.60	12.46	12.8	0.10	14.16	0.7
1998-99	0.10	14.16	0.7	1.76	12.18	14.4
1999-00	1.76	12.18	14.4	1.85	15.87	11.7
2000-01	1.85	15.87	11.7	4.37	19.10	23.0

Source: Gulbarga and Solapur Municipal Corporations Comparative Annual Accounts, Op.cit.

Table-5.14
Receipts and Payments of Water Supply Accounts

(Rs. in crore)

Year	Receipts [a]			Payments [b]		
	Gulbarga	Solapur	Percentage	Gulbarga	Solapur	Percentage
1991-92	0.35	7.39	4.7	0.65	7.60	8.5
1992-93	0.55	8.27	6.6	1.25	10.52	11.8
1993-94	0.65	10.10	6.4	1.40	12.06	11.6
1994-95	0.80	10.53	7.6	1.50	13.18	11.4
1995-96	0.90	10.50	8.6	1.40	10.98	12.7
1996-97	1.03	13.57	7.6	1.60	12.88	12.4
1997-98	1.23	12.80	9.6	1.75	16.789	10.4
1998-99	1.41	14.40	9.8	2.47	19.12	12.9
1999-00	0.61	20.04	3.0	1.50	25.72	5.8
2000-01	1.19	22.55	5.3	2.40	27.69	8.7

Source: Compiled from Gulbarga and Solapur Municipal Corporations Comparative Annual Accounts.

Note: a) The receipts on water supply account is combined total of revenue and capital accounts. The loan taken for purchase of machinery, equipments, etc. comes under capital receipts. Whereas the ordinary receipts include the water tax / rate collection and the grant in aid received from the state governments. This is revealed during discussion with the officials.

b) The payment head of the municipal account on water supply include current as well as capital expenditures, in other words the expenditures such as maintenance and repairs, salaries for staff, contingencies, power charges etc. The item from water supply account were Rs.7.39 crore in 1991-92 and this has been increased to Rs. 22.55 crore in 2000-01. There has been three times increase in water supply receipts during 1991 to 2000. The payments of corporation during 1991-92 were Rs. 7.60 crore. It increased to Rs.27.69 crore in 2000-01. There has been 3 times more increased in water supply payments.

If we compare the two cities corporations receipts and payments of water supply accounts, for example, the receipts from water supply account of Gulbarga Corporation were only 4.7 per cent during 1991-92 and such percentage in 2000-01 is 5.3 percent only. Whereas payments comparison of two cities corporations, for example during 1991-92, Gulbarga Corporation water supply accounts payments were only 8.5 percent of the payments of Solapur Corporation and this it increased to 8.7 percent. The comparison of water supply accounts reveals that the Solapur corporation has increased its expenditure by significant amount by the end of 2000-01.

The growth of opening and closing balance and the difference between the two existing in Gulbarga and Solapur have been noted in Table 5.15. It may be observed from the Table that the opening balance for the year 1991-92 was Rs. 1.20 crore in Gulbarga and it increased to Rs. 2.14 crore in 1995-96. Further this has been increased to Rs. 5.30 crore in 2000-01. Whereas the closing balance of water supply account of Gulbarga corporation during 1991-92, it was Rs. 1.22 crore, Rs. 2.65 crore during 1995-96 and it is increased from Rs. 2.65 crore to Rs. 5.88 crore during 2000-01.

Whereas in Solapur, the opening balance was Rs.3.47 crore in 1991-92 and it increased to Rs. 17.44 crore in 2000-01. There has been five times increase in opening balance of water supply account in Solapur Municipal Corporation during 1991 to 2000. While the closing balance was Rs. 3.90 crore in 1991-92 and it increased to Rs. 18 95 crore in 2000-01.

Inter-city and intra-city comparison of the differences between opening and closing balance on water supply account bring out the fact that Solapur has made tremendous increase over Gulbarga. The year to year differences between Gulbarga and Solapur also is very significant. The Solapur city spends considerably much higher on water supply account even on annual basis compared to Gulbarga.

Table-5.15
Opening and Closing Balances of Water Supply Accounts

(Rs. in crore)

Year	Opening Balance			Closing Balance		
	Gulbarga	Solapur	Percentage	Gulbarga	Solapur	Percentage
1991-92	1.20	3.47	34.6	1.22	3.90	31.3
1992-93	1.22	3.90	31.3	1.63	9.68	16.8
1993-94	1.63	9.68	16.8	2.08	10.15	20.5
1994-95	2.08	10.15	20.5	2.14	10.15	21.2
1995-96	2.11	10.08	21.2	2.65	14.47	18.4
1996-97	2.65	14.40	18.4	3.51	14.43	24.3
1997-98	3.51	14.42	24.3	4.00	16.14	24.8
1998-99	4.00	16.13	24.8	4.59	14.17	33.4
1999-00	4.59	13.76	33.4	5.30	17.85	30.4
2000-01	5.30	17.44	30.4	5.88	18.95	31.0

Source: Op.cit.

SECTION - V
CRITICAL LOOK

In addition to the comparison of sources and systems of water supply, the comparison of funding pattern, a true picture of macro level differences between Gulbarga and Solapur could be evaluated with the help of a) the cost of water supply, b) the cost of remodeling the water supply distribution systems, c) nature of meeting the cost of water supply and d) the comparative tap rate charges have been noted in the following.

Table-5.16
Water Supply Project Costs of Gulbarga and Solapur Cities

(Rs. in Lakh)

Glubarga		*Solapur*		*Difference*
Source	*Cost*	*Source*	*Cost*	
Bhosga	84.40	Ekruk	98.50	14.10
Bennethora	153.00	Bhima	303.0	150.0
Bhima	1286.00	Ujjani	9072.38	7786.38
Total	1513.40		9473.5	7960.10

Source: Compiled from Gulbarga and Solapur Municipal Corporations Records.

The Table-5.16 depicts water supply projects cost of Solapur city is six times more than that of Gulbarga. That means, the project cost of Gulbarga is Rs. 1513 lakh and that of Solapur is Rs. 9473 lakh. Therefore, in terms of water supply Solapur is far ahead of Gulbarga. The source wise comparison of project cost between Gulbarga and Solapur reveals that there is not much of difference in terms of small and divergent projects in both the cities. Whereas the common source i.e., Bhima water is concerned, the project cost of Solapur is Rs. 303 lakh as against Rs. 12.86 crore in Gulbarga. Therefore it may be concluded that the Solapur city is harnessing Bhima water more fully and giving marginal opportunities to Gulbarga city for exploiting Bhima river for drinking water supply.

The superiority of water supply system of Solapur compared to Gulbarga could also be understood by comparing the differences in remodeling costs. The remolding was undertaken in both the cities during the year 1997. The Solapur has spent Rs. 10.76 crore more than that of Gulbarga, the remodeling cost of water supply distribution in Solapur has been much wider than Gulbarga during the year 2000-01. It is evident from the Table-5.17 that the remodeling cost of Solapur is two time the recent cost of water supply scheme in Gulbarga.

Table-5.17
Remodeling Costs of Distribution Systems in Gulbarga and Solapur Cities

(Rs. in crore)

Year	*Gulbarga*	*Solapur*	*Difference*
1997-98	46.50	57.26	10.76
2000-01	57.98	125.28	67.30
Total	104.48	182.54	78.06

Source Compiled from Gulbarga and Solapur Water Supply Authorities and Corporations.

The funding pattern makes a significant difference for water supply systems. The own sources are the hard nut to crack. Therefore, the grant from state government is the source which does not place any burden on the water supply system of municipalities authorities. The loans are a kind of burden on the municipal authorities, because they call for not only repayment but also the debt servicing charges.

Against the background noted above the statistics of funding pattern in Gulbarga and Solapur could be seen from the following Table 5.18.

Table-5.18
Funding Pattern for Urban Water Supply Schemes in Gulbarga and Solapur Cities

City	*Financial Institution Loan*	*Govt. Grant*	*Local body share*
Gulbarga	66.67%	23.33%	10%
Solapur	76.67%	23.33%	Nil

Source: Gulbarga and Solapur Municipal Corporations.

The two cities have the same sources of funds. But the significant difference is that Solapur Municipal Corporation need not spend any amount for water supply projects. The entire cost is met through loans and grants from state government. Whereas in Gulbarga, the municipal corporations have to provide 10 per cent of the total cost from their own sources. Hence, Gulbarga corporation is placed at a disadvantage in terms of funding for water supply projects as compared to Solapur municipal corporation.

A true evaluation of the water supply systems at a macro level will be incomplete without the comparison of tap rates in the two cities under consideration. There are two differing rates i.e., domestic and non-domestic in both the cities. Further both cities have revised the rates between 1991-92 to 1998-99. However, there are some marginal differences in the two systems of tap rates. The Solapur does not discriminate very much on the basis of the size of the tap. Whereas in Gulbarga city instead of tap rates on size of tap pipes a flat amount is collected from water users. The following Table 5.19 provides the details of differing tap rates in two cities during from 1991 to 1998-99.

It is interesting to note that since Solapur supplies more quantity of water, it has also higher tap rates for domestic as well as non-domestic water users than the water users in Gulbarga, the highest domestic and non-domestic annual rates are Rs. 980 & 7000 respectively in Solapur as against Rs. 540 and 6480 in

Table-5.19
Annual Comparative Water Taxes

Year	Gulbarga		Solapur	
	Domestic	*Non-domestic*	*Domestic*	*Non-domestic*
1991-92				
½"	Rs. 60	Rs. 600	Rs. 700 per /yr	Rs. 2250
¾"		Rs. 900	Rs. 1650/-	Rs. 5000
1"		Rs. 1200	Rs.3 per kl-	Rs.12 per kl
1 ¼"		Rs. 1800	-	-
1993				
½"	Rs. 540	Rs. 2160	Rs. 980	Rs. 3950/-
¾"		Rs. 3240	Rs. 2250	Rs. 7000/-
1"		Rs. 4320	Rs. 3 per kl-	Rs. 12 per kl-
1 ¼"		Rs. 6480	-	-

Source: Gulbarga and Solapur Municipal Corporations.

Gulbarga. It is a noteworthy fact that in addition to that annual rate, the Solapur has adopted meter system and charges for 1 inch and above tap sizes Rs. 3 per 1000 litres for domestic users and Rs. 12 per 1000 litres for non-domestic users. Therefore the Solapur municipal corporation is placed at an advantage in terms of tap rate when compared to the lower or even the floor tap rates adopted in Gulbarga.

NOTES AND REFERENCES

1. Carhart Arthur H., "Water or Your Life", Lippin Coll, New York, 1951.
2. Gulbarga District Gazetteer, 1991, p.16.
3. MJP, Solapur, "General Information Brochure", 2000.
4. Solapur District Gazetteer, 1991.
5. Ibid, p.21.
6. Probably the Jagat tank was the source of water to the subjects of Bahamani ruler. It may be noted in passing that the tank was

used by the people inside and outside the fort and also by the people staying in Brahmpur, which is alongside the Sharanabasaveshwar temple.

7. Government of Maharashtra, "Solapur District Census Hand Book", 1991.
8. No doubt there are many theories of urbanization such as central place theory of business district. Gulbarga and Solapur and their location cannot fit into either of the two.
9. It is undesirable of the fact that growth of water for drinking purpose is no less important and it is also dependent on configuration and topography.
10. The marginal difference between Gulbarga and Solapur are clearly washed off if we take into account their location nearness to sea. The Solapur is closer to sea than Gulbarga it is true that the two cities are almost equal in their locations when compared to the sea.
11. The high temperature hosts up the upper layer of water in stored tanks this result in evaporation of oxygen context of drinking water, the water becomes tasteless and consequently useless. Similarly, if big steel or cement pipes are used in the process of water supply are exposed to the sun on the earthen surface also create the problems here.
12. During winter the minimum temperature will be 8^0 C to 9^0C.
13. For fun the people of healthy climate speak of hot, hotter and hottest days in the two cities under consideration.
14. This excludes the untimely and un-seasonal rainfall data which has not been recorded. But it is important under water supply. Further, there is no data relating to an improvement in water table due to this in the two cities.
15. It is no wonder that big cities in India faced with poor rainfall have been arranged with water supply by railway, but this has not been the case with Gulbarga and Solapur except the year 1992.
16. Gulbarga Urban Development Authority, "Comprehensive Development Report", 1997.
17. Solapur Municipal Corporation. "Feasibility Report", 2000.
18. KUWS & DB, Gulbarga, "Annual Report 2000".
19. MJP Solapur "Annual Report 2000".
20. Population covered under borewells in both the cities is not available.

21. As per the corporation rules of the two cities a households consisting of 5 members and 25 such households i.e., about 125 people should have to be covered by each public stand post. Against this, each stand post in both the cities cover few hundreds of people instead of 125 people. A note worthy point is that the stand posts are located in most of the slum areas in the two cities under considerations.
22. The development of airport, national highway from Bidar to Sri Rangapathanam via Gulbarga and bringing up new industries are the significant considerations for Gulbarga city whereas the Solapur being closer to Pune may have to experience the backwash effects.

6

Urban Water Supply in Gulbarga and Solapur Cities-The Households Survey

Introduction

In order to understand the ground realities, a survey of households is an essential point. The survey data provides the findings on key issues. The findings of the survey also provide a support to the policy that may be design by the water supply authorities. The merits of the findings of survey are also crucial in evaluating the household behaviour which is directed for welfare maximization. The important findings of the survey relate to methods and manner of water supply, behavioural findings, findings on management and health. The findings are contingent upon the important aspects of the very nature of the survey and sample design and size. The age, education, occupation, income which are all treated as the part of profile is the starting point. Therefore, the present chapter provides the findings of our survey.

For convenience, it is divided into the following sections. The **Section-I** describes the sample size and nature of questionnaire. The profile of households has been given in **Section-II**. The **Section-III** explains the method and manner of water supply. The behavioural findings are described in **Section-IV**. The **Section-V** examines findings on management and health aspects.

SECTION-I
SAMPLE SIZE AND NATURE OF QUESTIONNAIRE

For the purpose of micro level understanding of the economics of urban water supply, a household level survey has been adopted in our study. A detailed questionnaire has been administered to the households at Gulbarga and Solapur cities. The size of sample and nature of questionnaire has been discussed in the present part.

The two cities have a population of 4.30 lakh and 9.75 lakh respectively. It is not desirable to consider individual as the basis of the survey. Therefore, the population is divided into number of households. Hence, a household becomes an ideal base for the purpose of survey. The households located in different areas face differing problems in getting water. In order to select an ideal number of households which would reflect the problems, a detailed survey of wards have been undertaken as a starting point. The following Table 6.1 provides details of number of wards located in Gulbarga and Solapur cities.

Table-6.1
Area and No. of Wards in Gulbarga and Solapur Cities

City	*Area (sq.kms)*	*Total Wards*
Gulbarga	65	55
Solapur	180	90

Source: Compiled from Gulbarga and Solapur Municipal Corporations.

It may be observed from the table that, there are in all 55 wards in Gulbarga city providing an area of 65 sq kms while the Solapur city has as many as 90 wards spread in the radius of 180 sq km It is difficult to chose sample households from all the wards of the cities, it is also neither feasible nor desirable. For analytical purpose there is need for choice of wards and within each ward choice of households as the representative of area and households.

In order to arrive at a suitable judgment, the following Table 6.2 provides the details of number of wards and number of households within each ward in the two cities under consideration. It may be noted that for the purpose of present study 11 wards of Gulbarga city i.e., 20 per cent of the total wards and 22 out of 90 wards i.e., 24.4 per cent of the total wards in Solapur city have been selected.

Table-6.2
Sample Wards

City	*Total wards*	*Sample wards*	*Percentage*
Gulbarga	55	11	20.0
Solapur	90	22	24.4

Source: Field Survey.

The details of ward wise distribution of households are given in Table 6.3. It may be observed that a total of 150 households have been selected from Gulbarga and Solapur cities. However, to the popular view i e., unity in diversity was having selected differing number of sample households from each ward in each city. Numbers of households have been selected on the basis of the area, population and location of the wards (see maps 6.1 and 6.2).

For 150 sample households of each city, a detailed questionnaire has been designed. The questionnaire contains various questions relating to water supply aspects of the households. The important questions relate to general profile aspects such as, name, sex, age, education, occupation, annual income of the households, physical size of the house, size of the household, plants around the households, households with commercial establishments, and the quantity of water required, daily water supply, method and manner of water supply, behavioural findings, and management aspects.

The following Table 6.4 indicates an articulated distribution of questions relating to 5 aspects of the households. Since economics of urban water supply is largely dependent on management aspects, our questionnaire has largest number of questions listed in the questionnaire provide quantitative and qualitative data.

MAP-6.1 SELECTED WARDS IN GULBARGA CITY

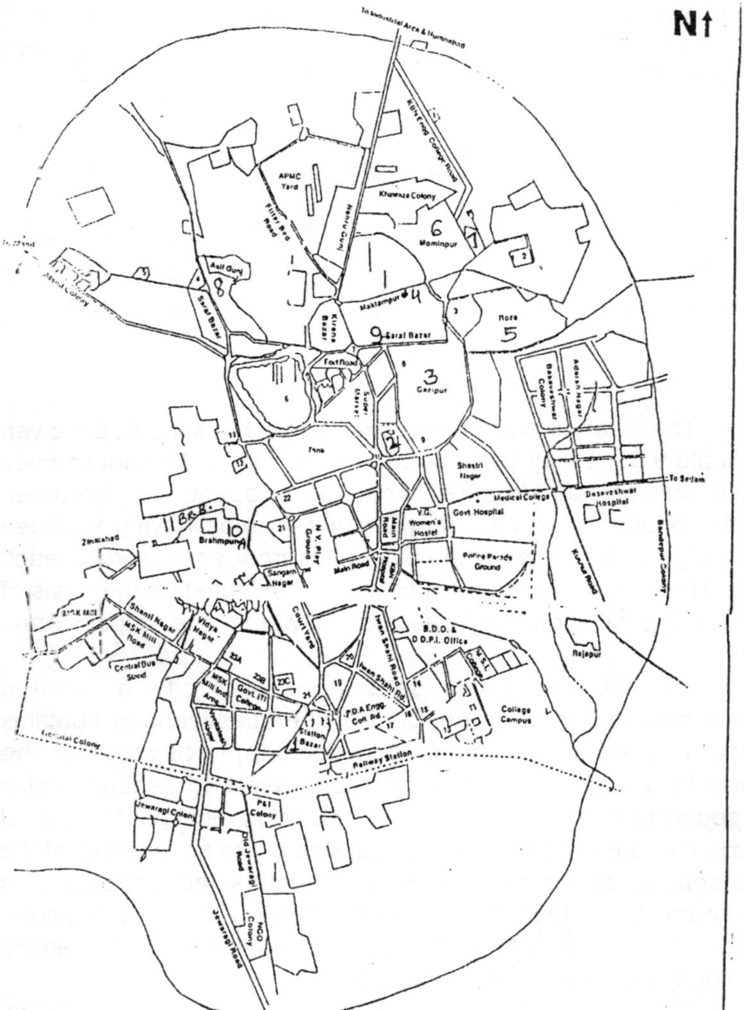

SAMPLE WARDS IN GULBARGA

1. Station Baazar
2. Jagat
3. Gajipur
4. Maktampur
5. Raja
6. Mominpura (A)
7. Mominpura (B)
8. Aasifgunj
9. Shahabazar
10. Brahmapur (A)
11. Brahmapur (B)

MAP-6.2 SELECTED WARDS IN SOLAPUR CITY

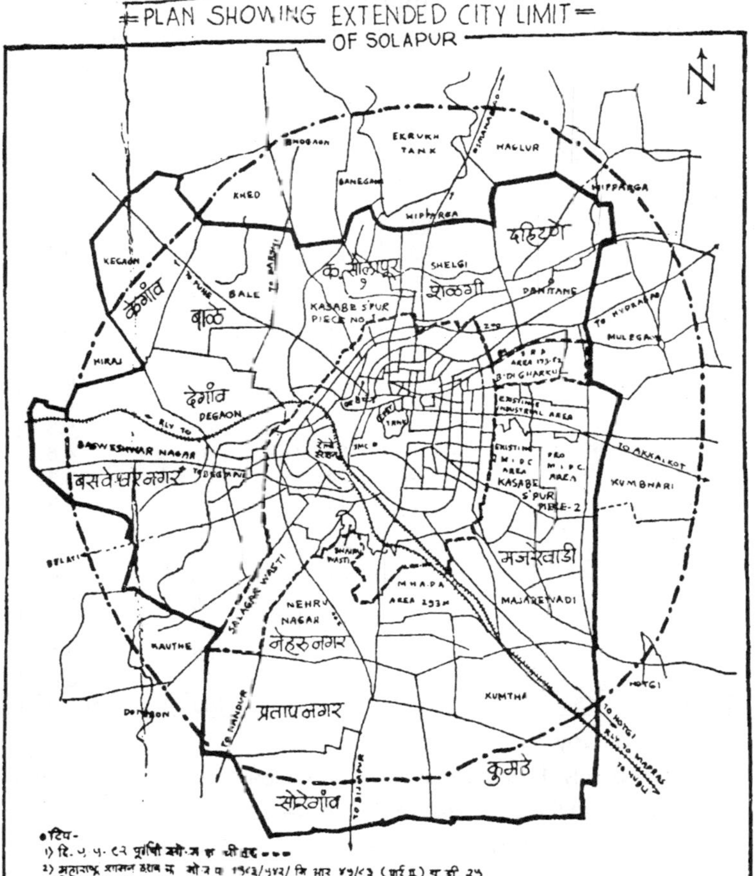

SAMPLE WARDS IN SOLAPUR

1. Bale
2. Shelgi
5. Murargi Pet
12. Soregaon
14. Degaon
17. Milind Nagar
86. Sunderam Nagar
24. Bhavani Pet
25. Mangalwar Pet
28. Ravivar Pet
31. New Pachh Pet
41. Nehru Nagar
50. Varadh Chala
87. Uttarkasba
56. Budhvar Pet
66. Sakh Pet
70. Datt Nagar
72. Shastri Nagar
79. Dasa Bazar
82. Railway Line
90. Begum Pet

Table-6.3
Ward Wise Distribution of Sample Households

Gulbarga			*Solapur*		
Ward No.	*No. of households*	*Percentage*	*Ward No*	*No. of households*	*Percentage*
01	25	16.6	82	10	6.6
02	11	07.3	50	05	3.3
03	20	13.3	90	08	5.3
04	08	05.3	72	10	6.6
05	16	10.6	79	07	4.6
06	10	06.6.	28	05	3.3
07	12	08.0	86	05	3.3
08	13	08.6	17	05	3.3
09	15	10.0	25	07	4.6
10	09	06.0	02	10	6.6
11	20	13.3	01	05	3.3
-	-	-	12	08	5.3
-	-	-	87	07	4.6
-	-	-	24	05	3.3
-	-	-	14	05	3.3
-	-	-	31	05	3.3
-	-	-	36	05	3.3
-	-	-	41	10	6.6
-	-	-	05	08	5.3
-	-	-	70	05	3.3
-	-	-	56	05	3.3
-	-	-	66	10	6.6
11	150	100.0	22	150	100.0

Source: Field Survey.

Note: There are only 11 municipal wards in Gulbarga, which have been selected from the city. Households have been selected from each ward based on size, population and location in the city.

Table-6.4
Nature of Questionnaire

Aspects	*No. of Questions*
Profile	11
Method and Manner of Water Supply	07
Household Behaviour	09
Management and Health	14
Assessment	05
Total	46

Source: Field Survey.

The following Table 6.5 provides information regarding the number of quantitative and qualitative questions contained in our questionnaire.

Table-6.5
Details of Quantitative and Qualitative Questions

Aspects	*Quantitative Questions*	*Percentage %*	*Qualitative Questions*	*Percentage %*	*Total Questions*
Profile	03	13.36	08	33.33	11
Methods & Manner	05	22.72	02	08.33	07
Household Behaviour	06	27.27	03	12.50	09
Management & Health	04	18.18	10	41.66	14
Assessment	04	18.18	01	04.16	05
Total	22	100.00	24	100.00	46

Source: Field Survey.

The large number of quantitative questions could be found in assessment and household behaviour and manner of water supply. While qualitative questions are more in profile and method and manner of water supply system faced by households.

SECTION-II
THE PROFILE OF SAMPLE HOUSEHOLDS

For proper micro level understanding of the economics of urban water supply a relevant household profile is a starting point. The water use or misuse and considerations relating to water and its importance will be reflected in the profile of each household. For example, more family members, big size of the house, high income, etc., point out the demand for more water. Therefore, the important aspects relating to the profile include age, education, occupation, income, location, physical size of the house, size of the household, and plants around the household, which have been discussed in the following.

The age of households is if not directly has a great connection to the quantity of water use[1]. The age differences reflect the changes in biological differences of generation. Accordingly the differences in the age profile of households in Gulbarga and Solapur cities have been given in the following Table 6.6.

Table-6.6
Age-wise Distribution of Sample Households

Age	*Gulbarga*		*Solapur*	
	No. of Households	*Percentage*	*No. of Households*	*Percentage*
25-35	20	13.3	25	16.6
35-45	55	36.6	40	26.6
45-55	45	30.0	55	36.6
55 & above	30	20.0	30	20.0
Total	150	100.0	150	100.0

Source: Field Survey.

Table-6.7
Level of Education

Education	*Gulbarga*		*Solapur*	
	No. of households	*Percentage*	*No. of Households*	*Percentage*
Illiterate	10	6.6	8	5.3
Primary	25	16.6	20	13.3
High School	60	40.0	60	40.0
Degree	45	30.0	55	36.6
PG & above	10	6.6	7	4.6
Total	150	100.0	150	100.0

Source: Field Survey.

Though the two are neighbouring cities our random selection of households, computed by range group indicate that the Gulbarga has highest 37 per cent of sample population in the age group of 35-45 as against the 37 per cent of the sample found in 45-55 range in Solapur, our findings are co-incidental[2].

A comparative educational profile of sample households could be found from Table 6.7

The higher level of education, ipsofacto ensure better use of water. However, it is a bit surprise that there is equal percentage of (40%) sample households with matriculation in Gulbarga and Solapur cities. As expected, there are more households with graduation in Solapur (37%) as against 30 per cent in Gulbarga[3].

The occupation is an important part of households profile[4]. The occupation profile of sample households in Gulbarga and Solapur cities have been noted in Table 6.8.

Table-6.8
Occupational Distribution of Households

Occupation	*Gulbarga*		*Solapur*	
	No. of Households	*Percentage*	*No. of Households*	*Percentage*
Private Employee	35	23.3	48	32.0
Govt. Employee	55	36.6	35	23.3
Any other business	60	40.0	67	44.6
Total	150	100.0	150	100.0

Source: Field Survey.

The main findings which emerge from the Table 6.8 are, a) there are more number of private employees in Solapur i.e., 32% of households as against 23% in Gulbarga, b) in Solapur, there are 45% of households with business activities as compared to 40% of Gulbarga, c) there are more percentage of households with govt. employment in Gulbarga.

It may be argued that the use of water after is having a significant relation to the level of income. The range of households with differing income of our sample in Gulbarga and Solapur have been given in Table 6.9.

Table-6.9
Annual Income of the Households

Income	*Gulbarga*		*Solapur*	
	No. of Households	*% Percentage*	*No. of Households*	*% Percentage*
Rs. 10,000-20,000	15	10.0	12	8.0
Rs. 20,000-30,000	23	15.3	25	16.7
Rs. 30,000-40,000	47	31.3	30	20.0
Rs. 40,000 & above	65	43.3	83	55.3
Total	150	100.0	150	100.0

Source: Field Survey.

There are maximum number of sample households in Gulbarga in the income range of Rs.40,000 and above and the same is true of Solapur city[6].

If we look at the size of house and distribution of sample households in Table 6.10, the important findings are, a) there are marginal differences in all sizes of houses of our sample households in Gulbarga and Solapur cities, b) there is heavy concentration of households in the size group of 40' x 60' in both the citieis[7].

Table-6.10
Physical Size of the House

Physical Size	***Gulbarga***		*Solapur*	
	No. of Households	*Percentage*	*No. of Households*	*Percentage*
20" × 30"	28	18.6	25	16.7
30" × 40"	55	36.6	50	33.3
40" × 60"	40	26.6	45	30.0
60" and above	27	18.0	30	20.0
Total	150	100	150	100

Source: Field Survey.

The size of family is an important but an independent variable determining the water use. Given this background, it may be seen from Table 6.11 that, Gulbarga has 50 per cent sample households whose family size is 4 - 6 members but there are only 43 per cent in Solapur. The two cities have equal percentage of sample households consisting of family members 6-8 (27%) of the total sample.

Table-6.11
Size of the Family

Size	*Gulbarga*		*Solapur*	
	No. of Households	*Percentage*	*No. of Households*	*Percentage*
2-4	15	10.0	20	13.3
4-6	75	50.0	65	43.3
6-8	40	26.7	40	20.0
8-10	20	13.3	25	16.8
Total	150	100.0	150	100.0

Source: Field Survey.

The gardens and trees as against play grounds require more water for their upkeep. If we see the Gulbarga and Solapur cities (Table 6.12), it is above board that there are few gardens and parks in Gulbarga than Solapur, whereas there are more number of sample households (43.3 per cent) in Gulbarga having trees than 40 per cent in Solapur. Therefore, tree planting in and around the house is more in Gulbarga than Solapur.

Table-6.12
Plants and Trees around the House

Type	*Gulbarga*		*Solapur*	
	No. of Households	*Percentage*	*No. of Households*	*Percentage*
Plants	80	53.3	75	50.0
Trees	65	43.3	60	40.0
Garden	05	3.3	15	10.0
Total	150	100.0	150	150.0

Source: Field Survey.

SECTION-III
METHODS AND MANNER OF WATER SUPPLY

The findings of households survey relating to method and manner of water supply is essential in the analysis of the economics of urban water supply. The views of households on method and manner of water supply include, type of arrangement, distance between house and water source, duration of water supply, tap size, type of connection, households with bore wells, pipe line system of water supply and drainage, road digging for water supply.

The desired quantity of water supply ease of water supply and households satisfaction largely depend on the very system of water supply. The three systems (methods) basically found in Gulbarga and Solapur cities are house connections, stand posts/ hand pumps and house service connections with borewells. The systems existing in Gulbarga and Solapur could be seen from the Table 6.13.

The striking points are that the Solapur has 77 per cent of households dependent on house connections and Gulbarga has one fourth of the total sample households dependent on HSCs with borewells. Hence, it may be concluded that the system of water supply in Solapur is far better than that of Gulbarga, because the bore wells and other sources call for additional efforts and cost for the households.

Table-6.13
Type of Water Arrangements

Type	*Gulbarga*		*Solapur*	
	No. of Households	*Percentage %*	*No. of Households*	*Percentage %*
House Connection	95	63.3	115	76.7
Stand Posts/hand pumps	20	13.3	15	10.3
HSCs with Bore wells	35	23.3	20	12.0
Total	150	100.0	150	100.0

Source: Field Survey.

The distance between house and source of water supply is another indicator in measuring the efficiency of the system of water supply. The nearer the source, it is convenient for the households to get water. The distance between house and source of water existing in Gulbarga and Solapur have been noted in Table 6.14.

Table-6.14
Distance between House and Water Source

Distance (Meters)	*Gulbarga*		*Solapur*	
	No. of Households	*Percentage*	*No. of Households*	*Percentage*
10-20	15	10.0	35	23.3
20-30	32	21.3	50	33.3
30-40	55	36.6	40	26.6
40 and bove	48	32.0	25	16.6
Total	150	100.0	150	100.0

Source: Field Survey.

The key points emerging from table that the large number of sample households in Solapur have to face a distance of 20-30 meters as against 37 per cent of total sample households facing the longer distance of 30-40 meters in Gulbarga city. Therefore, the Solapur households have advantage over the households of Gulbarga city.

The duration of water supply is an important element in evaluating the efficiency of system of water supply. The basic assumption here is that longer the duration, more water will be the quantity of water supply. The households Therefore, enjoy the benefit of the system of water supply, the duration of water supply in Gulbarga and Solapur have been compared in Table 6.15.

It is evident that the 67 per cent of sample households in Gulbarga get water between less than 1 hour as against 60 per cent of sample households getting water from 1-2 hours in Solapur. Thus, the result is clear cut that the households in Solapur get more water than the households in Gulbarga. The Solapur system is far more satisfactory as 30 per cent of sample households get water between 2- 3 hours of duration.

Table-6.15
Duration of water supply

Duration (Hours)	*Gulbarga*		*Solapur*	
	No. of Households	*Percentage*	*No. of Households*	*Percentage*
Less than 1	100	67.0	15	10.0
1-2	50	33.0	90	60.0
2-3	–	--	45	30.0
3 and above	–	--	–	--
Total	150	100.0	150	100.0

Source: Field Survey.

The quantity of water supply depends essentially on the size of taps used in water supply. The existing tap sizes in Gulbarga and Solapur include ½ , ¾ and 1 and above inches. The distribution of households on the basis of tap size in Gulbarga and Solapur has been given in Table 6.16.

Table-6.16
Tap Size of the Households

Tap size (in inches)	*Gulbarga*		*Solapur*	
	No. of Households	*Percentage*	*No. of Households*	*Percentage*
½	150	100.0	80	53.0
¾	--	--	50	33.0
1 and above	--	--	20	14.0
Total	150	100.0	150	100.0

Source: Field Survey.

The important findings of our survey are i) all the households in Gulbarga have the tap size of ½ inch only, ii) 53% of households depend on ½ inch size of taps in Solapur, iii) 33 per cent of households in Solapur gets water from tap size of 3/4 inches, and iv) 14% of households get water from 1 and above inch pipes in Solapur cities. Therefore, the households in Gulbarga get smaller quantity of water due to the small size of the taps and the largest tap sizes in Solapur provides more greater quantity of water to as many as 14 per cent of households.[8]

Besides tap connections bore wells are the alternative or additional source of water supply. No doubt, bore wells are independent but almost entirely private source of water supply. The sample households dependent on bore wells in Gulbarga and Solapur cities has been given in Table 6.17.

Table-6.17
Households with Bore wells

Opinion	*Gulbarga*		*Solapur*	
	No. of Households	*Percentage*	*No. of Households*	*Percentage*
Yes	55	36.6	10	6.6
No	95	63.3	140	93.4
Total	150	100.0	150	100.0

Source: Field Survey.

The main conclusion from the table is that as many as 55 sample households i.e., 37 per cent in Gulbarga depend on bore wells as the source of water supply which is very small in Solapur[9] city.

The pipeline system plays a significant role in the method of water supply. There are basically two types of tapping system existing in our study area. They are, underground system and surface system. The distribution of households subject to two different system of tapping in Gulbarga and Solapur has been indicated in Table6.18.

Table-6.18
Water Supply System

System	*Gulbarga*		*Solapur*	
	No. of Households	*Percentage*	*No. of Housholds*	*Percentage*
Under ground	60	40.0	140	93.3
Surface	90	60.0	10	6.7
Total	150	100.0	150	100.0

Source: Field Survey.

A noticeable fact is that the 93 per cent of sample households in Solapur have been provided with under ground pipeline system as against 60 per cent faced with surface system of tapping in Gulbarga.[10]

The efficiency and quantity of water supply depends, besides the underground and surface tapping systems, within the under ground, more deeper the taps more better the system of water supply. Because, deeper underground system is more safer than the pipeline system than those placed very close to surface system. The system of underground pipeline and the range of depth existing in Gulbarga and Solapur could be seen from the Table 6.19.

Table-6.19
Depth of Underground Pipes

Depth (Feet)	*Gulbarga*		*Solapur*	
	No. of Households	*Percentage*	*No. of Households*	*Percentage*
<1	20	13.0	--	--
1-2	40	87.0	35	25.0
2-3	--	--	45	32.1
3 & >	--	--	60	42.9
Total	60	100.0	140	100.0

Source: Field Survey.

It is a noteworthy fact that, there is poor underground pipeline system in Gulbarga when compared to Solapur. For example, 87 per cent of sample households in Gulbarga get water connection from the underground pipe line system which is placed between 1- 2 feet whereas 43 per cent of households followed by 32 per cent households get water facility with the underground pipes placed between 2-3 feet and 3 and above feets respectively. Thus, it may be concluded that the households in Solapur enjoy better underground pipe line system than Gulbarga.

Water supply is also connected to the drainage and sanitation system If there is no proper distance is maintained between underground water supply pipes and sanitary drainage pipes would create problems if one or two of them are subject to damage. For the purpose of safety, the distance between water supply pipes and drainage pipes is essential. The distance between water supply systems existing in Gulbarga and Solapur as faced by sample households has been noted Table 6.20. The distance between underground water supply pipes and drainage pipes is very close to 67 per cent of sample households in Gulbarga and 50 per cent of households in Solapur have greater distance between their water supply pipes and drainage pipes. Therefore, it is observed that Solapur households are placed more comfortably in terms of water supply and sanitary conditions.[11]

Table-6.20
Distance between Water Supply and Drainage Pipes

Distance (meters)	*Gulbarga*		*Solapur*	
	No. of households	*Percentage*	*No. of households*	*Percentage*
1-2	40	67.0	--	--
2-3	20	33.0	50	36.0
3-4	--	--	70	50.0
4 and above	--	--	20	14.0
Total	60	100.0	140	100.0

Source: Field Survey.

For providing water supply connections, road digging is a source of disturbance to the households. It is also the problem for easy commutation. The following Table 6.21 gives the opinion of households regarding road digging for water supply purposes in Gulbarga and Solapur.

It may be concluded that highest number of households (77%) have faced road diggings in Gulbarga city as against just 20 per cent households in Solapur. Besides frequent road diggings, the discussions with households revealed that after digging repairs are not undertaken by authorities. There has been considerable delay between digging and repair. Therefore, the sample households in Solapur enjoy better water supply system than Gulbarga[12].

Table-6.21
Road Digging for Water Supply

Opinion	*Gulbarga*		*Solapur*	
	No. of Households	*Percentage*	*No. of Households*	*Percentage*
Yes	115	77.0	30	20.0
No	35	23.0	120	80.0
Total	150	100.0	150	100.0

Source: Field Survey.

SECTION-IV
BEHAVIOURAL FINDINGS

As it is well known that in the ultimate analysis, the economics is the study of human behaviour in relation to scarce economic resources. Accordingly, the findings of households with regard to water supply are more important than the household views on the method and manner of water supply. The households basic objective is maximisation of utility with given budgetary and other constraints. The availability of sufficient water provided at the door step, clean and potable would help the households to maximise utility in the context of drinking water. Therefore, the findings relating to household view on the water supply are very important. These include: water demand, water supply, water storage system, problem of water leakages, public tap leakages, daily quantity of wastage water, no. of persons used for getting water from stand posts, time spent for getting water from public stand posts and monthly payment of water tax.

The macro level demand for water as a public good[13] suffers from the limitations that 1) It is difficult to know the preferences of the households, 2) There are numerous invisible[14] factors affecting demand of the individual household, 3) The family (including number of persons) cultural functions, festivals and other social events also affect demand for water[15], the demand for water as revealed by households of our survey in Gulbarga and Solapur cities have been noted in Table 6.22.

Table-6.22
Daily Water Demand

Demand (Litres)	*Gulbarga*		*Solapur*	
	No. of Households	*Percentage*	*No. of Households*	*Percentage*
300-400	45	30.0	15	3.4
400-500	60	40.0	20	13.3
500-600	35	23.4	70	46.7
600-700	10	6.6	55	36.6
Total	150	100.0	150	100.0

Source: Field Survey.

In all, we have taken 4 ranges of per day water demand, it may be observed that 40 per cent of households in Gulbarga have revealed demand for 400-500 litres per day as against 47 per cent which have demanded 500-600 litres per day in Solapur. As against demand, the actual quantity supplied to the households is very important. This indicates the responsibility of authorities in meeting the household demand for water.[16]

Table-6.23
Daily Water Supply

Supply (Litres)	*Gulbarga*		*Solapur*	
	No. of Households	*Percentage*	*No. of Households*	*Percentage*
300-400	117	78.0	5	3.4
400-500	20	13.4	45	30.0
500-600	10	6.6	60	40.0
600-700	03	2.0	40	26.6
Total	150	100.0	150	100.0

Source: Field Survey.

The actual supply of daily water as revealed by households in Gulbarga and Solapur may be glanced from Table 6.23. The 78 per cent of households get 300-400 litres per day as against 40 per cent which is 500-600 litres per day in Gulbarga and Solapur respectively. Therefore, it is clear that the water supply situation in Solapur is far better than Gulbarga.

The type of water storage greatly influence the water use. The method of storage also influence the sustainability of household for next days water supply a systematic storage means better use[17] of water supplied. The method of storage adopted by households in Gulbarga and Solapur has been given in Table 6.24.

Table-6.24
Water Storage System

Type of Storage	Gulbarga		Solapur	
	No. of Households	% Percentage	No. of Households	% Percentage
Water Tanks	50	33.4	80	53.3
Earthen Tanks	10	6.6	5	3.4
Drums	80	53.3	59	39.3
Pots	10	6.7	6	4.0
Total	150	100.0	150	100.0

Source: Field Survey.

It may be observed that due to uncertainty and poor quantity of water supply 53 per cent households in Gulbarga store the water in drums as against the systematic storage adopted by 53 per cent households in Solapur.

Besides the storage, the leakage of water reduces the water consumption of houses. The less leakage more will be the quantity available for consumption. The leakages reported by households has been noted in Table 6.25. It is evident that due to poor storage, 40 per cent of households as against 7 per cent of our sample have reported leakage in Gulbarga and Solapur cities respectively.

Besides leakages in the households storage the leakages in public pipes and stand posts greatly reduce the quantity of water available for use. It may be seen from Table 6.26 that 53 per cent of our sample households as against 13.3 per cent in Solapur have reported leakages in public water supply pipes and stand posts.

Table-6.25
Problem of Water Leakage

Opinion	*Gulbarga*		*Solapur*	
	No. of Households	*Percentage*	*No. of Households*	*Percentage*
Yes	60	40.0	10	6.7
No	90	60.0	140	93.3
Total	150	100.0	150	100.0

Source: Field Survey.

Table-6.26
Public Tap Leakages

Opinion	*Gulbarga*		*Solapur*	
	No. of Households	*Percentage*	*No. of Households*	*Percentage*
Yes	80	53.3	20	13.3
No	70	46.7	130	86.7
Total	150	100.0	150	100.0

Source: Field Survey.

The drinking water is indeed a very scarce commodity. Therefore, it has to be used very economically, but there are various reasons due to which there is a lot of wastage in collecting the water from public stand posts. For example, the public stand posts do not have locking system, there are no proper tap fittings, infighting among the households, lack of awareness are important causes for wastage of water[18]. As has been seen in Table 6.13 above, there are 20 and 15 households dependent on PSPs in Gulbarga and Solapur. According to our survey, the sample households have reported wastage of large quantity of water as could be seen from the Table 6.27.

For instance, in Gulbarga 40 per cent of households have reported the wastage of 700-800 litres per day against which 67 per cent of households have indicated wastage of 500-600 litres in Solapur. Though there is higher percentage of households in Solapur but the greater leakage is evident in Gulbarga city.

Table-6.27
Daily Quantity of Wastage Water

Wastage (Litres)	*Gulbarga*		*Solapur*	
	No. of Households	*Percentage*	*No. of Households*	*Percentage*
500-600	3	15.0	10	66.6
600-700	5	25.0	3	20.0
700-800	8	40.0	2	13.4
800-900	4	20.0	--	
Total	20	100.0	15	100.0

Note: Adjusted from Table 6.13 above.

In fetching water from PSPs, the households have reported used more number of persons as there is queing system. The number of persons used in Gulbarga and Solapur by the households is given in Table 6.28.

Table-6.28
Number of Persons Used for Getting Water from Stand Posts

Persons	*Gulbarga*		*Solapur*	
	No. of Households	*Percentage*	*No. of Households*	*Percentage*
1-2	15	75.0	12	80.0
2-3	5	25.0	3	20.0
3-4	--	--	--	--
4 and above	--	--	--	--
Total	20	100.0	15	100.0

Source: Field Survey.

It is evident from the Table 6.28 that the households in Gulbarga have to use more additional labour than that of Solapur. Besides parents even children have been asked to get water from the public stand posts. Infact fetching water from PSPs is a very big botheration is the opinion expressed by households in Gulbarga.

The time element is an important factor in getting water from public stand posts. In addition to additional labour, the time spent by households in getting water in Gulbarga and Solapur is noted in Table 6.29. Due to good amount of water supply through the pipes in Solapur the households spend less time (53% households spend 20-40 minutes) than that of Gulbarga. In Gulbarga 35 per cent of households spend 60-80 minutes per day to get water from PSPs.

Table-6.29
Time Spent for Getting Water from Public Stand Posts

Minutes	*Gulbarga*		*Solapur*	
	No. of Households	*Percentage*	*No. of Households*	*Percentage*
20-40	3	15.0	8	53.3
40-60	5	25.0	4	26.7
60-80	7	35.0	3	20.0
80 & above	5	25.0	-	-
Total	20	100.0	15	100.0

Source: Field Survey.

The payment of water tax is other important behavioural aspects of household. According to our survey, as could be seen from following Table 6.30. All the sample households in Gulbarga paid a monthly tax of Rs. 45 as against Rs.81.6 per month tax paid by households in Solapur. Thus, the households in Solapur pay more water tax compared to the households in Gulbarga.[19]

Table-6.30
Monthly Payment of Water Tax

Tax (Rs.)	*Gulbarga*		*Solapur*	
	No. of Households	*Percentage*	*No. of Households*	*Percentage*
40-50	150	100.0	-	-
50-60	-	-	-	-
60 –70	-	-	-	-
70 & above	-	-	150	100.00
Total	150	100.0	150	100.0

Source: Field Survey.

SECTION-V
FINDINGS ON MANAGEMENT AND HEALTH

As has been seen in earlier chapters that, the water supply is a debated issue as to consider it as a public utility a part of over all urban infrastructure.[20] If it is treated as an urban infrastructure than a general, state policy has to attend to this. However, in Gulbarga & Solapur, the water supply system is the responsibility of City Municipal Corporations. They have to provide drinking water to the residents. Therefore, it is needless to say, the type of problems that confront the system[21] of water supply are the most important. They considerably influence the households utility maximisation with respect to drinking water. How much quantity of water they get, what is the quality of water, how the water is supplied, what are the problems in the supply, how they are attended, are these attended satisfactorily are the important aspects. If quantity of water is poor or becomes poor or polluted, it would lead to many health problems. Thus, it may be noted that given the situation described above, the households are at a receiving end. The view of households relating to management are essential for evaluating the economics of urban water supply in the two cities under consideration. Accordingly, the important management issues are 1) Breakages and leakages in water supply pipes, 2) Breakages and leakages in drainage pipes, 3) Complaints to water supply authorities, 4) Households response regarding the complaints attended by authorities, 5) Payment of money for repairs, 6) Head wise payments for water supply, 7) Payment of un-official gratia to water supply staff, 8) Special water treatment, 9) Method of water treatment / purification, 10) Family members affected by drinking water, 11) Type of diseases affected, 12) Problems of health affected by authorities and 13) Amount of expenditure for water diseases treatment.

Though apparently the breakages and leakages are considered as minor problem in the system of water supply. But, if repairs to them are not attended from time to time, they would create water vands and water loggings all around the area of water supply. If the pipes are laid alongside and across the service roads of the residents, it is quite imaginable that, they inundate the road and cause inconveniences to the residents. The opinion of households regarding breakages and leakages in Gulbarga and Solapur have been tabulated in the Table 6.31.

Table-6.31
Breakages and Leakages in Water Supply Pipes

Opinion	*Gulbarga*		*Solapur*	
	No. of Households	*Percentage*	*No. of Households*	*Percentage*
Breakages	70	46.7	30	20.0
Leakages	45	30.0	35	23.3
Nil	35	23.3	85	56.7
Total	150	100.0	150	100.0

Source: Field Survey.

There are only a quarter of the sample of our households in Gulbarga have reported no breakages and leakages[22] in their water supply. But close to 50 per cent of the sample households in Gulbarga have express the opinion that there are 23 per cent of breakages[23] in the pipe line systems arranged by the corporation. There are 30 per cent of sample households in Gulbarga face the problems of leakages of water supply pipes at several points leading to reduction in the quantity received by households.

In Solapur city on the other hand, it may be noted from the table that, 57 per cent of sample households have reported no leakages and breakages. Therefore, it may be observed that the system of water supply according to households is more satisfactory (33 per cent) in Solapur than Gulbarga. Furthermore, there are also less breakages and leakages faced by households in Solapur city under the circumstances, it may be argued that the Solapur water supply system is sound and full proof than Gulbarga.

It is an inevitable situation to any urban city that to provide water supply and arrange drainage system side by side. Because, it may be for convenience or unavoidable. The opinion of households regarding the drainage pipes in the two cities have been given in Table 6.32.

Table-6.32
Breakages and Leakages in Drainage Pipes

Opinion	Gulbarga		Solapur	
	No. of Households	Percentage	No. of Households	Percentage
Breakages	70	33.4	10	6.7
Leakages	50	46.6	20	13.7
Nil	30	20.0	120	80.6
Total	150	100.0	150	100.0

Source: Field Survey.

As regards to breakages and leakages of drainage pipes only 20 per cent of sample households have reported in Gulbarga city. There are 33 per cent and 47 per cent households have reported breakages and leakages in drainage pipes respectively in Gulbarga city. Therefore, it may be observed that the drainage system is very poor in Gulbarga. While in Solapur only 20 per cent of households have faced the problems of breakages and leakages. An important conclusion that could be derived is that along with water supply, the sanitary system in Solapur is more satisfactory than Gulbarga.

The awareness and action of the household place an important role in the system of optimum water supply. This is very much true as the vast area which has to be attended by water supply authorities. This would also ensure timely action and prevention of wastage[24] of scarce water. The complaints regarding breakages, leakages disconnections due to blocks[25] and interception by others are very important which will help the authorities. The findings of sample households relating to the general complaints and specific complaints have been given in Table 6.33

It is evident that 10 per cent of samples households reported complaint about breakage of pipes, 7 per cent and households reported about leakages of pipes, 13 per cent of households reported disconnection due to blocks and 23 per cent of sample households reported about intercepted by neighbours and 47 per cent of households have not made any complaint. While on the other hand in Solapur. 23 per cent of sample households reported about breakages of pipes, 13 per cent households reported about leakages of pipes, 40 per cent of households reported about disconnection due to blocks, 3 per cent of households reported about intercepted by neighbours[26] and 20 per cent of households have not made any complaint.[27] Thus, it is clear that there is more awareness and interest among the households to complaint about their problems in Solapur than that of Gulbarga.

Table-6.33
Complaints to Water Supply Authorities

Reasons	*Gulbarga*		*Solapur*	
	No. of Households	*% Percentage*	*No. of Households*	*% Percentage*
Breakage of Pipes	15	10.0	35	23.3
Leakage of pipes	10	6.6	20	13.3
Disconnected due to blocks	20	13.4	60	40.0
Interesepted by neighbours	35	23.3	5	3.3
No response	70	46.7	30	20.0
Total	150	100.0	150	100.0

Source: Field Survey.

As against the complaint how often they have been attended by the authorities[28] is an important issue. Hence, the response of households regarding the complaints attended by authorities in Gulbarga and Solapur have been given in the Table 6. 34. It may be observed from table that, only 20 per cent of sample households reported about water supply authority attended their complaints. Whereas in Solapur 53 percent of sample households reported positively. Therefore, it is cleared that the complaints are well attended in Solapur than Gulbarga.

Table-6.34
Households Problems of Water Supply Attend by Authorities

Opinion	Gulbarga		Solapur	
	No. of Households	Percentage	No. of Households	Percentage
Yes	30	20.0	80	53.3
No	120	80.0	70	46.7
Total	150	100.0	150	100.0

Source: Field Survey.

The problems of water supply faced by sample households in the study areas have been given Table 6.35. If we read the Table 6.35 along with the Table 6.34, it is undoubtedly evident that, due to more awareness among the households in Solapur, the water supply authorities are kept on their tenterhooks,[29] thereby ensuring smooth supply of water to households.

Table-6.35
Problems of Water Supply

Problems	Gulbarga		Solapur	
	No. of Households	% Percentage	No. of Households	% Percentage
Repairing pipes	10	33.3	30	37.5
Fitting bolts	7	23.3	15	18.7
Removing blocks	13	43.3	35	43.8
Total	30	100.0	80	100.0

Note: Adjusted from Table 6.34

For example, 33.3 per cent of households in Gulbarga have reported about pipe repairs, 23.3 per cent have reported about fitting bolts, and 43.3 per cent of the sample reported about removing blocks as against 37.5 per cent, 18.7 per cent and 43.8 per cent of sample households in Solapur city.

Although there is need for repair to the public taps, if not attempted that will greatly disturb the house connections.

Therefore, willingness to pay for repairs by households becomes an important factor for ensuring smooth water supply. The payment of money made by sample households for repair purposes in Gulbarga and Solapur cities is given in Table 6.36.

Table-6.36
Payment of Money for Repair

Amount (Rs.)	*Gulbarga*		*Solapur*	
	No. of Households	*Percentage*	*No. of Households*	*Percentage*
100-200	--	--	--	--
200-300	5	16.6	25	31.3
300-400	10	33.4	40	50.0
400 and above	15	50.0	15	18.7
Total	30	100.0	80	100.0

Note: Adjustment from Table 6.34

As there is relatively poor pipeline system in Gulbarga, 50 per cent of households have paid Rs. 400 and above for the purpose of repairs as against 50 per cent of households have paid Rs. 300-400 in Solapur which is less as compared to Gulbarga.

Table-6.37
Headwise Payment of Water Supply

Heads	*Payment*	*Gulbarga*		*Solapur*	
		No. of Households	*Percentage*	*No. of Households*	**Percentage**
Pipes	Rs. 500	7	23.3	45	56.2
Bolts and nuts	Rs. 150	10	33.3	25	31.2
Digging charges	Rs. 75	13	43.3	10	12.5
Total		30	100.0	80	100.0

Source: Field Survey.

An item wise payment for repair reflects the quality of the system of public water supply, if we consider in this context Table

6.37 indicates that the maximum of 43 per cent of households pay a sum of Rs. 75 for the purpose of digging as against 56 per cent of households paying Rs. 500 for pipes repair in Solapur city. Therefore, the system of repair is very poor in Gulbarga as compared to Solapur.

It is an in explicable fact that corruption has been playing an important role all over the globe. Besides it has spread to almost all aspects of public life. Therefore, the public water supply system is not an exception to this. It is not difficult to imagine the inquisitiveness and eager to get water by the households. As a result to avoid delay in getting water they pay unofficial gratia to the water supply workmen and staff. The unofficial gratia payment reported by sample households has been given in Table 6.38.

Table-6.38
Payment of Un-official Gratia to Water Supply Staff

Amount (Rs.)	*Gulbarga*		*Solapur*	
	No. of Households	*Percentage*	*No. of Households*	*Percentage*
100-200	--	--	--	--
200-300	5	20.0	25	31.3
300-400	8	32.0	40	50.0
400 and above	12	48.0	15	18.7
Total	25	100.0	80	100.0

Source: Field Survey.

For example, nearly 50 per cent households have reported the payment of Rs. 400 and above in Gulbarga[31] as against the same 50 per cent of households have paid Rs. 300-400 in Solapur.[32]

The quality of water is very important in the health and hygiene of the people. The good quality of water greatly reduces the dangers of water borne diseases. A frequent treatment[34] after filtration is an integral part of providing safe drinking water.

In this context it may be visualised from Table 6.39 that there is high frequency of water treatment after filtration in Solapur than in Gulbarga. In fact a weekly treatment is reported in Solapur by the sample households. Whereas in Gulbarga the less frequency has been reported due to different quantities of water supplied by different rivers(i.e.Bhosga, Bennithora and Bhima). In general, according to our sample survey 53 per cent of households in Gulbarga have reported quarterly treatment as against 73 per cent households reported monthly special treatment in Solapur.

Table-6.39
Special Water Treatment Adopted

Frequency	*Gulbarga*		*Solapur*	
	No. of Households	*Percentage*	*No. of Households*	*Percentage*
Monthly	20	13.3	110	73.3
Bi-monthly	50	33.4	35	23.3
Quarterly	80	53.3	5	3.33
Total	150	100.0	150	100.0

Source: Field Survey.

In addition to the general filtration (to avoid contamination), further treatment of water with chemicals is specially needed for drinking purpose. The various chemical treatment apply to the drinking water are a) Bleaching Powder b) Poly Alumino Clhoride /Alum Powder c) Filtration, d) Liquid Chlorine Gas. Among these treatment with PAC Powder / Alum and Clorine are more safely but relatively costly. The chemical treatments reported by various sample households under different chemicals in Gulbarga and Solapur have been given in Table 6.40.

For example, in Gulbarga i) 57 per cent of sample households reported treatment done with bleaching powder, ii) 10 per cent households with PAC powder / Alum and iii) 33 per cent households with filtration. Thus majority of households get water with bleaching powder treatment. The treatment with different chemicals differs some what among the sample households in Solapur. For example, i) 30 per cent of households getting water with bleaching powder treatment, ii) 43 per cent households with

PAC Powder / Alum , iii) 7 per cent-households with filtration and iv) 20 per cent households are getting with chlorine gas treatment. There is thus favorably more better water treatment adopted in Solapur than Gulbarga.

Table-6.40
Method of Water Treatment/Purification

Treatment with	Gulbarga		Solapur	
	No. of Households	Percentage	No. of Households	Percentage
Bleaching powder	60	56.6	45	30.0
PAC Powder /Alum	25	10.4	65	34.3
Filtration	50	33.0	10	6.6
Liquid Chlorine Gas	15	10.0	30	20.0
Total	150	100.0	150	100.0

Source: Field Survey.

There has been by now, especially during the last decade specific international and national attention has been focused on the general health conditions of the masses.[35] No doubt the problems of health have not received greater attention at the local level. This does not mean that the urban people (including the poor and living in slum areas) are not suffering from health problems. The network for health care is very poor in developing countries. This may be due to not only non-availability of large number of doctors but also difficulties in getting appropriate instruments/machines and medicines. The cheap medicine to be consumed by masses is a hard nut to crack. Further more among the health problems, the quality of drinking water is considered as the major factor affecting the health of the people-be they haves or have nots?. The impure quality of water which is generally supplied has been pin pointed as the cause number of diseases attacking the people. There is at the same time no proper diagnosis and treatment for these disease inflicted by drinking water. The households being aware of or ignorant of these diseases have to pay from their nose orals in with prolonged illness have to end of their lives. In keeping with the ideas noted above, if not large but a few questions on drinking water and health and related problems of diseases and cost of treatment undertaken by households[36] have been noted in the questionnaire. The important data tabulated from the questionnaire relating to health and disease of our survey include, family members affected by drinking water, type of diseases, health problems attended by authorities, amount spending for treatment of water diseases, reasons for not attending health problems.

For example, for a qualitative question the answers of households in Gulbarga and Solapur have been noted in Table 6.41.

Table-6.41
Family Members Affected by Drinking Water

Opinion	*Gulbarga*		*Solapur*	
	No. cf Households	*Percentage*	*No. of Households*	*Percentage*
Yes	110	73.0	70	46.6
No	40	27.0	50	53.4
Total	150	100.0	150	100.0

Source: Field Survey.

The table is self explanatory. In the sense that, 73 per cent of households in Gulbarga and 47 per cent of households in Solapur have opined that they have been affected by drinking water.

It may be observed from Table 6.42 that, for example in Gulbarga 9 per cent of sample households are suffering from cholera, 13.06 per cent reported about jaundice, 54 per cent of households have suffered from gastroenteritis (dysentery and diarrhea) and 23 per cent of households are suffering from typhoid. While in Solapur 8.5 Per cent sample households are suffering from Cholera, 13 per cent reported about jaundice, 64 per cent of households are suffering from gastroenteritis and 14 per cent have suffered from typhoid.

Table-6.42
Type of Diseases Affected

Diseases	*Gulbarga*		*Solapur*	
	No. of Households	*Percentage*	*No. of Households*	*Percentage*
Cholera	10	9.0	6	8.5
Jaundice	15	13.6	9	12.8
Gastroenteritis	60	54.5	45	64.2
Typhoid	25	22.7	10	14.2
Total	110	100.0	70	100.0

Note: Adjusted from Table 6.41

The disease-wise relative difference between Gulbarga and Solapur is as follows; 1) with regard to the disease like cholera is affecting the same percentage people in Gulbarga and Solapur[39] as reported by our sample households, 2) it is also true of the fact that, there is only marginal difference but Gulbarga and Solapur with respect to the jaundice disease, 3) whereas the disease like gastroenteritis (dysentery and diarrhea) is very much high in Solapur than Gulbarga. The enquiry with the households revealed that they have admitted members of their family to the hospital for the treatment of diarrhea in Solapur city, 4) the other disease which may partly be related to drinking water is typhoid. According to our survey, the incidence of typhoid is very high in city. Some of the households have pointed out that, they are now adopted the method of boiling the water for drinking purpose due to the instructions from health authorities.

The civic awareness is an important factor affecting health through the drinking water. In many cases, as per our survey, it is found that complaining to authorities and getting solution is a no less important quality of civic awareness. Under such circumstances, the opinion of households relating to the action of the water supply authorities in the matter is given in Table 6.43.

For instance, only 13 per cent of sample households have responded positively as against 33 per cent in Solapur. Therefore, there is more health care awareness in Solapur with regard to drinking water supply than Gulbarga.

Table-6.43
Problems of Health Attended by Authorities

Opinion	*Gulbarga*		*Solapur*	
	No. of Households	*Percentage*	*No. of Households*	*Percentage*
Yes	20	13.4	50	33.3
No	130	86.6	100	66.7
Total	150	100.0	150	100.0

Source: Field Survey.

The amount of expenditure borne by sample households in Gulbarga and Solapur cities for treatment of water borne diseases are given in Table 6.44.

Table-6.44
Expenditure for Treatment of Water Diseases

Amount (Rs.)	*Gulbarga*		*Solapur*	
	No. of Households	*% Percentage*	*No. of Households*	*% Percentage*
100-200	15	11.5	10	10.0
200-300	10	7.7	70	70.0
300-400	70	53.8	20	20.0
400 and above	35	26.9	--	--
Total	130	100.0	100	100.0

Source: Field Survey.

It is noted from table that, 11.5 per cent of sample households spends Rs. 100-200 for treatment of water diseases, 8 per cent of households spend Rs. 200-300, 54 per cent households spend Rs 300-400 and 27 per cent of sample households spends Rs. 400 and above. While in Solapur, for example 10 per cent of sample households spend Rs. 100-200, 70 per cent. households spend Rs. 200-300 and 20 per cent households spend Rs. 300-400. Thus, relatively more money is spent by large number of households for treatment of water borne diseases in Gulbarga than the sample households in Solapur.

NOTES & REFERENCES

1. See, Kamen, C.S. and Dar.P., "Factors Affecting Domestic Water Consumption", Total Water Planning for Israil, Ltd Tel. Aviv, 1973.
2. The Gulbarga has younger people as heads of households supposedly dynamic and forward looking in their living standards than the older generation.
3. This could be attributed to the decadal higher literacy rate registered in Maharashtra. The Solapur city have, had more number of educational institutions in the past than Gulbarga.
4. The water use differs subsequently across the occupational groups. Understandingly, the trade, business and industry would use more water than others.
5. Because, located in the extreme part of the state Gulbarga city has been made as the administrative divisional headquarter.
6. These ranges have been constructed due to the fact that the minimum annual income of urban households will have to be Rs. 20000 according to the price situation prevailing in 2001. (For example, the rent, food and clothing, power are most essential urban minimum needs even for the below poverty line households in the urban areas).
7. These may be termed as lower middle and middle households for water use considerations.
8. It may be noted in passing that all the 150 households in Gulbarga are un-metered system of supply as against 90 un-metered and 60 metered in Solapur.
9. The bore wells are independent but much dearer source of water supply. Further the yield (quantity) depends greatly on the level of ground water. If table water is deep and low, the quantity of water supply will be very small. Hence tap system and house connection is far more better than bore wells which exists in Solapur city.

10. There are relative merits and demerits of the two systems but the underground system is consider to be convenient and safe as against the surface system being expose to dangers and breakages.
11. If the water supply pipes are very close in width and also in length, breakage and leakage among them may create health problems. The discussion in the field survey brought out the fact that there have been few cases of breakages and leakages in the two systems in Gulbarga and no case has been found in Solapur city.
12. The surface pipeline system faces an additional problem for water supply together the problems of frequent road diggings and uncared or delayed road repairs. The restoration of water supply with surface system bringing difficulties to the households in getting timely drinking water.
13. For detail see, Buchanan James.M., "The Demand and Supply of Public Goods", Rand Menally, Chicago, 1967,Arrow K.J.Social Choice and Individual preferences", 1951. Also see, Sen Amratya, "The Social Choice Theory A Re-examination, Econometrica, 1978.
14. For further discussion, see Hanke S.H., " Demand for Under Dynamic Conditions" Water Resources Research, Vol.6, No.5, Columbia Maryland, USA, 1970.
15. See, Daar, Feld Man and Kannen, "Socio-economic Factors Affecting Domestic Water Demand in Israil", Water Resources Research, 11(6) Dec., 1975, PP. 149-220.
16. Indeed the water wastage at household level is difficult for estimation. For further details see, Arceivala.S., "Percapita Water Consumption and Losses', E.E. Dept, MET, Ankare, Thurkey,.
17. In fact there is poor behaviour of households for reuse of water that we have found during the survey.
18. For more description, see, Linawear, F.P. et al., "A Study of Residential Water Use", Govt. Printing Office, Washington D.C 1967.
19. There is difference in the mode of water tax payment adopted in Gulbarga and Solapur cities. In the former it is monthly, while in the later it is collected annually.
20. See chapter two above, Review of Literature.
21. Vyas Anjan, and Anand P.B. "Some Issues in Management of Urban Water Supply system: A Case Study of Ahmedabad" Nagarlok, 1989.

22. It may be observed that relatively leakages cause less waste of water as compared to the breakages. Besides, the leakages are subject to simple and less expensive repair.
23. For further discussion see, Paramshivam.R., "Un-accounted for Water in Distribution System", Paper Presented at the National Seminar on "Water and Sewerage Tariffs", organised by the CPHEEO at Srinagar, during September 9-11,1986.
24. This is s particular complaint through related to public water supply system, some households make or mend something to the public pipes resulting in poor quantity of water supply to the neighbours or tail enders. However, this also has to be solved by water supply authorities.
25. For such problems see, Adhikari, M. and Gupta.C.K., "Problems in Municipal Water Supply: Their Remedies", Social Culture,41(6), June 1975.
26. It is a very common visual appearance in Gulbarga that households connect electric motors for driving more and more water to their house from public taps/house connections and thereby reduce the pressure and volume of water supply to other households.
27. It may be consider as a general apathy and formed opinion of the households that their complaints are not attended by the authorities. Therefore, they consider that why to complain?.
28. Desai, V.D., "Water Supply Management", Journal of Indian Water Works Association, 8(2) 1976.
29. David, Hohz and Scott Sehastain, "Municipal Water System the Change for Urban Management" Indian University Press, London, 1978.
30. There are more than 500 ditches digged at several places in Gulbarga city. In fact these ditches cause great hindrance to road traffic and great nuisance to residents in particular these ditches get filled with rain water and often get mixed up with water supply pipes. These things are hard to find in Solapur city.
31. Indeed corruption and economic development became a major thing for World Bank during the year 1998-99. There are two schools of thought arguing that corruption, (unofficial gratia) promotes economic development, while others argue that it is a hindrance to development and reduces the rate of growth. See World Bank Report 1998-1999.

32. In our field survey, it has been told by all the 150 households that they have paid unofficial gratia to the water supply staff at one time or the other, but only 30 households have furnished the information.
33. It is due to high literacy and great awareness, very less amount is paid Solapur by the households. Therefore, as against 30 in Gulbarga only 10 out of the total sample of 150 households in Solapur have paid unofficial gratia.
34. A particular mention may be made of the fact that surface water that too river water specially during the rainy season require daily treatment which is beyond the capacity of the authorities. This has been reported by official during the discussion with them.
35. See logan, John., "The International Municipal Water Supply Programme-A Health and Economic Approaisal", A.J. Tropical Medicine and Hygine, 9(5), Sept 1960.
36. For some relevant ideas see, Logan "Investment in Water Supply Program-A Health Economic Approaisal", American Journal of Water Works Association, 1960.
37. See Rao S.Subba, "National Water Supply and Sanitation Programme, With Special Reference to Cholera Endemic Areas", Indian Journal of Public Health, 19(1) 1975.
38. Esrey, S.A., J.B.Potash, L. Roberts and C. Shiff, "Effects of Improved Water Supply and Sanitation on Ascariasis, Diarrhoea, Dracunacuhiagic, Hookworm, Infection, Schistosmia and Trachoma", 1991.
39. The eradication of cholera, bringing the disease under control (during rainy season) is a common national health programme implemented in both the cities. But the intensity of the compaign is very high in Solapur.
40. During the discussion with the households have pointed out few cases of immediate deaths due to no proper diagnosis of the disease Jaundice / Cholera in both the cities.

7

URBAN WATER SUPPLY IN GULBARGA AND SOLAPUR CITIES – A CRITICAL EVALUATION

Introduction

Against a macro level assessment coupled with the micro level articulation of the findings of survey, a critical evaluation of the comparative economics of urban water supply is an inevitable step. But the evaluation is largely dependent on the system of water supply arrangement made at the local level which is decided by the State Governments are an influential factor.

For example, it may be recapitulated briefly from Chapter-IV that 1) KUWS&DB and MJP's responsibility is to conceive, planning, prepare and execute the water supply and sewerage/ drainage schemes in the states, 2) there is beneficial system of financing in Maharashtra than Karnataka, 3) the funding pattern is more efficient in Maharastra, 4) the bulk water supply programme suffers from the problem of shortage of funds in Karnataka, 5) operation and maintenance of water works is the responsibilities of the local bodies, since it is their prime responsibilities, 6) non backlog municipal water supply and sewerage schemes are highest in Maharastra, sewerage schemes are not included in Karnataka, 7) Maharastra state policy reserving a water source for drinking purpose, 8) 10 LPCD more water per day in Maharastra than that of Karnataka, 9) there are more plan allocations in Maharastra specially during VIIth and IXth plan, 10) better coverage of urban population (6% more) in Maharashtra, 11) 13 water supply projects are maintained by Board in Karnataka and 52 & 20 water works are maintained by the MJP on ownership basis in urban areas of Maharashtra, 12) level of taxation is very low in Karnataka and Maharashtra states, 13) partial privatisation is being tried by MJP in the form of entrusting operation and maintenance of water works to private organisational contractors, 14) MJP is attempting to improve billing system and timely recovery, wherever MJP supplies water directly to the consumers, the recovery is around 85 per cent.

While the macro level examination lends the following important points as a supplement to present evaluation. For example, 1) Solapur is an industrial town, 2) the two cities have not been founded in the bank of any river nearby, 3) increasing industrial cultural demand for water in the two cities, 4) hot climate in both the cities, 5) higher average rainfall in Solapur city, 6) 8 and 12 urbanised villages incorporated in both the cities, 7) low capacity of water supply in Gulbarga, no pipeline system in extension areas, 8) Solapur has more house service connections, and non domestic connections than Gulbarga, 9) poor coverage of households and less number of public stand posts in both cities.

Given the above background, this chapter attempts a critical evaluation of the comparative economics of urban water supply in Gulbarga and Solapur cities. The major points of evaluation are a) normative view, b) the household view, c) the redesign (remodeling) and d) question of adopting new technology, which help for analysing the comparative welfare gains of an urban utility i.e. water supply. The testing of hypotheses have been systematically twined under these heads.

For convenience the chapter is divided into the following sections. **Section-I** examines the normative view of the economics of urban water supply. The household view which is most crucial in the evaluation of the economics of urban water supply (a positive approach) has been examined in **Section-II**. The remodeling of water supply system conceived by the authorities in Gulbarga & Solapur has been noted in **Section-III**. The problems and prospects of adopting new technology and new techniques so as to improve water supply in the two cities has been examined in **Section-IV**. The **Section-V** gives the picture of suggestions and scope for further study has been explained in **Section-VII**.

SECTION -I
NORMATIVE VIEW

A normative approach based on normative indications, it has been argued[1] in the literature that it gives better results than welfare comparisons. The indictors are more exact scale, quantity or units of comparison indicators permit less scope for value judgements. The normative indicators are dynamic and greatly support the policy making. The normative comparison is therefore a widely used method of decision making particularly in the field of public choice and public utility. The important normative comparisons of indicators of water supply in Gulbarga and Solapur consists of a) minimum domestic water consumption for high income groups, b) minimum domestic water consumption for weaker sections and low income groups, in small Indian towns and cities, c) water requirements of individuals institutions and commercial establishments.

A first step before proceeding to the normative comparison of indicators the latest list of indicators on their simple look is an essential. Table 7.1 gives the description of various indictors of water supply existing in Gulbarga and Solapur during the year 2000-2001. There are as many as 16 indicators. These include (a) geographical area, (b) density of population, (c) number of wards, (d) number of water supply zones, (e) year of becoming a municipalities, (f) gradation of corporations, (g) number of bore wells, (h) average annual rainfall, (i) temperature, (j) daily water supply, (k) per capita water supply per day, (l) number of public stand posts, (m) number of house service connections, (n) number of non domestic connections, (o) population served by public stand posts, (p) population served by house service connections, (q) population dependent on each public tap, (r) ratio of public stand posts to house service connections and (s) ratio of non domestic connections to house service connections (see Table 7.1) .

Table-7.1

Indices of Selected Indicators on Water Supply and Distribution in Gulbarga and Solapur Cities - 2000-01

Indicator	*Gulbarga*	*Solapur*	*Difference*
Geographical area (in sq. km.)	65	180	115
Density of population (per sq. km.)	7796.9	5416.6	2380.3
Gradation of corporation	1981	1964	17
Number of wards	55	90	35
Number of zones	3	6	3
Number of households	81250	195000	113750
Number of slum areas	34	225	191
Number of bore wells	1301	2300	999
Average annual rainfall(mm)	624.1	706.9	82.8
Temperature	43.0	42.0	01.0
Daily water supply(lakh gallons)	67.5	275.0	207.5
Per capita supply per day(gallons)	15.7	28.2	12.5
Number of public stand posts	2000	2300	300
Number of house service connections	19663	48300	28637
Number of non domestic connections	345	3500	3155
Ratio of PSPs to HSCs	0.10	0.05	0.5
Ratio of NDCs to HSCs	0.02	0.07	-0.5

Source: Compiled from City Municipal Corporations Records, 2000-2001.

The above 16 indicators without loss of generality, may be grouped into five heads viz., 1) Physical indicators; includes geographical area, no. wards, zones of the city, 2) Social indicators; density of population, no. of households, populations served by PSPs, HSCs, and population dependent on each PSPs, 3) Economic indicators; no. of bore wells, HSCs, NDC, PSPs, Ratio of PSPs to HSCs, NDCs to HSCs, 4) Natural indicators; average annual rainfall, temperature and 5) Management indicators; no. of wards, zones, year of becoming a municipality, gradation of corporation.

As a starting point, one can obtain the results of comparative efficiency of water supply systems if the actual supply is compared to the normatively fixed quantity of supply. For example, according to international system of code[2] there are two upper quantities of water which have been fixed for high and low income families[3]. For high income families, the item wise water requirement is for drinking 5 litres per capita per day (LPCD), cooking 5 LPCD, bathing 75 LPCD, washing of clothes 25 LPCD, washing of utensils 15 LPCD, washing and cleaning of houses and residences 15 LPCD, lawn watering and gardening 15 LPCD, flushing of water closets, etc. 45 LPCD.

It is evident from Table 7.2 that Gulbarga provides very small quantity of water either for high income households or for the low income households. Whereas the water supply in Solapur city is very close to the international standard norm. Hence, it is an obvious conclusion that the water supply system of Solapur is very efficient than Gulbarga.

Table-7.2
Minimum Domestic Water Consumption for Indian Towns and Cities with Full Flushing System as per IS Norm

Use	*Consumption (LPCD)*		
	IS Norm	*Gulbarga*	*Solapur*
Drinking	5	5	5
Cooking	5	5	5
Bathing	75	50	65
Washing of clothes	25	20	25
Washing of utensils	15	10	10
Washing and cleaning of houses and residences	15	10	15
Lawn watering and gardening	15	10	10
Flushing of water closets, etc.	45	40	45
Total	200	150	180

Source: Santoshkumar Garg, "Water Supply Engineering" , Khanna Publishers Delhi, Vol.1, 1999. p. 8.

The same is true of the comparison with normative indicators applied for low income families. For example, in Gulbarga as against 135 LPCD required per day only 71 litres pr capita per day is actually supplied. Thus there is a shortfall of 63.8 litres which is just half of the IS norm. Whereas in Solapur as against 135 LPCD required, the actual supplied by corporation is 128 LPCD i.e. very close to IS norm. (see Table 7.3).

Table-7.3
Minimum Domestic Water Consumption for Weaker Sections and Low Income Group Colonies in Small Indian Towns and Cities

Use	*Consumption (LPCD)*		
	IS Norm	*Gulbarga*	*Solapur*
Drinking	5	5	5
Cooking	5	5	5
Bathing	55	25	50
Washing of clothes	20	10	18
Washing of utensils	10	5	10
Washing and cleaning of houses and residences	10	5	10
Flushing of water closets, etc.	30	16.2	30
Total	135	71.3	128

Source: Ibid, p.9.

Against household comparison the institutional water demand and actual supply may be treated as an additional but no less important measure of efficiency of water supply. In accordance with IS norm the institutional water requirements[4] has been noted in Table 7.4 and the actual supply in Gulbarga and Solapur have been compared therein.

As per IS norm 1) offices require 45-90 LPCD, 2) factories where bath rooms are provided 45-90 LPCD, where bathrooms are not provided require 30-60 LPCD, 3) in schools for day scholars required 45-90 LPCD, residential 135-225 LPCD, 4) hostels needed 135-180 LPCD, 5) hotels average water consumption is 180 LPCD per bed, 6) restaurants consumption is 70 LPCD per seat, 7) hospitals (including laundry), number of beds not exceeding 100,

Table-7.4
Water Requirements of Individual Institutions and Commercial Establishments

Sl. No.	Type of Institution or Commercial Establishments	Average Water Consumption (LPCD)		
		IS Norm	Gulbarga	Solapur
1	Offices	45-90	20-50	35-80
2	Factories			
	a) Where bath rooms are provided.	45-90	30-65	40-80
	b) Where no bath rooms provided	30-60	20-40	25-50
3	Schools			
	a) Days scholars	45-90	25-60	30-70
	b) Residential	135-225	65-150	110-200
4	Hostels	135-180	65-110	120-160
5	Hotels	180/bed	90	150
6	Restauranls	70/bed	45	60
7	Hospitals(including laundry)			
	a) Number of beds not exceeding 100	340/bed	250	320
	b) Number of beds exceeding 100	450/bed	380	430
8	Nursing homes and medical quarters	135-225	65-105	100-190
9	Railway stations:	70	40	60
	a) Junctions and intermediate stations where mail and express trains stop.	45	20	35
	b) Intermediate stations where mail and express trains do not stop	23	13	20
	c) Terminal roadway stations	45	25	35
10	Airports-international and domestic	70	-	-
11	Cinema halls & theaters (per seat)	15	5	10

Source: Ibid, p.11.

water requirements is 340 LPCD per bed, number of beds exceeding 100 water consumption is 450 LPCD per bed, 8) nursing homes and medical quarters consumption is 135-225 LPCD, 9) railway stations require 70 LPCD with bathing facilities, 45 litres for without bathing facilities, 10) airports (international and domestic) needed 70 LPCD, and 11) cinema halls and theaters consumption is 15 LPCD.

It may be noted from Table 7.4 that for example in Gulbarga, water requirements for offices is 20-50 LPCD, factories required 30-65 LPCD and 20-40 LPCD for schools 25-60 and 60-150 LPCD, hostels required 65 - 110 LPCD, restaurants needed 70 LPCD per seat, hospitals required 250 & 380 LPCD, nursing homes and medical quarters required 65-105 LPCD, railway stations 70 LPCD, and cinema halls 5 LPCD. While in Solapur, office requirement is 35-80 litres, factories 40-80 litres, hostels required 120-160 LPCD, hotels required 150 LPCD, hospitals (including laundry) required 320 & 430 LPCD, nursing homes and medical quarters demand is 100-190 LPCD, railway stations 60 LPCD, airports requirement 6 LPCD and cinema halls and theatres requirement is 10 LPCD.

Thus, the other normative institutional water requirements and actual supply clearly demonstrate the fact that the system of water supply in Solapur is very efficient than that of Gulbarga. The supply in Gulbarga is 65.0 per cent of the IS norm as against 88.0 per cent in Solapur (see Table 7.4)

Table-7.5
Break up of Per capita Demand for water an Average Indian City

(LPCD)

Particulars	*Domestic*	*Industrial*	*Commercial*	*Civil or Public*	*Wastes & thefts*
National	200	50	20	10	55
Gulbarga	135	25	10	3	50
Solapur	175	40	15	6	20

Source: Ibid.

Lastly, the relative efficiency of water supply systems may also be evaluated with the help of normative indicators such as the national requirements of water for domestic use (200 LPCD), Industrial use (50 LPCD), commercial use (20 LPCD), civil or public use (10 LPCD) and wastes and thefts (55 LPCD) as against actual supply. The following Table 7.5 provides the actual supply of water for different activities in Gulbarga and Solapur cities.

For example in Gulbarga, for example, the actual supply for domestic use is 135 litres, industrial use 25 litres, commercial use 10 litres, civil or public use 3 litres and for wastes and thefts 50 litres, while in Solapur, the supply for domestic use 175 LPCD, industrial use 40 LPCD, commercials required 15 LPCD, civil or public use 6 LPCD and wastes and thefts etc. is 20 LPCD.

The comparison with national norms fixed for a city, Gulbarga meets only 67 per cent of water supply as against 90 per cent met in Solapur. Therefore, the system of water supply in Solapur is superior to Gulbarga.

It is in this context could be kept in mind that the hypothesis relating to" The present system of water supply has outlived demand for water in the study areas" is proved positively for Gulbarga and negatively for Solapur. The above normative comparisons give an actual proof of the hypothesis.

SECTION-II
HOUSEHOLD VIEW

For a systematic evaluation of the economics of urban water supply against normative the positive approach is also essential. The ultimate objective is the household (which includes also individual) welfare maximisation in the context of drinking water supply. The ideas of the households provide a policy base for drinking water supply.

As an adjunct to positive views of the households, there are a number of issues aspects and problems confronting the question of household welfare maximisation, these have been noted in the following. For example, forecasting the urban residential drinking for water, trends in residential water uses, the demand for water some empirical evidence on consumers response to a commodity uncertain in supply, municipal water demand: statistical and management issues, income and price elasticities of demand for water in developing countries, estimation of household consumption of water, future water demands, the impact of growth of water on use patterns in selected sectors of Gujarat's economy 1969-2000, user specific water demand elasticities and per capita water consumption and losses.

With the given background aspects, besides for evaluation and testing of formulated hypotheses concerning household views have been discussed below. The important positive views of the households are a) difference between demand and supply, b) difference between per capita demand and per capita supply, c) amount of expenditure on tap connection, d) distance between house connection and service reservoir, e) amount of more willingness to pay for improved water supply and f) water borne diseases.

The macro level forecasting of water demand has to be based on the micro level household data. This is apparently uncalculative but indirectly influences the household welfare maximization view. Further, the often used normative indicators fail to reflect the desires of the households for water demand. Thus, the difference between demand and actual supply brings out the inequilibria which has to be tackled with the help of the policy[6]. The difference between demand and actual supply of water in Gulbarga and Solapur cities as desired by households has been given in Table 7.6.

Table-7.6

Difference between Demand and Actual Supply

Litres	*No. of Households (1997-98)*				*No. of Households (2001-2002)*			
	Gulbarga	*%*	*Solapur*	*%*	*Gulbarga*	*%*	*Solapur*	*%*
300-400	10	20	-	-	15	18.7	-	-
400-500	25	50	-	-	30	37.5	-	-
500-600	15	30	18	45	35	43.7	11	36.7
600 & above	-	-	22	55	-	-	19	63.3
Total	50	100	40	100	80	100	30	100

Source: Field Survey, excludes households 100 in Gulbarga and 110 in Solapur with no extra demand for water during 1997-98 and 70 households in Gulbarga and 120 households in Solapur during 2001-02.

It may be noted from Table 7.6 that, for example during the year 1997-98, there are 10 households comes under the range of 300-400 litres in Gulbarga, 25 households in the range of 400-500 litres, and 15 households have expressed their difference of 500-600 litres between demand and supply. Where as the remaining households (100) have expressed their satisfaction with existing quantity of actual water supply, while such difference for the year 2001-02 is 15 households in the range of 300- 400 litres, 30 households fall in the range of 400-500 litres, 35 households 500-600 litres.

Whereas in Solapur, such difference[7] during 1997-98 is 18 households in the range of 500-600 litres, and 22 households in the range group of 600 litres and above, and such difference for the year 2001-02, 11 households comes under 500-600 litres, 19 households in the range of 600 and above litres. The 120 households in Solapur have expressed satisfaction over the quantity of water actually supplied.

Therefore, it is evident from the Table 7.6 that both in Gulbarga and Solapur cities the demand for water among the larger households is increasing as against its supply[8]. Further, it is also evident that the difference in the range of water demanded by number of households has also increased. Therefore, it may be concluded that there is substantial difference between demand and supply for number of households and the difference is increasing over a period of time. Accordingly the hypothesis that" The gap between demand and supply of water in Gulbarga and Solapur cities has been widening". This hypothesis is proved positively by the positive views of the households of our survey.

The Table 7.7 gives the information about per capita demand and supply[9] of sample households of the study areas. For example, during 1997-98, per capita demand of Gulbarga city is 115 litres and actual supply is 81 litres, and the difference is 34 litres and in 2001- 02, per capita demand is 135 litres and supply is 72 litres, the difference is 63 litres. The difference between per capita demand and per capita supply has been widening in Gulbarga city for the sample period.

Where as in Solapur, per capita demand is 125 litres and supply is 120 litres for the year 1997-98, and the difference is 5 litres, while during 2001-02, such difference is 12 litres i.e., per capita demand is 140 litres and per capita supply is 128 litres per day.

Table-7.7
Difference between Per Capita Demand and Supply

(LPCD)

City	1997- 98			2001-02		
	Per capita demand	Per capita supply	Difference	Per capita demand	Per capita supply	Difference
Gulbarga	115	81	34	135	71.3	63.7
Solapur	125	120	5	140	128	12

Source: Field Survey.

Thus, the analysis of the survey findings relating to per capita demand per capita supply data also supports the view that the gap between demand and supply is widening, which in terms may be consider as additional proof of the hypothesis noted above.

The tap connections to the households may be considered as more systematic method of water supply. The tap connection helps to the households in various ways such as saving time, controlling wastage and economic use for different purposes other than drinking. But for this, the tap connection expenditure is very important in influencing the decision of the households, whether to go or not to go for tap connection. The existing tap connection expenditure for households in Gulbarga and Solapur has been noted in Table 7.8. For example, 23.3 per cent of households expenditure is Rs 1000 -2000, 13.3 per cent of households expenditure is Rs.2000-3000, 43.3 per cent households expenditure is Rs. 3000-4000, and 20.0 per cent households expenditure is Rs. 4000 and above.

Whereas in Solapur, for example, 33.3 per cent of households spend Rs. 1000-2000 for tap connection, 23.3 per cent of households spend Rs. 2000-3000, 13.3 per cent households expenditure is Rs. 3000-4000, and 30 per cent households spend Rs. 4000 & above for tap connection.

Thus, it may be observed that due to poor system of water supply in Gulbarga there is more expenditure on tap connection as faced by 43 per cent households as (Rs 3000-4000) against expenditure incurred by only 33 per cent households in Solapur (Rs. 1000-2000). Bureaucratic methods in giving tap connections are no less serious considerations.

Table-7.8
Expenditure on Tap connection

Expenditure (Rs.)	*Gulbarga*		*Solapur*	
	No. of Households	*Percentage*	*No. of Households*	*Percentage*
1000-2000	35	23.3	50	33.3
2000-3000	20	13.3	35	23.3
3000-4000	65	43.3	29	13.3
4000 & above	30	20.1	45	30.0
Total	150	100.0	150	100.0

Source: Field Survey.

There is yet another point for evaluation of the system of water supply based on households view. It was found during the field survey that the pressure and volume of water is available more to those households which are very close to the service reservoirs. This is nothing but the problems of tail enders. If the

Table-7.9
Distance between Service Reservoir and House Connections

Distance (In Km.)	*Gulbarga*		*Solapur*	
	No. of Households	*Percentage*	*No. of Households*	*Percentage*
Less than 1	5	3.3	15	10.0
1-2 km	15	10.0	30	20.0
2-3 km	25	15.5	40	26.6
3-4 km	50	33.3	65	43.3
4 and above	55	36.6	5	3.3
Total	150	100.0	150	100.0

Source: Field Survey.

underground pipelining is poor then it is worst for the tail enders located far from service reservoirs. Besides, smaller the number of reservoirs more distance that it needs for getting house connection, the problems of households with distance from service reservoirs may be noted from the following Table 7.9. For example, Gulbarga has highest 37 per cent of households in the distance range of 4 km and above as against 43.3 per cent sample households found in the distance range of 3-4 km in Solapur.

The important cognitive point is that there are 16 service reservoirs in Gulbarga as against 23 in Solapur. Hence, to improve the system there is need for constructing more service reservoirs.

As could be seen from the Table 7.10 that there are 80 households out of 150 sample in Gulbarga and 30 out of 150 sample households in Solapur which are willing to pay more for more quantity of water. The willingness to pay, the range of amount per annum by number of households is given in the Table 7.10. For example in Gulbarga, maximum number of households i.e. 44 per cent of sample households are willing to pay more amount in the range of Rs. 1500-2000 as against 67 per cent of sample households in the range group Rs. 500-1000 in Solapur.

Table-7.10
Annual Willingness to Pay for More Amount

Willingness to pay (Rs.)	*Gulbarga*		*Solapur*	
	No. of Households	*Percentage*	*No. of Households*	*Percentage*
500-1000	10	12.5	20	67.0
1000-1500	15	18.7	8	27.0
1500-2000	35	43.7	2	6.0
2000 & above	20	25.1	-	-
Total	80	100.0	35	100.0

Source: Field Survey.

Therefore, one may accept the hypothesis that there is high income elasticity of demand for water, the range of willingness to pay[10] is over and above the tax that the households pay.

Table-7.11(a)

Water Borne Diseases in Gulbarga City

Particulars	*Years (1995-96 to 2000-01)*					
	95-96	*96-97*	*97-98*	*98-99*	*99-2000*	*00-01*
Cholera						
Cases	17	25	20	15	05	55
Deaths	01	-	02	02	-	01
Typhoid						
Cases	90	85	105	250	302	455
Deaths	03	01	03	09	06	05
Gastroenteritis						
Cases	800	755	889	895	785	662
Deaths	18	20	25	12	08	18
Jaundice						
Cases	65	70	72	75	80	70
Deaths	15	13	18	13	09	08
Dysentery						
Cases	140	125	140	15	65	60
Deaths	03	04	02	01	03	02
Diarrhea						
Cases	09	12	15	13	15	08
Deaths	-	-	-	1	2	-

Source: Compiled from Gulbarga Municipal Corporation Records.

Apart from the quantity of water, its demand and supply and other connected issues, the quality of water is also very important point for critical evaluation. It is a well recognized fact that the quality of water gets affected by various factors, the quality therefore has implications for health and hygiene of the people. The water borne diseases seriously affect the health even leading to deaths. There are number of findings in the households survey relating to a) breakages and leakages in drainage pipes, b) pipeline system of water supply and drainage, c) methods of water treatment/ purification, d) special water treatment adopted, e) problems of health, f) family members affected by drinking water, g) types of water borne diseases affected by households, h) amount of expenditure for treatment of water borne diseases.

As an end result of the number of points noted in the survey findings, the important water borne diseases in Gulbarga and Solapur cities have been noted in Table-7.11 (a) & (b).

It may be observed from Table 7.11(a) & (b) that, there are maximum 800 gastroenteritis cases recorded and 18 deaths has been reported in Gulbarga, 140 dysentery cases and 3 deaths due to dysentery has been reported, 90 typhoid cases reported and 3 deaths due to typhoid during 1995-96. While in 2000-01, there are 55 cholera cases and only one death has been reported, there are as many as 255 persons suffering from typhoid and 5 people have ended the life due to typhoid, there are 662 gastroenteritis cases have been reported and 18 deaths due to gastroenteritis disease, there are 70 jaundice cases and 18 deaths due to jaundice, 60 dysentery cases and 2 deaths have been reported in 2000-2001. Gastroenteritis diseases are common in Gulbarga during rainy season and number of water borne diseases reported in rainy season.

Whereas in Solapur, there are also water borne diseases such as, chloera, typhoid, gastroenteritis, jaundice, dysentery and diarrhea cases have been reported during 1995-96. For example, 15 cholera cases, 85 typhoid cases and 1 death, 745 gastro cases and 15 deaths, 60 jaundice cases and 20 deaths due to jaundice, 150 dysentery cases and 2 deaths and 6 diarrhea cases have been reported in Solapur in 1995-96. While in 2000-2001, 44 cholera cases, 210 and 1 typhoid cases and death, 746 and 10 gastro cases and deaths, 57 & 5 jaundice cases and death, 41 and 6 dysentery and diarrhea cases are reported.

For example, during 1994-95, water borne diseases like cholera, gastro enteritis, jaundice, typhoid, dysentery and diarrhea cases are recorded in Gulbarga 13,1184,88, 239, 6 and 8 respectively and only one death is recorded due to jaundice for the same year, and in 1997-98, 2, 1044, 61,195,4 and 2 cases such as cholera, gastro enteritis, jaundice, typhoid, dysentery and diarrhea recorded in Solapur, and there is no deaths due to any water borne diseases during 1997, and during 2000-01, there are 20 cholera cases recorded and one death, 665 gastro enteritis cases, 71 jaundice cases, 221 typhoid cases, recorded in Solapur, there are no cases recorded such as dysentery, diarrhea.

There have been only 6 persons suffering from diarrhea. While in 2000, there are 44 cholera, 210 typhoid cases, 746 gastro cases, dysentery 41, 6 diarrhea cases have been recorded. Further, the disease causalities are typhoid 1, gastro 10 and jaundice 5.

There are more number of water borne diseases recorded in Gulbarga than Solapur, because the water supply network in Gulbarga is absolutely poor and bad. The parallel water supply and sewerage pipes, cris-cross of the two and breakages and leakages are so important in age old city of Gulbarga. Cholera and gastro diseases affected in rainy season. There are more gastro and typhoid cases recorded in Gulbarga and Solapur respectively. The water supply authorities have greatly neglected the health and hygienic aspects of drinking water in Gulbarga whereas in Solapur city, large number of diseases and cases have been reported. It is evident from the table that the very record is a complement to the hypothesis that along with more quantity and better network, the water supply authorities have neglected the health and hygiene considerations of the people. Therefore, we may thus conclude that the hypothesis" The considerations of health and hygiene in water supply in the study areas have been greatly neglected" , is testified from the facts and conditions prevailing in the study areas.

There is also additional evidence for the proof of the hypothesis. For example the incidence of diseases, that means

Table-7.11(b)
Water Borne Diseases in Solapur City

Particulars	*Years (1995-96 to 2000-01)*					
	1995-96	*1996-97*	*1997-98*	*1998-99*	*1999-2000*	*2000-01*
Cholera						
Cases	15	23	-	10	-	44
Deaths	-	01	-	01	-	-
Typhoid						
Cases	85	122	117	239	265	210
Deaths	01	-	01	02	03	01
Gastroenteritis						
Cases	745	646	437	861	452	746
Deaths	15	12	07	09	06	10
Jaundice						
Cases	60	88	66	67	53	57
Deaths	20	17	04	02	05	05
Dysentery						
Cases	150	136	44	08	50	41
Deaths	02	01	-	-	-	-
Diarrhea						
Cases	06	-	04	08	02	06
Deaths	-	-	-	-	-	-

Source: Compiled from Solapur Municipal Corporation Records.

occurrence of disease per 10000 population is an important indicator. If we see Table.7.11(c) & (d), it is clear that there are more water borne diseases (all types) per 10000 population in Gulbarga than Solapur, but the difference is not very substantial, (except the only disease gastroenteritis).

While in Gulbarga during 1997-98, there are 889 gastro enteritis cases recorded, 1998 769 gastro enteritis cases, 1 jaundice case, and 3 cholera cases recorded. In 1999, 565 only gastro enteritis cases, recorded in Gulbarga city, and during 2000-01 662 and 1 gastro enteritis and cholera cases recorded.

More than that of the facts noted from the table above there are some points worth recording. For example, with regard to water borne diseases the municipal corporation of Gulbarga has not put on record the cases systematically, no record keeping undertaken of the people affected by various diseases. Only those which are serious and registered in Government Hospital has given as information to us. Further, the city gets water from three different sources. Therefore less number of diseases may be anticipated.

Table-7.11(c)
Incidence of Water Borne Diseases per 10000 population in Gulbarga

Particulars	*Years (1995-96 to 2000-01)*					
	95-96	*96-97*	*97-98*	*98-99*	*99-00*	*00-01*
Cholera	0.3	0.6	0.5	0.3	0.1	1.3
Typhoid	2.1	3.6	2.4	5.8	7.0	5.9
Gastroenteritis	18.6	17.6	20.6	20.8	18.3	15.4
Jaundice	1.5	1.6	1.7	1.7	1.6	1.6
Dysentery	3.2	2.9	3.3	0.3	1.4	1.3
Diarrhea	0.2	0.3	0.3	0.3	0.3	0.2

Source: Adjusted from Table-7.11(a).

The water of Bhima river has been recently added to the network of water supply in Gulbarga. The Gulbarga city also has more number of bore wells. Accordingly one may anticipate some what better quality of water and less prone to diseases noted in the table above. The awareness of people and their less inclination for reporting is another point for reportedly less number of people affected in Gulbarga (see Table.7.11a).

Not with standing the small number of cases and no deaths, the water supply network in Gulbarga is absolutely poor and bad. The parallel water supply and sewerage pipes cris-cross of the two, breakages and leakages are so important in age old city of Gulbarga, the water supply authorities have greatly neglected the health and hygienic aspects of drinking water.

Table-7.11(d)

Incidence of Water Borne Diseases per 10000 population in Solapur

Particulars	*Years (1995-96 to 2000-01)*					
	95-96	*96-97*	*97-98*	*98-99*	*99-00*	*00-01*
Cholera	0.1	0.2	-	0.1	-	0.4
Typhoid	0.8	1.2	1.2	2.4	2.7	2.1
Gastroentertis	7.6	6.6	4.4	8.8	4.6	7.6
Jaundice	0.6	0.9	0.6	0.6	0.5	0.5
Dysentery	1.5	1.3	0.4	0.1	0.5	0.4
Diarrhea	-	-	-	-	-	-

Source: Adjusted from Table-7.11(b).

In the Solapur city large number of diseases and cases have been reported. It is evident from Table 7.11(b) that the very record is a complement to the hypothesis that along with more quantity and better network, the water supply authorities have neglected the health and hygiene considerations of the people.

Therefore, we may thus conclude that the hypothesis that" The considerations of health and hygiene in water supply in the study area have been greatly neglected", is testified from the facts and conditions prevailing in the study areas.

SECTION-III
THE SCOPE FOR REMODELING

The study of physical aspects of water supply is not independent of its financial aspects. The demand and supply, the physical network and quantity and quality of water supplied are (as noted above) no doubt important but their existence is dependent on the available financial resources and their utilisation. The critical evaluation will be incomplete without an examination of the financial aspects. The financial aspects also lend support to the idea or reject the scope for remodelling. The financial aspects and scope for remodeling have been discussed in the following.

An examination of the basic elements of financial position[11] in water supply activities such as, unaccounted water, average water rate, maintenance and repair expenditure, power charges, staff salary, total collection charges would provide an indirect idea relating to the scope for remodelling. The relative position of Gulbarga and Solapur Municipal Corporations with respect to various sub activities and their financial aspects has been given in Table 7.12.

Table-7.12
Operational Expenses - 2000-01

Item	*Gulbarga*	*Solapur*	*Difference*
Unaccounted water (%)	20.0	10.0	10.0
Average water rate (per1000 ltrs) (Rs)	2.79	5.25	2.46
Maintenance & repairs (Rs. in lakh)	55	135.45	80.45
Salaries & over heads (Rs. In lakh)	85	254.10	169.1
Power charges (Rs. in Lakh)	75	1026.90	951.90

Source: Gulbarga and Solapur Municipal Corporations Records

It may be understood from the Table 7.12 that there is 20 per cent unaccounted water in Gulbarga, average water rate per kilo litre is Rs. 2.79 maintenance and repairs expenditure is Rs. 55.0 lakh, salaries and overheads of the water supply staff is Rs. 85 lakh and power charges is Rs. 75.00 lakh. Whereas in Solapur, unaccounted water is 10%, average water rate per kilo litre is Rs. 5.25, maintenance and repairs expenditure is Rs.135.4 lakh, salaries and overheads expenditure is Rs. 254.10 lakh, and power charges Rs. 1026.90 lakh.

It is to be understood from the examination of the operational expenses, differences between Gulbarga and Solapur cities that not only Solapur provides water to more households but also more water to the city dwellers. Consequently, it has higher magnitudes of expenditures but also more revenue collections on water supply account.

Besides the financial evolution of sub systems, the unaccountability in water resources management and efficient management policies[13] for urban water supply systems are at the heart of the matter. In the absence of detailed financial statistics, the statistics of corporations with regard to total accounts and accounts on water supply provide an insight sufficient for evaluating the scope for remodeling. The current financial performance of Gulbarga and Solapur on water supply accounts has been given in Table 7.13.

Table-7.13
Percentage Differences of Water Supply Accounts Receipts and Payments to Total Corporations Receipts and Payments in Gulbarga and Solapur Cities.

Year	*Receipts*			*Payments*		
	Gulbarga	*Solapur*	*Percentage*	*Gulbarga*	*Solapur*	*Percentage*
1991-92	8.8	21.5	12.7	16.4	22.2	5.8
1992-93	12.4	19.7	7.3	27.4	24.9	2.5
1993-94	14.5	20.8	6.3	34.5	24.9	9.6
1994-95	17.2	19.2	2.0	35.8	24.1	11.7
1995-96	11.7	15.0	3.3	18.3	17.3	1.0
1996-97	12.4	18.3	5.9	22.7	16.2	6.5
1997-98	14.6	17.7	3.1	17.7	23.3	5.6
1998-99	11.4	17.6	6.2	19.0	23.5	4.5
1999-00	6.8	19.1	12.3	19.1	24.5	5.4
2000-01	7.9	17.6	9.7	14.1	22.1	8.0

Source: Compiled from Gulbarga and Solapur Municipal Corporations Records.

As our attention is placed on water supply the water supply account as a per cent to the total accounts of the corporations provides an insight into the magnitude of the problem of water supply[14]. In this respect, it could be seen from Table 7.13 that for example, the receipts of water supply accounts in Gulbarga 8.8 per cent to the total receipts of corporation in 1991-92, 12.4 per cent in 1992-93, 17.2 per cent in 1994-95 and declined to 7.9 per cent in 2000-01. While the payments of water supply accounts to total corporation was 16.4 per cent in 1991-92, 35.8 per cent in 1994-95 and in 2000, it is 14.1 per cent to total corporation.

Whereas in Solapur, the receipts of the water supply account to total corporation account form 21.5 per cent in 1991-92, 20.8 per cent in 1993-94 and it is declined to 17.5 per cent in 2000. The payments of water supply accounts to total corporation during 1991-92 was 22.2 per cent, 24.9 per cent in 1993 and it declined to 22.1 per cent in 2000-01.

The examination of water supply accounts of Gulbarga and Solapur corporations indicate that payments are more than the receipts. Besides payments form a higher per cent of total corporations account of the cities. Therefore, it is hard to think of the capability of corporations to take up any new project or programme for water supply. Added to this, if the rules of the game are taken into account, under the existing circumstances the corporations can never imagine to go in for new water supply schemes. Because, there is the statutory requirement that 10 per cent contribution to new schemes should be arranged by corporations and they will get 66.67 per cent of the new project cost in the form of loan which bears interest charges. The two conditions along with existing poor maintenance account, the corporations cannot think of incurring capital expenditures. Thus, the data supplements the hypothesis that" The financial performance of water supply accounts of the municipal corporations does not favour the expenditure of urban water supply in both the cities" .

The expansion of city corporation limits have forced the authorities to cover more and more households in their programmes of water supply. The existing systems are hard to dispense with. Further, they have obvious limitation of small capacity. Therefore, remodeling is considered as an essential aspect of water supply. It is difficult sometimes to redesign for the purpose of capacity expansion. The redesign also require very huge amount of resources. Therefore, the remodeling programmes of Gulbarga and Solapur city corporations have been noted in following.

Remodeling of Water Supply Distribution System in Gulbarga

For upgrading water distribution system of Gulbarga city including extension areas Gulbarga Municipal Corporation prepared" Remodeling of Water Supply Distribution System" in 2000-01, costing Rs. 57.98 crore from KUWS & DB Gulbarga.

Remodeling includes;

a) Construction of 11 service reservoirs, b) construction of 0.5 lakh gallons for booster stations, c) construction of booster pumping station, d) construction of 50 pumping masonry, e) construction of 10 lakh gallons capacity mother tank, f) providing and laying feeder main from old filter bed to Alandnaka, g) providing and laying feeder main from HSR to GLSR at Roza, i) providing and laying feeder mains in Gulbarga city, j) providing and laying distribution lines in various zones of city, k) providing water supply arrangements to extension areas, l) providing and erection of fire hydrants (LS), m) provision towards fencing and compound wall to the reservoir and pumping stations (LS) etc.

Funding pattern for remodeling

HUDCO Loan 80%	-	Rs. 46,38,29,000.00
Govt. Grant 10%	-	Rs. 5,79,79,000.00
Local Body Share 10%	-	Rs. 5,79,79,000.00
Total	-	**Rs. 57,97,87,000.00**

After completing remodeling of Gulbarga city water supply distribution system, the city get 120 lakh gallons of water, and 5.0 lakh population get 24 GPCD of water as against 35 GPCD, this is better than present existing level of water supply (15.7 GPCD)

Remodeling of Transmission and Distribution System in Solapur

For upgrading water distribution system of Solapur city including extended areas, Solapur Municipal Corporation prepared"

Remodeling of Transmission and Distribution system" in 2000, costing Rs. 125.28 crore from MJP. This scheme will be constructed in two phases. First phase costs Rs. 47.64 crore and second phase costs Rs.77.64 crore. For implementing this scheme Solapur Municipal Corporation requires loan as below.

For First Phase	-	Rs. 36.52 crore
For Second Phase	-	Rs. 56.92 crore

The Remodeling scheme consist a) construction of sump, b) pump house, c) master balancing reservoir at H.S.R, d) 30 new E.S.R's in city, 13 E.S.R. will be constructed in extended area and transmission, distribution system upgrading. After completion this scheme pumping station at a) Sadhu Vasvani b) Nehru Nagar E.S.R, c) High Level Area, d) Bidi Gharkul E.S.R. etc will be deleted. Only pumping H.S.R & Bhavani Peth Water Works will continue. For implementing the above scheme Solapur Municipal Corporation requires immediately Rs. 15.00 crore loan in 2000-01.

The abstracts of remodeling given by authorities point out clearly that the Solapur corporation has better remodeling programme than Gulbarga, because not only higher amount has been fixed but also the remodeling is device to complete in a phase-wise manner.

SECTION-IV
ADOPTION OF NEW TECHNIQUES & TECHNOLOGY

There has been growing demand for water in urban areas. Added to this, there are physical and financial constraints for increasing water supply. With respect to this public policy of urban water supply, the household welfare maximisation could be possible if the scarce water is used efficiently and optimally. Therefore, in addition to the use of existing water, the application of new technology and new techniques of water supply, use and re use have become the basic ingredients of the economics of urban water supply. A critical evaluation would be complete then and then only after the examination of new technology and techniques and their adoption in our study areas. The present section attempts to discuss the issues relating to new techniques and technology and their adoption in Gulbarga and Solapur cities. The important aspects discussed here are a) the need, b) waste water c) reuse and recycling, d) a blue print of new master plan for water supply (including essential restraints), e) change in financial approach. Besides the discussion of these aspects, the supportive normative data and test of hypothesis relevant to new techniques and technology in our study has been undertaken.

The Need

The need for adoption of new techniques and technology of water supply arises from the following considerations. For example, there are three sources of water supply in Gulbarga and Solapur cities. These provide regular water supply to the cities but Bhima river is the common source for both cities and Ujjani dam is constructed across Bhima river at Ujjani place. Whereas the same Bhima water in the down stream acts as a source of water supply of Gulbarga city (from Jewargi) when there are poor days of rain fall it is hard to expect water supply even for drinking purpose to the people of Gulbarga. The people of Gulbarga not only have to get irregular supply, the quantity supplied is also very limited as against growing demand. The mercipitation from Karnataka Government to Maharashtra Government do not yield satisfactory results even to get drinking water to the people. Therefore, there is urgent need for adopting new techniques and technology in Gulbarga city than Solapur. The techniques of waste water treatment, recycling or the older approaches which help for reducing burden on drinking water, while the new technology of natural water harvesting would ensure additional source of drinking water supply. Therefore, these have to be taken up specially in the context of Gulbarga city.

Waste Water Treatment

The waste water treatment[15] and use of treated water is of less significance to Solapur city. Because, the Ujjani Dam not only acts as a source of irrigation but also part of the water goes to Solapur for drinking water purpose. Whereas in Gulbarga city, there is an urgent need for application of waste water treatment with varying expenditure requirements, namely, Activated Sludge Treatment Plant (ASTP), Oxidation Ponds (O.P), Aerated Lagoons (AL), Upward Anaerobic Sludge Blanket (UASB).

Among the four techniques of waste water treatment the oxidation ponds system has greater relevance to Gulbarga city. This method ensures the treatment of 80 per cent of daily drinking water system. The details of the technique may be understood with the help of following Table 7.14.

Table-7.14
Costs of Domestic Wastewater Treatment

Technology	*Land Requirement*	*Capital Cost*
Activated Sludge Treatment Plant (ASTP)	0.5 acres / mld	Rs. 25-30 lakh / mld
Oxidation Ponds	2.5 acres / mld	Rs. 7.5 lakh / mld
Aerated Lagons	1.5 acres / mld	Rs. 15 lakh / mld
Upward Anaerobic Sludge Blanked (UASB)	0.5 acrs / mld	Rs. 16 lakh / mld with post-treatment.

Source: Kirit S.Parikh, Jyoti Parikh, and Tata L. Raghu Ram, Air and Water Quality Management, India Development Report 1999,p.91.

Note: Capital cost is exclusive of land costs

Thus, it is evident from the table that for adopting wastewater treatment technology the land is (which is very scarce) the only major component of the cost in particular. But there is plenty of land fallen vacant in and around Gulbarga City Municipal Corporation. Therefore, it is obvious to think that, if the waste water treatment technology[16] is adopted for Gulbarga city, a minimum of 15-20 lakh gallons can be given treatment and supply to the city dwellers. This is an essential and inevitable water supply method applicable to Gulbarga city. In particular, the oxidation ponds technique can be put into place. As per Table 7.14, with oxidation ponds techniques, the land requirement is 1.5 acres/ mld and the capital investment needed is Rs. 7.5 lakh per mld.

The reuse and recycling of urban water are indispensable part of urban water in Gulbarga and Solapur cities as there is scarcity[17] and drought conditions from time to time as experienced by the cities could help in the economic use of urban water. The reuse may be considered for less domestic but more non-domestic purpose. The quantity of reuse and cycling of water in Gulbarga and Solapur cities-the scope could be understood from the following Table 7.15.

Table-7.15
Reuse and Recycling of Wastewater

Method	*Gulbarga*	*Solapur*
Daily water supply	67.5 lakh gallons	275.0 lakh gallons
Re-use	7 lakh gallons	20 lakh gallons
Recycling	20 lakh gallons	54 lakh gallons

Source: City Municipal Corporations, 2000-01.

It is worthwhile to note that the cost of reuse and recycling and its benefits require further detailed study. However, apparently one could think that the recycling of waste water will help to irrigate hundreds of hectares of land around Gulbarga and Solapur cities. It is unfortunately to note that the figures have been furnished by authorities but there is no plan in existence or have any future plan for reuse and recycling of water in both the cities.

Rain Water Harvesting

The rainwater harvesting is of utmost urgent and important more for Gulbarga city than Solapur. Because, the Bhima river and Ujjani dam being closure to Solapur city naturally collect the rainwater through the river lets. Besides the topography of city provides less opportunity for rainwater harvesting scheme.

As against this it is to be noted that, Gulbarga on an average receives 624 mm rainfall during 45-55 days in an year. Furthermore, there are untimely sporadic and heavy rainfall during the summer season specially in Gulbarga. Therefore, there is scope for rainwater harvesting at a micro level and macro level.

A Micro View of Rain Water Harvesting

The micro level scheme and the macro level schemes have been discussed in the following for Gulbarga city.

A prototype micro level water harvesting technique to be adopted by households in Gulbarga city has been recapitulated[18] as follows.

RAIN WATER COLLECTION AND STORAGE

NOT JUST A STRUCTURAL ENGINEERING PROBLEM ! MANY OTHER DETAILS NEED ATTENTION.

- ADEQUATE ROOF SUFACE AND AREA
- ADEQUATE CAPACITY BASED ON HYDROLOGICAL DATA
- BYPASS ARRANGEMENT FOR INITIAL RUN-OFF
- COVER ON STORAGE TANK (AEDES MOSQUITO)
- DRAINAGE AROUND TANK (CULEX MOSQUITO)
- NO BITUMINOUS PAINTS INSIDE
- CLEANING AND EMPTYING ARRANGEMENT

EDUCATION OF THE USERS

It is an adopted figure and is self explanatory.

Source: Adopted from WHO," Low Cost Water Supply and Sanitation Technology : Pollution and Health Problems" , Searo Regional Health Papers No.4, New Delhi, 1984, p.11.

Table-7.16
Pollution and Health Problems Related to the Use of Simple, Appropriate and Low-Cost Technologies for Water Harvesting for Households

System Component	*Likely nature of pollution or health problem*	*Precautions / Remedial measures*
Rainwater collection from roofs and ground surfaces followed by storage in tanks or reservoirs	Wash-down of dirt, bird dropings, etc., from roof and ground surfaces Contamination of stored water	Provide bypass arrangements for the initial run-off of the season. Educate householders Provide cover on storage tank. Provide taps for tanks above ground and hand pumps for underground tanks. Provide cleaning / emptying arrangements. Avoid the use of bituminous paints on the inside surface of tanks. Teach people not to dip buckets or hands in stored water, and not to use unclean utensils at home. Provide slow-sand filters
	Mosquito nuisance Use of other water sources of unsafe quality to supplement meager rainwater supplies	Provide drainage around tank and netting on any overflow pipe (Aedes mosquito is known to breed even in covered tanks) Based on hydrological data, provide adequate capacity of rainwater collection system. Educate Householders

Source: Reproduced from WHO (1984)" Low Cost Water Supply and Sanitation Technology: Pollution and Health Problems, New Delhi, 1984. pp.31-32.

The rain water (roof) harvesting techniques are slowly underway in India. For instance, these technologies have been effectively implemented in Manipur (Holly area) and Kerala. It may be remembered that on a conservative estimate (if not the quantity of water), the roof water harvesting will help the households to have daily quantity of water lasting for minimum of 25-30 days.

Macrolevel Rain Water Harvesting

A macro level rain water harvesting is desirable and feasible for Gulbarga city on the considerations of rainfall, water scarcity and its topography. If there is a rainfall 624 mm, it is the experience of Gulbarga city that it receives 4 - 6 centimeter of rain fall on some days during the summer and rainy season. There is marginally sloppy vast land in Gulbarga. Indeed the ring road

Table-7.17

Two Rain Water Harvesting Schemes in Gulbarga City

Particulars	*Scheme-I Dharmapur*	*Scheme-II Biddapur*
Size of the pond	1 ½ km	1 km
Height of the pond	25 feet	20 feet
Catchment area	10 sq. km	6 sq. km.
Quantity of surface water	½ TMC**	¼ TMC
No. of service reservoirs required	2	1
Daily water supply	3.0 lakh gallons	0.50 lakh gallons
No. of days covered	35	20
Cost of harvesting and supply*	--	--
Treatment and purification pond	6 furlongs	2 furlongs
Height of treatment and purification pond.	30 feet	30

Note : *-This is the engineering aspect, hence not attempted here.

**-TMC-Thousand Million Cubic

Source: Compiled from Water Supply Authorities in Gulbarga and Solapur Cities.

constructed by Gulbarga Development Authority has a very big canal type system in many parts which runs into kms. Under these circumstances, the two area schemes for Gulbarga city are really a suitable device, the two schemes have been described in the following.

Thus, it may be observed that if rain water harvesting scheme is implemented in Gulbarga, given the existing size of the city, the water demand can be met easily. Further in the year of scarce rainfall the surface water harvesting through the ponds will help to provides 3 lakh gls[19] of water per day may be supplied to the Gulbarga city dwellers. Thus, it abundantly clear that the rain water harvesting programme should be firmly nailed to the corporation authorities. It is supportive of the fact that getting water from Bhima has cost more than Rs. 100 crore to the Gulbarga Municipal Corporation. The rain water harvesting programme will not be this much costly affair.

The Bore wells

The bore wells are though limited but alternative means of urban water supply. The cost and need for bore wells have outlived in Solapur city. Therefore, there are only 2300 bore wells in the whole Solapur city against this even with low table water many households in Gulbarga city have gone for drilling bore wells, this is very much true of hundreds of households being beyond the reach of corporation water system.

Undoubtedly the bore wells are independent but costly source of water supply, the rich can only afford it. The yield from many bore wells in Gulbarga city very low[20], because the city being constructed on a big rock. The bore wells have bleak chances of success in providing water to the households[21]. If rain water harvesting programme is implemented at several points in the city, the table water would likely to go up and can help to yield more water from bore well. The field survey indicated that many households have suggested that the corporation should take up a programme which will help to increase underground water table.

Changing the Financial Structure

There is an urgent need for bringing about changes in the financing system for water supply in Gulbarga and Solapur. The corporations cannot afford to make any surplus on their revenue account. Hence 10 per cent contributing for new water supply schemes by the corporations goes very handy. The loans are other source with full of difficulties such as, small amount long interval in the release of installments and heavy interest charges loaded on the finances of corporations. The grants and the magnitude of grants are reduced year after year for corporation. Therefore, the State Government should consider urban water supply as an important infrastructure and provide budgetary support (meeting entire cost at least once) to the corporations[22].

SECTION- V
SUGGESTIONS

After an indepth study of" The Economics of Urban Water Supply in Karnataka and Maharashtra: A comparative study of Gulbarga and Solapur cities", there are a number of suggestions which may be put in place. But it is essential to remember that our study has been very exhaustive in beginning with a chapter on Urban Water Supply System in India, followed by a separate treatment of urban water supply systems in Karnataka and Maharashtra and tailored by a chapter on macro analysis of water supply system in Gulbarga and Solapur cities. Accordingly, the important suggestions have been grouped into three broad heads such as general suggestions, area specific suggestions and suggestions relating to micro aspects of the economics of urban water supply in the context of households.

General

The following suggestions are considered as general in the sense that they are a complement to the present study and have emerged from a more broad based approach. These are;

- India spends only 1.3 per cent of GDP on water supply while America spends 4.6% of GDP. Therefore, more per cent of GDP has to be spent on water supply in India. Further, it may be noted that Rakesh Mohan committee suggested investment of Rs. 28,000 crore in which the country-India spent only Rs. 2000 crore, which is grossly inadequate.

- More plan funds for urban water supply by the government is necessary and water supply should be treated as a part of Indian urban infrastructure and Rs 20750 crore needed for 100% coverage of urban population for safe drinking water.
- In order to sustain the urban water supply, ground water resources should be judiciously used. Over exploitation of ground water should be avoided. Water conservation awareness programme is essential. The government should prepare a comprehensive program in this context. The programs of Gujarat and Rajasthan are worth emulating here.
- Community bore wells control and regulation of ground water in the municipal areas-laws are necessary. This is an unexplored area which cause great damage to the table water and its proper use.
- Provision of soft loan for drinking water purposes and also provision of market loan is to be strengthened to corporations authorities .
- Revision of tariff rates and fixing high rates should be done on the basis of economic considerations rather than political compulsion.
- Privatisation of water supply and sanitation sector to improve efficiency, effectiveness, reliability and sustainability. Govt. should take the role of macro distribution (i.e., wholesaling) rather than individual system. Within-colony distribution can be handed over to either consumer forums, societies, etc.
- Diarrhea and child death will have to be controlled. This is possible only if potable drinking water supply for urban areas is seriously undertaken.

Area Specific

There are number of policy suggestions which will help to improve the economics of urban water supply in Karnataka and Maharashtra. A comparative study of Gulbarga and Solapur cities. However,, it may be noted at the outset that Maharashtra is a rich state and has a better approach for urban water supply. Similarly, it is no doubt that the system of water supply in Solapur is far more better than that of Gulbarga. The suggestions noted here are area specific but more directed towards the supply system in Gulbarga. Some suggestions are also towards Solapur City Corporation as well.

- Water Supply in Gulbarga has to be increased by 128.8 LPCD to meet 200 LPCD for high income group which is almost satisfactory in Solapur and Gulbarga corporation it has to supply 135 LPCD for low income groups, which is less by 63.8 LPCD.
- Activities like domestic, industrial, commercial and public use, get only 67 per cent of the IS norm in Gulbarga is very low. Therefore, the corporation has to make efforts to come closure to the IS norm of water supply important activities. Unless this is done, Gulbarga remains an industrially backward city.
- There is need for reducing tap connection charges which are very high in Gulbarga compared to Solapur.
- Gulbarga Corporation has to construct more service reservoirs to store more water.
- Gulbarga Corporation has to reduce atleast 10 per cent of unaccounted water.
- Heavy rates should be fixed for water users. That means, water rate has to be increased atleast by Rs. 4 per 1000 litres. This will enable greatly the water supply account of Gulbarga Corporation.
- It is not possible to generate surplus in the operating expenses of water supply. Therefore, the state or central governments should not expect any contribution from corporations for taking new programmes.
- Besides they also need huge amount of one time loan without interest. This has to be provided by urban development ministry of Government of India.
- There is an urgent need for remodeling water supply system in Gulbarga. This would require additional funds to the corporations. This should also be provided by the state governments. Because there have been emerging of large number extension areas (which are known as colonies) in Gulbarga. There is mounting pressure for water supply in them and corporation cannot can not give deaf ear to this.

- There is urgent need for recycling waste water in Gulbarga city because the recycled water can be used for agriculture as well as industrial purpose.
- The rain water harvesting is indispensable for Gulbarga city. Micro level and macro level rain water harvesting schemes are very very essential activities to be undertaken by City Corporation and encourage the households in this regard.
- Similarly, there is need for improving the pipeline system of water supply. The unauthorised wholes / unauthorised connections and use of electrical machines are the common features to be found in morning hours in Gulbarga city. This is properly checked and controlled.
- There should be thorough check on the leakage of distribution lines. The leakages should be corrected immediately. If necessary more staff may be employed for watching and reducing the wastage of water in Gulbarga.

SUGGESTIONS RELATING TO HOUSEHOLDS

The following suggestions relating to household survey are considered as essential. Because the ultimate objective is the study of economics which aims at household welfare maximisation in the context of water supply.

1. The large number of higher age members would likely need more water than the members of younger age. Therefore, there is need for additional demand for water in Solapur and Gulbarga. Water is already scarce and it is likely to become more and more scares in coming future. Rational use of water is essential in both the cities.
2. There are more higher income households and therefore may put pressure for additional supply of water in both the cities.
3. Both cities are commercially, administratively and industrially growing cities with large per cent of high income households, due to bigger physical size of the house (40" x 60") and large number in the households would naturally require more quantity of water for drinking and other domestic purposes.
4. The watering of trees in the house and upkeep of gardens need additional quantity of water in Gulbarga and Solapur

respectively. It may be noted that these are essential specially during the summer when the temperature goes up to 41^{0}- 45^{0}C.

5. There is need for extending house connection system of water supply in Gulbarga. This would considerably help to conserve and reduce wastage of water use.
6. There is need for increasing the duration of water (1 to 1 ½ hrs) specially in Gulbarga, because the water supply size of tap is very small (1/2 inch only).
7. The community bore well concept has to be introduced in Gulbarga by the corporation (with regulation of ground water use).
8. Metering and billing of water supply is essential in Gulbarga city. The households should be made to pay water charges. The meters should be fixed for measuring quantity of water use by rich and big households.
9. Gulbarga Corporation has to create distance between water supply pipes and drainage pipes which is far better in Solapur city. Because large percentage of sample reported about breakages in drainage pipes affecting water supply system.
10. The Gulbarga Corporation should adopt underground pipeline system for better water purpose.
11. The road digging for various purposes often disturbed water supply system which is very common in Gulbarga. Therefore the authorities should take care of this problem to ensure smooth water supply.
12. It is essential for attending the complaints of households regularly in Gulbarga city.
13. The survey reveals that demand for more quantity of water to the households in both the cities. But the households in Gulbarga deserve serious attention as there is great difference between households demand and actual supply.
14. The public water supply pipes need timely repair to reduce water leakage in Gulbarga.
15. There is need for locking system and better tap fitting in both the litres regarding public stand posts.
16. More time spent by households in getting water from public stand posts on Gulbarga this has to be reduced and also

big tanks with more number of taps may be a worthwhile step. This is also not so expensive arrangement.

17. There is need for increasing water tax on households in Gulbarga city. Further our survey indicates that high income families are prepared to pay more for it additional quantity of water is supplied to them.
18. The repairs for house connection is poorly attended both in Gulbarga and Solapur. More money is charged in Gulbarga for these repairs. Therefore, authorities should fix proper cost of road digging and the digging should be undertaken by the corporation.
19. The Gulbarga corporation should control corrupt practice of repair personnel and house corporation section. The system should be mode more transparent.
20. Frequent water after filtration is needed in Gulbarga city. This will help to avoid more water borne diseases entering the city.
21. The health care awareness programme regarding water supply is to be undertaken by the Gulbarga Corporation. Because going to the depth of the water supply pipe drilling holes and getting unauthorised connection is very common in the city. The rain water often get mixed up with water supplied by the corporation. Water theft and unauthorized use should be regulated immediately, regulating misuse of public taps is also very essential.
22. Public awareness campaigns be started to conserve water i.e., to make economic use of water.
23. The micro level rain water harvesting culture to the households should be imparted in the city in line with the system in Kerala and Manipur.

SECTION - VI
LIMITATIONS AND SCOPE FOR FURTHER STUDY

LIMITATIONS

A vast study of comparing the economics of urban water supply is likely to have a number of macro level and micro level limitations. For convenience these are noted in the following.

1) It may be observed form our analysis that the treatment of urban water supply has dual problems. First is that should it be treated as a part of urban infrastructure?. If so, how that should be financed?. Similarly how the cost should be recovered?. What pricing should be adopted? all these are questions for which our study has no solution to offer.
2) If, in case it is considered as a public utility the municipal corporations face number of problems of finance and maintenance. The taxes and fees do not come easily. Therefore, the quantum of investment and long run rate of return on this public utility is not possible to work out. Hence, no attempt is made in this study either with regard to pricing or regarding the long run rate of return. Besides the corporation authorities do not provide sufficient data in this regard.
3) The municipal corporations of Gulbarga and Solapur have beset with the serious problem of city expansion. They are also attempting for the broad based foundation for industrilisation. Added to these, the central and state activities are expanding day by day. The establishment of airport construction of new railway roots and other public service demand more and more quantity of water. In the absence of exact nature of expansion it is not possible to make an exact calculation of demand and supply of urban water. The data provided by corporations is only a rough estimate. Accordingly no particular effort can be made in our study in meeting this challenge.
4) At the micro level too there are number of limitations; a) For example, the waste water at the household level is very difficult for estimation, b) The willingness of the households to pay for more water is really a difficult task for estimation, c) The existing pipelines are incapable of meeting the growing demand. As such how to cope with this problem is difficult for investigation because the new schemes call for a root and branch change in the approach. Therefore, this is treated as beyond the scope of the present study.
5) The estimation of the quantity of rain water, its collection, treatment and distribution is not only the new technique but

is highly technical. It needs not the complete economic but the engineering approach. Therefore, an engineering study of rain water harvesting is not attempted in the present study.

6) There are also financial constraints, political interferences an corruption in various aspects of urban water supply. These are not only difficult for identification but are more difficult for finding an acceptable solution.

SCOPE FOR FURTHER STUDY

There are a number of areas in the economics of urban water supply, which need a further detailed study. These are considered as beyond the scope of our approach are as follows;

Because of growing demand for drinking water (including extension areas) in Gulbarga and Solapur cities, the municipal corporation have been attempting to prepare a more comprehensive plan. For example in Gulbarga, an additional six barrages have been planned for construction at the already existing place i.e., Jewargi. Similarly, additional pipeline system from Ujjani to Solapur for water supply is contemplated by the corporation. These programmes i.e., project planning intend to adopt a though cost benefit analysis. This approach would help to increase water supply in Gulbarga and Solapur. Therefore, there is scope for further detailed study on Project planning in both the cities.

It has been found difficult to ensure proper distribution of water both in Gulbarga and Solapur cities, there are thefts and unauthorised connections. There is tax evasion and irregular payment of water tax. Therefore, similar to electricity (in Karnataka distribution has been handed over to private organisations) the government can assign distribution and tax collection function to the private sector which will help the corporations greatly. Further more the private sector investment, captive water supply plants (for industries) would help to increase water supply. The implications for public policy under these circumstances call for a further detailed study.

An exact estimation of the quantity of waste water, its storage, collection, treatment and distributions is, indeed a very frontier approach in the context of increasing the supply of water.

Therefore, a further detailed study specially with regard to waste water treatment is very essential more so in the context of Gulbarga city.

Similar to the above, the recycling and reuse of daily of water supply may be considered as additional responsibility for city corporation. The existing systems require remodeling for this purpose. A detailed project cost and benefits require a further detailed study. The recycling of water after reuse could be used for irrigational and non-domestic purposes. This scheme therefore, besides reducing demand for more water would help to increase agricultural production in the vicinity of Gulbarga and Solapur cities. Therefore, the amount of investment and benefit to urban dwellers (in the quantity of water) and increase in agricultural production is a fertile but essential part of the scope for further study.

The two city corporations are dependent on three sources of water supply. In which two sources depend largely on the rainfall and storage. These are Bhima and Bennithora in Gulbarga city, while Ekruk tank and Bhima river in Solapur. The other sources have natural constraints in increasing the storage and supply capacity. Therefore, there is an urgent need for adoption of rain water harvesting techniques more in Gulbarga and lesser extent in Solapur. The method of storage treatment estimate of quantity, nature of benefits all of them need further detailed study. The techniques and technology also provide a detailed engineering calculations. The scanty rainfall, untimely heavy rainfall is capable of providing huge quantity of surface water on the rainy days. The construction of tanks (for storage and treatment ponds), construction of reservoirs are the important aspects require an in-depth study. The two corporations cannot ignore the buffer stock of water to be used at the time when there are the days and years of scanty rainfall.

If Gulbarga and Solapur are consider as past growing corporations, besides industrial needs, the additional demand for water based on family income requires a serious rethinking, the cost of additional water supply to high income groups and industrial units and the resulting benefits also is an upcoming issue for further detailed study. The establishments of airports, new industrial units and high income families with (elastic demand for water) require a detailed study with an application of simulation models and detailed cost benefit analysis. This is beyond the scope of present study.

In addition to demand for household and industrial use the cultural demand for water (including parks, gardens and tree plantation) and its cost manner and method of supply also require a detailed study. The study is very urgent if considering the extreme hot weather reducing surface water, drying up ground water are considered in Gulbarga and Solapur. In addition to affecting temperature, the trees, plants, parks and gardens would help the city dwellers greatly. The construction of swimming pools may be treated as cultural demand for water. Similarly, establishment of public tanks during summer for drinking purpose by the floating people is other essential aspect of cultural demand for water. These aspects require a detailed study with environmental approach.

NOTES AND REFERENCES

1. The Finance Commission, Commission of Enquires generally adopt normative indicators for a comparison of various methods to obtain optimum decision. For discussion of the role of normative indications see, Amartya Sen, Social Choice Theory Area Examination, Econometrica 1978.
2. See, Santosh Kumar Garg," Water Supply Engineering", Khanna Publishers, Delhi, 1999.
3. 200 LPCD upper limit high income groups households is based on full housing system adopted in the toilets.
4. Bollard, J.J.," Water Requirements or Water Demands", Journal of American Waterworks Association, Vol.63, No.5, May 1971.
5. Raman. A.," Norms and Standards for Urban Water Supply and Sewerage Services Document", TCPO, Ministry of Works and Housing, New Delhi, November 1980.
6. Sewell W.R. and Bower B.T (Ed.)," Forecasting Demands for Water", Queen Printers, Ottawa, 1968.
7. Hanson R. and Hudson H.E.," Trends in Residential Water Uses" , Journal American Water Works Association, Vol.48, 1956, pp.1347-1358.
8. Turhosky Stephen," The Demand for Water-Some Empirical Evidence on Consumer Response to a Commodity Uncertain in Supply" , Water Resources Research, 5(2) 1969, p.350.

9. Andrews R.," Estimation of Household Consumption of Water", Water Resources Research, Centre of University of Hampshire, James Hall, Durhman, N.H.03824, U.S.A.
10. See Katzman Martin," Income and Price Elasticity of Demand for Water in Developing Countries", Water Resources Bulletin, 13:47-45, 1977.
11. Vyas Anjana and Anand P.B.," Some Important Financial Aspects Relating to Unaccounted Water, Maintenance and Repairs and Power of Urban Water Supply Systems: A Case of Ahmedabad", NAGARLOK, 1989.
12. Fourt, "The Impact of Policy Variables on Residential Water Demand and Related Investment Requirement", Water Resources Research, Vol. VII No. 4, pp.13-15, 1968.
13. David J. Allee," Efficient Management Policies for Urban Water Supply", Water Resources Research, Vol. VII, No. 4, pp.774, 1971.
14. Devi P. Rama," Accountability in Water Resources Management", Sing M. (Ed.) 1992.
15. Briggs R.," Monitoring and Control in Water and Wastewater Treatment: The Need" , Public Health Engineering 10(2) 1982.
16. Unvala, S.P.," Aspects of Water Treatment Technology Applied to Indian Public Water Supplies", Civic Affairs, September 1981.
17. Poster Saundra," Water: Rethinking Management in an Age of Scarcity" , World Watch Paper 62, September 1985.
18. Adopted from World Health Organisation," Low Cost Water Supply and Rain Water Harvesting Technology", New Delhi, 1984.
19. In Some Years the People of city have been supplied water once in two days and that to for less than hour. Under these circumstances the harvested rain water will be a great help and security. For detail see, Daroga J.D.," The Rains and Bombay's Water Supply", the Bombay Civic Journal (5), 17-18, 1954.
20. In an estimated total of around 10,000 bore wells (including 1301 of the corporation), during summer as many as 6000 do no yield even 20 litres of water per day, further at least 3000 of them become totally dry during the prolonged summer.
21. To drilling bore well is a costly affair, the single bore well drilling would cost Rs. 6-8 per feet, it is found during the survey that some households have drilled two to three bore wells in their premise to get water. In some places the drilling is proved to be in vain.

22. During the discussion with water supply authorities in Solapur suggested that the government should provide soft loan to the corporation, which will enable the water supply scheme, a viable one.

8

Summary and Conclusions

Water is an essential requirement for living beings, it is the vital fluid essential for human existence on the globe. It may be said that access to drinking water is human right, water is precious, use it properly. It is observed and also the fact that water is not using carefully and properly. Therefore, it is very important to create awareness among the users about the importance of water for present use as well as for the future. Water, though a gift of nature is becoming scarce, insufficient and unsafe for human consumption. Though demand for water is increasing tremendously, water is wasting so much, water is necessary part of infrastructure, required to achieve the goals of social and economic development. Till recent years, water supply to the households was not treated as an economic commodity. The water supply is a public good. The huge investments have been made in public water supply schemes by various governments. Thus, it has become the responsibility of governments to produce, collect, process and supply safe drinking water as a service to the community through budgetary resources.

The drinking water has become a scarcity in various cities. In the whole nation there is no any city in which water supply is assured all the 24 hours a day. Cities like Chennai, Hyderabad, Rajkot, Ajmer and Udaipur get water from municipal sources for less than an hour a day. Most towns and cities which normally get good rain every year have been undergoing the agony of acute water shortage in the last 90 years. Unfortunately, we do not have a well planned and an efficiently workable national water policy. States like Tamil Nadu and Karnataka, clash between themselves almost every year on the water issue. It has been estimated that at least 30 per cent of the people living in cities are consuming "unsafe" water. However, the 2001 Census report says that only 10 per cent of the people living in cities are not supplied with "safe" drinking water.

There is an incisive increase in the demand for water in urban areas. Because, the increase in population has put pressure on increase in the demand for drinking water. There is demand for water not only for domestic use but also for industrial and commercial uses. Similarly, on the supply side, there are great many problems. For instance, the natural rivers and tanks may not be close to urban areas and traditional wells do not have enough potential. The distance of water supply becomes expensive and difficult. The economics of urban water supply needs special attention because the household demand and supply cannot be met easily.

As per the review of literature attempted in this study, the important research gaps or the important aspects of urban water supply which need their incorporation or inclusion in our empirical study. Besides, since we have the empirical study the state of art question is kept in mind.

In terms of philosophy and practice, there are divergent views to consider urban water supply as a public utility within or one of the ingredient of urban infrastructure. This has a point blank problem of pricing, supply and maintenance of urban water. Besides, is it possible to have full cost pricing or supply. Urban water as a welfare measure is the fundamental issue.

The foremost aspect of urban water is its demand. The literature indicates that there is an ever increasing demand, and needless there are technical studies dealing with the forecasting and modeling aspects of demand for urban water.

If we look into the supply side, the important issues having an eye on our empirical study are providing potable water how and why, the economies of scale and scope in water supply, future water supply in Indian cities.

Besides, demand and supply the distribution is and has been treated seriously in the literature which need their reference in our present study. For example, planning inputs for water distribution, selection of water distribution stations, a biological growth in water supply, some control measures with special reference to demand systems.

The cost of water supply, how to finance and what should be the nature of investment have received sufficient attention in the literature, what is the situation specially in our study areas with respect to water distribution has to be taken into account. Similarly, as it is a public investment, how to finance (tax/charge collections, borrowing etc.) and how to recover this investment poses serious problem, specially if the water supply is considered either as a public utility or infrastructure. It is of almost interest if the disinvestment policy of the government in the recent past is taken into account. Needless to say, the municipal authorities have been compelled to think of devising the urban water supply plan to be handed over to private enterprises.

The growing urbanisation and increasing demand for water has been accepted as a subject of national planning. Further, the need for alternative sources of water supply, better utilisation of water is also treated very seriously. Under the circumstances, the governments have been forced to think on new, and newer policies as the days go by. What then is the idea of public authorities in our study areas is no less important aspect.

The review of our literature is clear that the pricing of urban water is and will be a million dollar question. The principles of economics will have to be thrown to the winds. Because the water charges, application of meter, cost recovery are the economic aspects. But the social welfare, supply of infrastructure and local political considerations loom large. Therefore, to gain salt from the review of literature, we will have to examine the question of pricing urban water in our study areas. The household use and consumption of water is related to its taste and preference. Besides, the income has its own influence. Hence, what sort of situation prevails in our study area is a gap that to be investigated.

The traditional method of water supply, its quantity and quality often have a crises cross underground relationship. In the modern days the underground electricity supply and telephone lines also get mixed up. How is the problem solved or to be solved in our study areas assumes greater importance. The drainage, sewage and sewerage also have to be looked into systematically.

With an eye to empirical research, there is need to study various techniques and technology of water supply in Gulbarga and Solapur cities. Because our review of literature points to the fact that reuse, recycling, treatment of supplied water, rain water harvesting have and will be serious aspects specially in our study area where there is irregularity, un seasonality and scanty rainfall.

There has been a point blank problem of pricing, supply and maintenance of urban water. The foremost aspect of urban water is its demand. If we look into the supply side the important issues having an eye on our empirical study are providing potable water how and why, the economies of scale and scope in water supply, future water supply in Indian cities. For example, planning inputs for water distribution, selection of water distribution stations, a biological growth in water supply. 73.6 per cent of urban households having access to safe drinking water by tap source in 1986. In the process of planning and management of urban water supply incorporating the slum dwellers is creating an overall problem of water supply. In recent times, water quality has deteriorated due to rapid industrialization, population growth as they generated increasing quantities of industrial waste water, domestic waste water respectively. The environmental related health problems concerned with water supply are very serious.

The importance of urban water supply in the planning process, it is true that the absolute amount spent on urban water supply has increased. Keeping with the requirements, the outlay on urban water supply increased from Rs. 5982 crore in Eighth Plan to Rs. 20750 crore in Ninth Plan. Therefore, it has been a four fold increase in the outlay on urban water supply.

The water supply aspects in Karnataka and Maharashtra are supplement to the study of water supply in Gulbarga and Solapur cities. The percentage of households having safe drinking water is very important. Karnataka covered 194 cities, towns and provides water supply to 144 lakh people. If we look into the latest demand for water, in Karnataka the demand for drinking water is 20 billion cubic meter, the water demand for agriculture is highest and the industrial water demand is 26 km cub. In Karnataka, the level of water in 208 urban areas ranges from 40 LPCD to 135 LPCD. A macro level aspect of water supply in Gulbarga and Solapur is essential and complementary to the micro approach. Therefore, the study examines a macro analysis of water supply in Gulbarga and Solapur cities. Gulbarga city incorporated 8 and Solapur city incorporated 12 villages. Gulbarga city has 3 sources of water supply. The scheme is designed to supply 2 MGD of water to the city. Third stage water supply scheme Bhima river as a source started in 1993. The scheme has been designed to the pumping capacity of 4.30 lakh and water supplied to city is 6.75 MGD and per capita water supply is 15.7 GPCD. The Solapur city is also having three sources of water supply, namely Ekruk tank, Bhima river and Ujjani dam. In 1882 Ekruk tank was started to supply water to Solapur city. The second stage water supply scheme Bhima river as a source started in 1968. The water supplied from two sources is 112.50 MLD.

The sources of water supply are important for providing drinking water to the people of urban areas. The population of Solapur is double the population of Gulbarga. There were 13017 HSCs, 592 PSPs and 260 NDCs in Gulbarga city. In terms of population covered, households served, the Solapur stands on a much better fruiting in the coverage of water supply. The receipts from water supply account of Gulbarga between 1991 and 2000 is Rs. 0.35 crore and Rs. 1.19 crores and payments is Rs. 0.65 crore and 2.40 crores between the same period. The Solapur city enjoys a very high level of financial soundness in terms of receipts and payments of water supply account. The two cities comparison between opening and closing balance of water supply account brings out the fact that Solapur has made tremendous increase over Gulbarga. The Solapur city spends considerably much higher on water supply account even on annual basis compared to Gulbarga. The water supply project cost of Solapur is six times more than that of Gulbarga. The remodeling cost of water supply projects in Solapur have been much wider than Gulbarga during 2000-01. The remodeling cost of Solapur water supply schemes is two times more than that of Gulbarga. The significant difference between Gulbarga and Solapur Corporation is that Solapur Municipal Corporation need not spend any amount for water supply projects. There are some marginal differences in the two cities water supply systems of tap rates.

A primary survey carried out in Gulbarga and Solapur for under standing the economics of urban water supply at a household level has been discussed in the study. The house households in Solapur get more water than the households in Gulbarga. The Solapur system is far more satisfactory as 30 per cent of sample households get water between 2- 3 hours of duration. As many as 55 samples (37 per cent) in Gulbarga depend on bore wells as the source of water supply which is very small in Solapur. Solapur households are placed more comfortably in terms of water supply and sanitary conditions. The highest number of households (77 per cent) have faced the problem of road digging in Gulbarga city as against just 20 per cent households in Solapur. The sample households in Solapur enjoy better water supply system than Gulbarga.

Due to uncertainty and poor quantity of water supply 53 per cent households in Gulbarga store the water in drums as against the systematic storage water tanks adopted by 53 per cent households in Solapur. The 53 per cent of our sample households as against 13.3 per cent in Solapur have reported leakages in public water supply pipes and stand posts. Due to good amount of water supply through the public stand posts in Solapur, the households spend less time than that of Gulbarga. In Gulbarga 35 per cent of households spend 60–80 minutes per day to get water from public stand posts.

The households in Gulbarga pay a monthly tax of Rs. 45 as against Rs. 980 (annual) Rs. 81.6 per month tax paid by households in Solapur. Thus the households in Solapur pay more water tax compared to Gulbarga.

There are 30 per cent households in Gulbarga face the problems of leakages of water supply pipes at several points leading to reduction in the quantity received by households. The system of water supply all to households is more satisfactory (33 per cent) in Solapur than Gulbarga. While in Solapur, 20 per cent of households have faced the problems of breakages and leakages water supply the sanitary system in Solapur is more satisfactory than Gulbarga. In Gulbarga, the less frequency of water treatment have been reported due to different quantities of water supplied by different rivers.

The 30 per cent of the households getting water with bleaching powder treatment, 43 per cent of households treatment with PAC powder, and 21 per cent households are getting water with Clorine and Alum treatment in Solapur. There is thus favorably more good water treatment adopted in Solapur than Gulbarga. The disease like Gastro Enteritis is very much high in Solapur than Gulbarga, only 13 per cent of sample households have responded positively as against 33 per cent of Solapur regarding complain to water supply authorities. Relatively more money is spent by large number of households for treatment of water diseases in Gulbarga than the sample households in Solapur.

Gulbarga provides very small quantity of water either for high income households or for the low income households. It is an obvious conclusion that the water supply system of Solapur is very efficient than Gulbarga. In Gulbarga and Solapur cities, the demand for water among the larger households is increasing as against its supply. There are 80 households out of 150 sample in Gulbarga and 35 out of 150 sample households in Solapur are willing to pay more for more quantity of water. The parallel water supply and sewerage pipes cris–cross of the two, breakages and leakages are so important in age old city of Gulbarga, the water supply authorities have greatly neglected the health and hygienic aspects of drinking water. As our attention is placed on water supply, the water supply account as a per cent to the total of the corporation provides an insight into the magnitude of the problem of water supply. The examination of water supply account of Gulbarga & Solapur corporations indicate that payments are more than the receipts. The waste water treatment and use of treated water is of less significance to Solapur city. If the waste water treatment technology is adopted for Gulbarga city, a minimum of 15-20 lakh gallons can be given treatment and supply to the city dwellers. This is an essential and inevitable water supply method applicable to Gulbarga city. The recycling of waste water will help to irrigate hundreds of hectares of land around Gulbarga and Solapur cities. The rain water harvesting is of utmost urgent and important more for Gulbarga city than Solapur. The bore wells are though limited but alternative means of urban water supply. India spent more per cent of GDP on water supply, for covering 100 per cent of urban population under safe drinking water Rs. 20750 crore needed. Average water rate has to be increased at least Rs. 4 per 1000 liters. This will enable greatly the water supply account of Gulbarga Corporation. There is need for increasing the duration of water supply (1 to ½ hours) specially in Gulbarga. Gulbarga corporation should adopt underground pipeline system for better water supply purpose. There are higher income households and therefore may put pressure for additional supply of water in both the cities. Water is a scarce resource rational use of water is essential in both the cities. A frequent water filtration is needed in Gulbarga city. This will help to avoid more water borne diseases entering the city.

Bibliography

BOOKS

Anil Agarwal, James Kiwondo, Gloria Moreno, Jon Tinker, "Water, Sanitation and Health for All?", An Earthscan Publication, London, 1981.

Bharadwaj R, "An Economic Analysis of Water Requirements of Bombay Region", Book, Bombay University, 1967.

Blake Nelson M. "Water for the Cities", Surcuse University Press, Syracusa, New York, 1976.

Bonbright, James C., "Principles of Public Utility Pricing", Columbia University Press, New York, 1961.

David, Holtz & Scott Sebastian, "Municipal Water Systems: The Change for Urban Management", Indian University Press, London, 1978.

Eckstein, O., "Water Resources Development: The Economics of Project Evaluation", Harvard University Press, Cambridge, 1958.

Elizebeth, S., Holfman, "Water for the World", Pyramid Publications, New Delhi, 1963.

Gehmud Jacob, Bergman, I., "Hand Book of Water Resources and Pollution Control",

Van Nostrand Rein hold company, New York, 1976.

Grima, A.P., "Residential Water Demand: Alternative Choices for Management", University of Toronto Press, Toronto, 1972.

Gupta, N.L., (Ed.), "Urban Water Supply", Rawat Publications New Delhi, 1994.

Hall W.A., and Draup, J.A., "Water Resources Systems Engineering", Mc Graw Hill New York, 1970.

Hollman, Kenneth .W. and Walter, J. Primeaux, Jr., "The Effect of Price and Other Selected Variables on Water Consumption", Bureau of Business and Economic Research, University of Mississippi, Oxford, 1973.

Howe, C.W., and Easter, K., "Inter Basin Transfers of Water: Economic Issues and Analysis", the John Hopkins Press, Baltimore, 1970.

Hufsechmidt, M.M. and Fiering, M.B., "Simulation Techniques for Design of Water Resource Systems", Harvard University Press, Cambridge, 1966.

Jack Hirshleifer, DeHaven, J.C. and Jerome W. Milliman., "Water Supply - Economics, Technology and Policy", 4th ed. University of Chicago Press, Chicago, 1969.

Jacob, John. "Economics of Public Water Supply: With Special Reference to Kerala", Rawat Publications, New Delhi, 1997.

James, Leonard Douglas and Robert. R. Lee., "Economics of Water Resources Planning", McGraw Hill, New York, 1971.

John W. Clark, Warran Visseman and Mark J. Hammer., "Water Supply and Pollution Control", International Text Book Company, London, 1971.

Kamen, C.S., and Dar P., "Factors Affecting Domestic Water Consumption", Total Water Planning for Israel Ltd., Tel Aviv, 1973.

Kheese and Blair.T. Bower, "Managing Water Quality Economics, Technology Institutions", John Hopkin Press Baltimore, 1968.

Kulkarni, G.J., "A Text Book of Water Supply and Sanitary Engineering", 1962.

Lee, Terence, R., "Residential Water Demand and Economics Development", Research Publication -II, Department of Geography, University of Toronto Press, Toronto, 1969.

Linaweaver, F.P., et al., "A Study of Residential Water Use", Govt. Printing Office, Washington, D.C.1967.

Linsely, Ray K., and Jospeh B., Franzini, "Water Resources Engineering", Mc Graw Hill New York, 1964.

Michael, Megarry and Duncan Mara (Ed.), "Water, Wastes and Health in Hot Climate", John Wiley and Sons, London, 1968.

Nageshwar Rao, K., "Economics of Water Supply", Himalaya Publishing House, New Delhi, 1993.

Nageshwar Rao, M., "Studies in Urban Public Sector", Ashish Publishing House, New Delhi, 1985.

Narayana Swamay, K., "Water to Bangalore", Maruti Publishing House, Bangalore, 1978.

Rathore, M.S.and Ratna ReddyV., (Ed.)., "Urban Water Management", Rawat Publications, New Delhi, 1996.

Saleth. R., Maria, "Water Institutions in India"; Economics, Law and Policy", Institute of Economic Growth, Common Wealth Publishers, New Delhi, 1996.

Sewell, W.R., and Bower, B.T (Ed.)., "Forecasting the Demands for Water", Queen Printers Ottawa, 1968.

Smith, S.C., and Castle, E.N (Ed.)., "Economics and Public Policy in Water Resource Development", Lowa State University Press, Ames, 1964.

Towrt, A.C., "A Text Book of Water Supply", Edward Arland Ltd, London 1963.

Turneavre, F.E. and H.L.Russel, "Public Water Supply", John Willey and Sons, New York, 1960.

Utton, Albert, E. and Ludwik, Teclaff, (Ed.), "Water in a Developing World: The Management of a Critical Response", Westview Press, U.S.A., 1978.

White Gilbert,F., David J. Bradley and Anne.U. White., "Drawers of Water; Domestic Water Use in East Africa", University of Chicago Press, Chicago, 1972.

ARTICLES

Abraham, Amrita., "Drinking Water for the Poor" Economic and Political Weekly, Vol.15, No.35, August 1980.

Abrol, Madavi Mohan., "A New Plant for Delhi Water Supply: Hyderpur Plant", Civic Affairs, 25(I) August, 1977.

Ackerman, Edward and George., "Technology in American Water Developmen", Baltimore, 1959.

Adhikari M., and Gupta, C.K., "Problems in Municipal Water Supply: Their Remedies", Social Culture, 41(6); June, 1975.

Afifi, Handy H.A., "Economic Evaluation of Water Supply Pricing in Illinois" – Journal of American Water Works Assoication, Vol 61, No.1, 1969.

Agarwal, A.K., "Urban Infrastructure: Problems and Other Associated Issues: A Study of Mizoram, "Southern Economist, January 1, 1997.

Agarwal, Anil and Others, "Prospects for the International Drinking Water Supply and Sanitation Decade 1981 – 90", Study of International Institute for Environment & Development, London, 1981.

Agarwal, R.C, "Urban Water Supply: Issues and Approaches", In N.L. Gupta, Ed. "Urban Water Supply", Rawat Publications, New Delhi, 1994.

Alikhan Fatima, "Water Supply to Hyderabad: The Role of Ground Water", Urban Crisis in India, K.Vithal Reddy and Ram Mohan Road, (ed.). pp. 43-48, 1985.

Amitabh and Irudaya Rajan, "Urban Growth and Infrastructural Development in India", Productivity, Vol.36, No.2, July – September, 1995.

Ananda Krishna.R., "Water Supply and Sanitation in Bangalore", Civic Affairs, 24(5) 1976.

Andrews, R.I., "Estimation of Household Consumption of Water", Water Resources Research, Central University of Hampshire, James Hall, Durhaman, U.S.A., 1988.

Apprai.T., "Water Supply in the South Indian Cities", Civic Affairs, 18(5) December 1970.

Arar-Nedal-Hamdi, "Cultural Response to Water Shortage Among Palestinians in Jordan: The Water Crisis and Its Impact on Child Health", Human Organisation, 5(3), 284-91, 1998.

Arceivala,S., "Per Capita Water Consumption and Losses", E.E. Dept, MET Ankare, Turkey, 1987.

Archana Ghosh, "Status of Water Supply and Sanitation Facilities in Urban India – An Overview", Urbanization in Developing Countries, 1993, pp.147-232.

Arunachalam, P., "The U.N. Water Decade", Meghalaya (1981-90) Civic Affairs, 28(7) February 1981.

Aslam,M., Parvaiz, "Why a National Policy for Water Management" Yojana, May 1-15, 1986.

Avadesh Kumar and Sukhatankar, G.A. "Selection of Water Distribution Stations", Journal of Indian Water Works Association, 8(1) 1976.

Azad, Harnamsingh., "Potable Water Supply in India: Retrospective and Perspective", Civic Affairs, 28 (6) January 1981.

Baale Rao.B.B and Algarsamy., "Cost Estimates for Various Treatment Systems in India", Proceedings of the Symposium on Low Cost Water Treatment, CPHERI, Nagpur, 1973.

Badhe G.S., "Water Supply as a Public Utility Service in the Bombay City", Quarterly Journal of Local Self Government Institute, 38(3) January – March, 1968.

Bajpai, Ganesh Dutt., "Water for the Millions", Civic Affairs, 26(3) October, 1978.

Barharas, A.P., "The Expenditure of Citizens in Getting Water Supply Connections", Indian Institute of Public Administration, New Delhi, 1965.

Barnabas, A.P., "Sanitation and Drinking Water Supply", Study Indian Institute of Public Administration, New Delhi, 1978.

Barnea Joseph, "Water Costs in Developing Countries", Departments of Interior, Washington, 1965.

Barnea Joseph, "Water Costs in Developing Countries", Dept. of Interior, Washington, 1965.

Basu, Amit., "Some Thoughts on Water Supply, Sewerage and Waste Water Systems", Urban India 2(1) March, 1982.

Batchelor, R.A., "Household Technology and the Domestic Demand for Water", Land Economics, August, 1975.

Bellubbi, P.R, "Water Supply in Karnataka", Water World Journal, January – March, 1980.

Belsare.S.V., "Augmentation of Water Supply for Nagpur", Journal Indian Water Works Association, 8(1) 1976.

Bernd H, Dieterich and John M, Henderson, "Urban Water Supply Conditions and Needs in Seventy Five Developing Countries", 1969.

Bhaumik, Kirit, "Rajasthan's New Strategy for Combat Water Scarcity", Times of India, 7 July 1976.

Bhise, D.R., "Water Quality and Public health", Quarterly Journal of Local Self Government, 1979.

Bisilani, H.U. and P.S.N.Rao, "Water Supply and Sanitation in India", New Delhi, 1990.

Bonem, Gilbert, W., "On the Marginal Cost Pricing of Municipal Water". Water Resources Research, Vol. IV No. 1, 1969, p.191.

Bora, L.N., "Water Scarcity in North – East – India", Assam IVF, 21 August 1977.

Bowonder,B., and Chettri, R., "Urban Water Supply in India: Environmental Issues", Urban Ecology, 1984.

Briscoe, John., "Poverty and Water Supply: How to Move Forward", Finance and Development, 29(4), PP. 16.19. 1985.

Brown. Gardner, Jr and C.B.Mc Guire, "A Socially Optimum Pricing Policy for a Public Water Agency", Water Resources Research, 1969.

Brutan laor, "Future Water Supply in India Cities". Vol. 3 and 4 Decea, Geography, 1965.

Buta Singh, "Seventh Plan Strategy for Safe Drinking Water", Kurukshetra, Vol.34 No.10, July 1986.

Central Pollution Control Board, "Status of Water Supply and Waste Water Collection Treatment and Disposal in Class I Cities", New Delhi, 1998, p.8.

Central Water Commission (CWC), "Rates for Surface Water in India", Ministry of Water Resources, Government of India, New Delhi, 1988.

Chandrashekhar.S., "Water Supply and Sanitation: Integrated Approach", Civic Affairs, 16(11) June, 1969.

Charles, W.Howe and F.P.I. Linawaver, Jr., "The Impact of Price on Residential Water Demand and Its Relation to Systems Design and Price Structure", Water Resources Research, Vol.III, No.1, 1967. p.8.

Chaturvedi A.C., "Water Supply and Sewerage: Social Service or Development Activity",? Civic Affairs 19(7) February, 1972.

Chhabria, B.C., "From Sewage to Clean Water", Civic Affairs, October, 1970.

Chicoine, David, L, and Ganapathi, Ramamurthy., "Evidence on the Specification of Price in the Study of Domestic Water Demand", Land Economics, Vol.62, No.1, February 1986.

Clark, Robert, M. and Richard.G.Stevie., "A Water Supply Cost Model Incorporating Spatial Variables", Land Economics, Vol.57, No.10 February 1981.

Clark.Robert.M., "Water Supply Economics", Journal of the Urban Planning and Development Division, August 1976.

Courtney, Riordan, "Multistage Marginal Cost Model for Investment Pricing Decisions; Applications to Urban Water Supply Treatment Facilities", Water Resources Research, Vol. VII, No.3, 1971, p.497.

Crew.M.A., and G.Robert, "Some Problems of Pricing Under Stochastic Supply Conditions: The Case of Seasonal Pricing for Water Supply", Water Resources Research, Vol.6, No.5, 1970.

Daksha.C.Barai, "The Augmentation of Water Supply to Meet the Rapidly Growing Metropolitan Cities of India". Rawa Publications, New Delhi, 1993.

Dal, A.K., "Co-ordination of Regional Water Resource Supply and Demand Planning Model",Yojana, , 1979, pp.11-20.

Daniel M.D., "Water Re-use: A Flexible and Efficient Management Alternative for Municipal Water Supply", Water Resources Research, 1975.

Dar, Feldman and Kannen., "Socio – Economic Factors Affecting Domestic Water Demand in Israel", Water Resources Research, 11(6) December 1975, pp.149 – 220.

Daroga, J.D., "The Rains and Bombay's Water Supply", The Bombay Civic Journal"(5), 1954.

David J. Allee, "Efficient Management Policies for Urban Water Supply", Water Resources Research, Vol.VII, No.4, P-774. 1971.

Deora, Muris, "Civic Efforts for Augmenting Bombay's Water Supply", Bombay Civic Journal, 24(11) January 1978.

Desai, V.D., "Providing Potable Water How and Why", Bombay Civic Journal 25(1) March 1978.

Desai V.D., "Water Supply Management", Journal of Indian Water Works Association, 8(2), 1976.

Devi, P.Rema, "Accountability in Water Resources Management", M.Singh (ed.), 1992.

Devi.P.Rema, "Ground Water Development and Legal Regulation". Journal of the Indian Law Institute, Vol.33, No.4, 1991.

Dhadke.V.S, and K.V.S. Rao., "Domestic Water Supply to Greater Bombay – A Geographic Perspective", N.L.Gupta (ed.) 1994.

Dhar, V.K., "A Better Water Delivery System", Yojana, Vol.33, No.3, February 1989.

Dinesh Chand, "Does India Need Protection of Water Resources?", Kurukshetra, Vol.36, 1988.

Dwivedi, K.N., "Asia's Biggest Underground Drinking Water Pipeline", Civic Affairs 25(11) June 1978.

Egyptian – German Seminar., "Water Re – use in Urban and Rural Areas". February 27 to March 2, Cairo University Report Cairo, 1982.

Esrey, S.A, J.B., Potash, L., Roberts and C.Shiff., "Effects of Improved Water Supply and Sanitation on Ascariasis, Diarrohea, Dracunchiagic, Hook Worm Infection, Schistosmia and Trachoma", 1991.

Frandra, Marcus, F., "Drilling for Drinking Water in Drought Prone India", American Universities Field Staff Reports, South Africa Series, Vol.XIX, No.11, (India) 1975.

George,W., Reid, "Multi Structural Municipal Water Demand Model", Water Resources Bulletin, Vol.VII.No.5,1971, p.1238.

Ghatpande, M.M., "Application of Network Technique in Executing a Water Supply Scheme", Journal of Indian Water Works Association, 8(3) 1976.

Gottleb, "Urban Domestic Demand for Water – A Kansas Case Study", Land Economics, 39(1), Vol.39, May 1963.

Government of India, "National Water Policy", Ministry of Water Resources, New Delhi, 1987.

Grewal, N.S. "Water Quality in Punjab", Journal of Water Works Association, 8(4) 1976.

Grima, A.P., "The Impact of Policy Variables on Residential Water Demand and Related Investment Requirement", Watet Resources Bulletin, Vol.9, No.4, 1973.

Haijkens.J, (Ed.), "Drinking Water Supply by Public Hydrants in Developing Countries", WHO, Indian Roads Congress – Centre for Urban Studies, Veerberg, the Hagye, 1977.

Hammad, Syed M., "Drinking Water Supply and Sanitation Decade – Task Ahead", Civic Affairs 17(11) June 1980.

Hanke, S.H., "Demand for Water Under Dynamic Conditions", Water Resources Research, Vol 6. No.5, Columbia Maryland, U.S.A, 1970.

Hanke.S.H., "Some Behavioural Characteristics Associated with Residential Water Price Changes", Water Resources Research, 6(07), 1970.

Hanson, R and Hudson H.E., "Trends in Residential Water Uses", Journal of American Water Works Association, Vol.48, 1956, pp.1347 – 1358.

Headly, Charles J., "The Relation of Family Income and Use of Water for Residential and Commercial Purposes in the San Francisco Oakland Metropolitan Area", Land Economics, Vol.39, November 1963, America, pp. 441-449.

Heljkens .J (Ed.), "Drinking Water Supply with Public Hydrants, U.S.A., 1977.

Hellman, Associates, "Forecasting Municipal Water Treatments", U.S.A., 1969.

Howe Charles. W., "Benefit Cost – Analysis for Water System Planning", Water Resources Management, No.2, 1971.

Howe, Charles W, Smith, Mark–Griffin., "Incorporating Public Preferences in Planning Urban Water Supply Reliability", Water Resources Research, 29(10) October 1993, p.3363-69.

Howe, Charles W, "Benefit-Cost Analysis for Water Systems Planning", Water Resources Monograph No.2, 1971.

Hubbel, L.K., "Public Policy Issues in the pricing of Water in Urban Areas of Less Developed Countries", NAGARLOK, 19(2) April – June 1978.

Hubbel. L.K., "The Residential Demand for Water and Sewerage Service in Developing Countries: A Case Study in Nairobi", Urban and Regional Report 77 – 14, Water Bank Economics Dept. Washington, D.C. Processed, 1977.

Huganty and Mackay, "The Impact of Large Temporary Rate Changes on Residential Water Use", Water Resources Research, 11(6), P-791, December 1975.

Jacoby, H.D., and Loucks, D.P, "Combined Uses of Optimization and Simulation Models in River Basin Planning', Water Resources Research, Vol.8, No.6, 1972.

Jones, C.V., Boland, J.E., Crews, C.F., Dekay and J.R. Morris., "Municipal Water Demand: Statistical and Management Issue", Boulder, Colo, Westview, 1984.

Kameth M.V., "Not Enough of Clean Water: Will U.N. Conference Find an Answer?", Times of India, Tata Institute, March 1977.

Katzman, Martin, "Income and Price Elasticities of Demand for Water in Developing Countries", Water Resources Bulletin 13: pp. 47-55, 1977..

Kaushalya Babel, and N.L.Gupta, "Problems and Prospects of Water Supply – A Case Study of Udaipur City", N.L.Gupta, (ed.) Rawat Publication, New Delhi, 1994.

Keig.N.G., C.W.Fristoe, and C.W.,Goddard, "Structure of Policy: Owned Water Utilities", Journal of the American Water Works Association, 1970.

Khurana,S.N., "Safe Water on Tap by 1980 Made Possible", Civic Affairs 8(1) August, 1980.

Kim-H-Youn, Clark, Robert-M, "Economies of Scale and Scope in Water Supply". Regional Science and Urban Economics, 18(4) 479 – 502,1988.

Krishnamoorthi, K.P., RamanV, and Gadkari, A., "Biological Growth in Water Supplies: Some Control Measures with Special References to Distribution Systems", Journal of Indian Water Works Association, 7(3) 1975.

Kshirasagar,S.R., "Environmental Sanitation and Safe Drinking Water", Southern Economist, 18(7),April 1977.

Kusumker, A., "Bangalore City Water Supply", Civic Affairs, August 1963.

Lahiri.A., "Planning Water Use for 2000 A.D", Commerce, 131 (3372) 1975.

Lauria.D.T., Schelenger, D.L. and Wentworth, R.W., "Models for Capacity Planning of Water Systems", Journal of the Environmental Engineers Division, April 1975.

Leonard, R.Brown, "Social Well Being of Water Resources Planning", Water Resources Bulletin, Vol XII, No.6, 1976.

Logan, John, "The International Municipal Water Supply Program: A Health and Economic Appraisal", American Journal of Tropical Medicine and Hygiene, Vol.9, No.5, September 1960.

Logan., "Investment in Water Supply Program – A Health Economic Appraisal". American Journal of Tropical Medicine and Hygiene, Vol.10, No.5, September 1960.

Loughlin.J.C., "The Efficiency and Equity of Cost Allocating Methods for Multipurpose Water Projects" Water Resources Research, VOL.13, No.1, 1977.

Marcus H., Monench, "Chasing the Water Table Equity and Sustainability in Ground Water Management", 1992.

Mc Phail, A., "The Five Percent Rule for Improved Water Service: can Households Afford More?", World Development, 21(6) 1993.

Mikkols Donollos, Jean Webler and Luician Dukestine, "Problems in Forecasting Water Requirements", Water Resources Research, Vol.XII, No.2, 1976.

Milliman.J.W., "Policy Horizons for Future Urban Water Supply", Land Economics, Vol.39, May, 1963.

Morgan W.D., "Residential Water Demand: The Case from Micro Data", Water Resources Research, 9(4), 1973.

Murugan, G., "Pricing Public Utilities: A Study of Drinking Water", M.Phil Dissertation, (JNU Delhi), Centre for Development Studies, Kerala, 1993.

Muttagi, P.K., "Tariff Studies for Water Supply and Sewerage Service of the Municipal Corporation of Greater Bombay", Research Study of Tata Institute of Social Science, Bombay, 1976.

Nambiar, R.G., "Future Water Demands: The Impact of Growth on Water Use Patterns in Selected Sectors of Gujarat 1969-2000 ", ARTHAVIKAS, Vol.XIII, No.1, 1977, pp. 1-3.

Nanjunda Swamy.P.L., and Ramaswamy, M.V., "Water Supply and Sanitation Programme for the Decade in Karnataka", Civic Affairs (Annual Number) 29 (1) August 1981.

Nickum – James.E., Easter, K. William (Ed.), "Metro Politan Water Use Conflicts in Asia and the Pacific", United National Center for Regional Development, 1994.

Niyathi, N., "Urban Water Supply in Kerala", Southern Economist, Aug. 15, 1988.

Panikar, J.T., "India's Water Needs for the Next 25 years – Hope or Disaster? Journal of Science – Today, Vol.II, No.2, 1976.

Patwardhan, S.V., "Set up for Sanitation and Water Supply Schemes Needs: An Overhaul", Civic Affairs 18(1) August 1971.

Pescod, M.B, and Lkun, D.A, (Ed.), "Water Supply and Waste Water Disposal in Developing Countries", Asian Institute of Technology, Bankok, 1971.

Pradhan, R.C., "Protected Water Supply", JANATA (Independence Day Number) 30(25) 1975.

Pyatt, Edwin E and Rogers Peter P, "On Estimating Benefit Cost Rates for Water Supply Investments", Journal of American Public Health, Vol.52,1962,pp.1729-1742.

Rajawanshy, P.S., "Economic & Technological Issues in Urban Water Supply", In Rathore and Reddy (Ed.), "Urban Water Management" Rawat Publication, New Delhi 1996.

Ramarao, S. and Nageswar Rao M, "Urbanization- Its Impact on Present and Future Urban Public Service Systems in Karnataka by 2001 A–D", NAGARLOK, Vol. XI, No.1, 1979, p.43.

Rao.S.Subba, "National Water Supply and Sanitation Program with Special Reference to Cholera Endemic Areas", Indian Journal of Public Health 19(1) 1975.

Rogers Sheick, "Benefit Cost Analysis for Municipal Water Supply", Land Economics,Vol.40, pp. 444-449.

Roma. "Treating Water for the City's ill – Health", Economic Times, 21 November, 1982.

Saha, P.K., "Self – Financing Urban Water Supply – A Model for Assansole – Durgapur" Economic and Political Weekly, 26th June, 1974.

Saha,P.K., "Planning Inputs for Water Distribution System Design in Urban Areas", Journal Institute of Public Health Engineers, 4(1) 1975.

Scartato,R.F., "Time Capacity Expansion of Urban Water Systems",Water Resources Research,Vol.5, No.5,1969.

Schneider,M.L., and E.E.Whitliach, "User-specific Water Demand Elastities", Journal of Water Resources Planning and Management 17,No.1,52-73,1991.

Sethi,J.L., "Safe Drinking Water at Every Door-Step", Hariyana Revenue 3(4) October-December, 1969.

Sewell,W.R., et al., "Forecasting the Demand for Water", Department of Energy, Mines and Resources, Queen Printers, Ottawa, 1968.

Sharma, K.S.R.N., "A Study of Metering of Municipal Water Supply". Study, Indian Institute of Public Administration, New Delhi, 1976 – 77.

Sharma, K.S.R.N., "Urban Water Supply tariffs Issues in Determination and Administration", A Study Sponsored by CPHEEO & Ministry of Urban Development, Government of India, Indian Institute of Public Administration, (Restricted) pp. 77 – 81, 1991.

Sheela Prasad, V.G., "New Economic Policy: Implications for Water", Economic and Political Weekly, May 22, 1999, pp. 1251-56.

Sleeman, J.F., "The Economics of Water Supply", Scottish Journal of Political Economy, Vol.2, 1965, pp. 231-235.

Steve, Hanke.H., "Water Rates: An Assessment of Current Issues", Journal of American Water Works Association, Vol. 67, 1975.

Stobber, W.J. and Falk, L.H., "A Benefit Cost Analysis of Local Water Supply", Land Economics, Vol.43, No.3, pp.329-335, 1967.

Subramaniam Arun, "Bombay's Water Supply Faces Toxic Threat", Business India, pp.46-55, 1987.

Thomas R.H., "Urban Water Supply; Symposium on the Use and Control of Water", New Zealand Institute of Engineers, 1964.

Thomas, R.G., and H.P. Young, "Forecasting Water Use for Policy – Making: A Review". Water Resources Research, Vol. 9, No.4, 1973.

Thomas, Robert H, "Importance of Opportunities in Urban Treatment Technology" Journal of India Water Works Association, 12(1) January – March, 1981.

Trivedi, V.N., "Water Treatment in Hill Water Supply Schemes" Civic Affairs, 27 (11) June 1980.

Turhousky, Stephen, "The Demand for Water – Some Empirical Evidence, One Consumer's Response to a Commodity uncertain in Supply", Water Resources Research, 5(2), 1969, p. 350.

Turvey Ralph, "Analysing Marginal Cost of Water Supply". Land Economics, Vol. 52, No.2, 1976, pp. 158-168.

Tyagi, Paritosh C and Ganga Bishan, "Economic Aspects of Potable Water Supply in India", Civic Affairs, 19(2) September 1971.

Unavala, S.P., "Aspects of Water Treatment Technology as Applied to Indian Public Water Supplies", Civic Affairs, 9(2) September 1981.

Vidyavathi K, "Drinking Water Problem in Bangalore Urban Area", Southern Economist, June 1998, pp.18-20.

Viraghavan T., and Paramashivam.R, "Drinking Water Quality, Guidelines Past Practices, Present Status and Future Trends", Journal of Indian Water Works Association, 14(1) January 1982.

Vyas Anjana, and Anand P.B., "Some Issues in Management of Urban Water Supply Systems: A Case Study of Ahmedabad" Nagarlok, 1969.

W.H.O., "Low Cost Water Supply and Sanitation Technology, Pollution and Health Problems", New Delhi, 1984.

Wadia, P.S., "Pretreated and Remainder Ancillary Equipment for Water Treatment Plant", Civic Affairs 29 (6) January 1982.

Warford J.J, "Water Requirement: The Investment Decision in the Water Supply Industry", Manchester School of Economic and Social Studies, Vol.34, January 1966.

Whittington, Dale et al,. "Estimating the Willingness to Pay in the Developing Countries: A Case Study of contingent Valuation

Surveys in Southern Haiti", Economic Development and Cultural Change, 38(2) January, 293 – 311, 1990.

World Bank, "Water and Sanitation: Toward Equitable and Sustainable Development", A Strategy for the Remainder Decade and beyond Mimeo 1988.

REPORTS AND OTHER PUBLICATIONS

Central Public Health and Environmental Engineering Organisation, Government of India., "Manual on Water Supply and Treatment", CPHEEO, 1984.

Gallagher, D.R. and R.W. Robinson, "Influence of Metering, Pricing Policies and Incentives on Water Use Efficiency", Australian Water Resources Council, Technical Paper No.19, Australian Government Publishing Service, Canberra, 1977.

Government of India (WHO), "Report of Seminar on Financing and Management of Water and Sewerage Works", Proceedings and Recommendations". Op.cit, 1964.

Government of India, "Report of the National Water Supply and Sewerage Disposal", Ministry of Works and Housing, New Delhi, 1961.

Government of Maharashtra, "Economic Survey, 1998 – 99", Planning Commission, Mumbai.

Government of Maharashtra, "Solapur District Census Handbook 1991".

Govt. of Karnataka, "Karnataka at a Glance 1999 – 2000", Directorate of Economics and Statistics, Bangalore.

Gulbarga City Municipal Corporation, "Administrative Reports".

Gulbarga City Municipal Corporation, "Comparative Annual Accounts".

India Development Report 1999 – 2000, "Cost of Providing Drinking Water, Sanitation and Waste Water Treatment".

Karnataka Urban Water Supply & Drainage Board Gulbarga, "Details of Water Supply Schemes and Remodelling and Feasibility Reports 1999 & 2000".

Karnataka Urban Water Supply and Drainage Board, Bangalore, "Annual Report 1998 – 99", Bangalore.

Karnataka Urban Water Supply and Drainage Board, Bangalore, "Information Brochure 2000".

Lovei, Laszlo, and Dale Whittington, "Rent Seeking in the Water Supply Sector: A Case Study of Jakarta Indonesia". Infrastructure and Urban Development – Discussion Paper 85, World Bank, 1991, Washington D.C. Processed.

Maharashtra Jeevan Pradhikaran, "Annual Reports 1996–1997 & 1997–98", Government of Maharshtra, Mumbai.

Maharashtra Jeevan Pradhikaran, Solapur, "Annual Reports and Remodelling Reports", 1999 & 2000.

Maharashtra Jeevan Pradhikaran, Solapur, "Details of Existing Water Supply Schemes, Remodelling and Annual Reports".

Maharashtra Jeevan Pradhikaran, "Maharashtra State Urban Water Supply and Sewerage Systems Outline 1999 – 2000", Government of Maharashtra.

Maharashtra Water Supply and Sewerage Board Report, "The Project Implementation Report of the Maharashtra Water Supply and Sewerage Board's New Bombay Project Bombay". Chief Engineer, MWS & SB, 1986, (Mimeo) p. 21.

Planning Commission, "Five-Year Plan Documents", Government of Maharashtra, Mumbai.

Planning Commission, "Five Year Plan Documents", Government of Karnataka, Bangalore.

Pushpangadhan K,. & Murugan.G, "Pricing with Changing Welfare Criterion: An Application of Ramsey – Wilson Model to Urban Water Supply", Working Paper, Kerala Centre for Development studies.

Rees J.A., "Factors Affecting Metered Water Consumption", Final Report to the Social Science Research Council, August 1971.

Saunders, Robert. J. et al. "Alternative Concepts of Marginal Cost for Public Utility Pricing: Problems of Application in the Water Supply Sector", World Bank Staff Working Paper No. 259, Washington, D.C., May 1977.

Solapur City Municipal Corporation, "Comparative Annual Accounts".

UNDP, "Safe Water 2000: A Global consultation on Safe Water and Sanitation", Conference Documents, New Delhi 1990.

UNDP, "Safe Water 2000: A Global Consultation on Safe Water and Sanitation", Conference Documents, New Delhi, 1990.

World Bank, "Water Resources Management, "A World Bank Policy Paper Washington D.C., 1993.

Index

S

T

U